GLOBAL STRATEGY AND ORGANIZATION

ANIL K. GUPTA
The University of Maryland

VIJAY GOVINDARAJAN
Dartmouth College

JOHN WILEY & SONS, INC.

Acquisitions Editor   *Jeff Marshall*
Marketing Manager   *Charity Robey*
Senior Production Editor   *Patricia McFadden*
Senior Designer   *Karin Gerdes Kincheloe*
Production Management Services   *Argosy*

This book was set in 10/12 Times Roman by Argosy and printed and bound by Courier Corporation.
The cover was printed by Phoenix Color Corporation.

This book is printed on acid-free paper.

ISBN: 0-471-25029-5

Printed in the United States of America

10 9 8 7 6 5 4 3 2 1

PREFACE

WHAT IS THIS BOOK ABOUT?

What do we mean when we say that we live in an increasingly global world? If you are a Hollywood producer, it means that you care not only about whether your movie will be a box office success in the home market, but also, and perhaps even more so, about whether it will be a successful export, as it can earn several times as much beyond North American shores. If you are the CEO of Black & Decker, it means that, when you review your strategy for the North American power tools market, you look at both domestic and international strategies of competitors such as Makita and Bosch. If you are the CEO of Ford Motor Company, it means that, as you enter and expand into emerging markets such as China or India, you do not need to design new cars entirely from scratch; you can enter these markets faster and more economically by leveraging on existing global platforms. And, last but not least, if you are a recent MBA and a junior manager at Procter & Gamble, it means that you do not have any hope of making it into the top ranks of the company unless you combine superb on-the-job performance with extensive international experience.

The twin forces of ideological change and technological revolution are making globalization one of the most important issues facing companies today. The makeover from state-dominated isolated economies to market-driven globally integrated economies is proceeding relentlessly in all corners of the world, be it Brazil, China, France, India, or South Africa. Accelerating developments in the information and transportation technologies are making real-time coordination of far-flung activities not only more feasible but also more reliable and efficient. Also, many emerging industries (e.g., software, computers, and telecommunications) themselves tend to be born global, thereby further transforming the worldwide economic landscape.

In the emerging era, every industry must be considered a global industry and every business a knowledge business. In this context, distinctions such as "international," "multinational," and "transnational" are becoming less and less meaningful. Today, globalization is no longer an option but a strategic imperative for all but the smallest corporations. This is as true of firms in industries such as cement, construction, and health care, which have traditionally been regarded as multidomestic, as it is of firms in industries such as semiconductors, televisions, and automobiles which globalized many decades ago. The only relevant question today is: Is your company a leader or a laggard in engineering and exploiting the ongoing globalization of your industry? The central premise of this book is that, no matter what the industry, only those companies that successfully lead the global revolution within their industry arenas will emerge as the winners in the battles for global dominance.

Over the last ten years, we have studied over one hundred global corporations through a variety of research methods: large scale surveys, case studies, and in-depth discussions with several hundred executives. We have also served as advisors and consultants to dozens of companies in their efforts to review, redesign, and recreate their global strategies and organizations. Building on this knowledge base, we provide herein a roadmap for smart globalization. We identify and focus on four tasks essential for any company to emerge and remain the globally dominant player within its industry:

1. *You must ensure that your company leads the industry in identifying market opportunities worldwide and in pursuing these opportunities by establishing the necessary presence in all key markets.* In some cases, these opportunities entail creating a new industry, as illustrated by Yahoo! which pioneered the Internet portal market in many parts of Asia and Europe. In other cases, these opportunities might be in transforming an existing industry, as illustrated by Wal-Mart, which is changing the rules of the retailing industry in every corner of the world.

2. *You must work relentlessly to convert global presence into global competitive advantage.* Presence in the strategically important markets gives you the right to play the game. However, it says nothing about whether and how you will actually win the game. Doing so requires identifying and exploiting the opportunities for value creation that global presence offers.

3. *You must cultivate a global mindset.* You must view cultural and geographic diversity as opportunities to exploit and be prepared to adopt successful practices and good ideas wherever they come from.

4. *You must constantly strive to reinvent the rules of the global game.* This process is captured in continually revisiting answers to three perennial questions: Who are our target customers? What value do we want to deliver to these customers? How will we create this value?

ROAD MAP FOR THE READER

Chapter 1 examines platform questions, such as: What is globalization? What is driving it? Why it is here to stay? What it means for companies and managers? Chapter 2 presents an organizing framework and set of conceptual ideas to guide firms in approaching the strategic challenge of casting their business lines overseas and establishing global presence. In Chapter 3, we utilize this conceptual framework to analyze and derive lessons from the myriad of decisions that Wal-Mart made in the process of its globalization during the 1990s. Chapter 4 focuses on the strategic challenge of converting global presence into global competitive advantage. In particular, this chapter identifies and analyzes the six distinct opportunities for the creation of global competitive advantage: adapting to local markets, capturing economies of global scale, capturing economics of global scope, optimizing the choice of locations for activities and resources, leveraging knowledge across subsidiaries, and playing the global chess game. In Chapter 5, we shift from content to process, and address the following questions: Why does mindset matter? What is a global mindset? What is the value of a global mindset? What can companies do to cultivate a global mindset? Chapter 6 continues the focus on process and addresses the challenge of converting the global corporation into an effective knowledge machine. In this chapter, we propose that building an appropriate social ecology is a crucial requirement for effective knowledge management. We explicitly uncover the pathologies and pitfalls which prevent companies from realizing the full potential of knowledge management, and we present a general framework for building the necessary social ecology for effective knowledge management. Chapter 7 focuses on the dynamics of creating and managing high-performing global business teams by addressing two key issues: why global business teams can fail and what steps can be taken to make such teams more effective and efficient. Chapter 8 looks at why firms must cultivate a bias for changing the rules of the global game. In this chapter, we derive generalizable lessons from the analyses of how three firms (Dell Computer, Tetra Pak, and Canon) changed the rules of the global game in their respective industries by discovering new answers to one or more of the following three questions: Whom should our targeted customers be? What customer value should we aim to deliver? How should we go about creating this value? Chapter 9 examines the opportunities and challenges associated with globalization in the digital age. In this chapter we address the following issues: How is digitization reshaping the economic landscape? How should newly formed information technology driven firms—operating at the leading edge of the digital revolution—deal with the imperative to globalize? How will the digital revolution transform the established global enterprise?

The architecture of the book reflects two design criteria. One, we wanted the book to be broad in its coverage of issues relevant to creating and exploiting global presence. Thus, the book focuses about equally on key "content" issues (such as choice of markets, entry strategies, and impact of the digital revolution) as well as on key "process" issues (such as cultivating a global mindset, creating knowledge networks, and managing global business teams). Two, we wanted each chapter to focus on a specific action-oriented issue (such as building global presence, cultivating a global mindset, or the dynamics of global business teams). Our hope is that this approach will make the contents of the book reasonably comprehensive and yet highly accessible and usable for the reader. They can read the entire book at one stretch or go directly to a particular chapter that holds immediate relevance.

ACKNOWLEDGMENTS

No one lives and works alone and no work is ever perfect. We are well aware that this book, like every other book that has ever been written, is a work in progress. While we are solely responsible for any weaknesses and limitations that might be reflected in these pages, we are deeply grateful to our many colleagues and friends who have helped shape our ideas over the last decade and nurtured and assisted us in bringing this book to fruition. In particular, we wish to acknowledge Jay Anand, Milton Bennett, Vincent Duriau, Mike Knetter, Ed Locke, Lee Preston, Ravi Ramamurti, Jorma Saarikorpi, Tapani Savisalo, Craig Schneier, Anant Sundaram, Chris Trimble, Haiyan Wang, and Sri Zaheer who read and gave us feedback on specific chapters.

This book would not have been possible without the cooperation of many global corporations and their executives who generously gave their time and shared their insights. We owe them a substantial debt of gratitude.

Our sincere thanks to Judy Marwell who skillfully edited the manuscript, to Joyce Kenison and Kristy Snow who professionally managed hundreds of pages of original manuscript and revisions with invaluable secretarial and computer skills, and to Michaela Cervenkova who conducted excellent library and web-based research for us. We also thank Jeff Marshall, Editor at John Wiley & Sons, for his enthusiasm and commitment to this project.

Anil Gupta received funding support for work on this book from the Center for Global Business, the Robert H. Smith School of Business at The University of Maryland, College Park. Vijay Govindarajan received funding support for this project from the William F. Achtmeyer Center for Global Leadership, the Tuck School of Business at Dartmouth College. He gratefully acknowledges the generosity of Bill Achtmeyer, a personal friend and role model.

In writing this book, we hope that you will share our enthusiasm for the rich subject of globalization. We would value your comments and thoughts about the book. Please free to contact: Anil K. Gupta (Smith School of Business, University of Maryland, College Park, MD 20742; tel: 301-405-2221; fax: 301-951-0262; agupta@rhsmith.umd.edu) or Vijay Govindarajan (Tuck School of Business, Dartmouth College, Hanover, NH 03755; tel: 603-646-2156; fax: 603-646-1308; vg@dartmouth.edu).

Anil K. Gupta
Bethesda, MD

Vijay Govindarajan
Hanover, NH

August 2002

ABOUT THE AUTHORS

Anil K. Gupta is the Ralph J. Tyser Professor of Strategy and Organization and a Distinguished Scholar-Teacher at the Smith School of Business, The University of Maryland at College Park. He has served as a visiting faculty at Stanford University and Dartmouth College. A two-time winner of the Krowe Award for Excellence in Teaching from the University of Maryland, Anil has been recognized by *Business Week* as an Outstanding Faculty in its *Guide to the Best B-Schools* and serves as a consultant, executive program faculty, and keynote speaker with multinational corporations and other organizations worldwide. In 2001, Anil coauthored (with Vijay  Govindarajan) *The Quest for Global Dominance: Transforming Global Presence Into Global Competitive Advantage* (Jossey-Bass, 2001). He is also the author of more than 60 highly cited papers in major journals and has been honored with inclusion in the *Academy of Management Journal*'s Hall of Fame (under the "Honorable Mention" category). In 1994, he was ranked by *Management International Review* as one of the "Top 20 North American Superstars" for research in strategy and organization.

Vijay Govindarajan (VG) is the Earl C. Daum 1924 Professor of International Business and the Director of the William F. Achtmeyer Center for Global Leadership at the Tuck School of Business at Dartmouth College. For two consecutive years, the *Wall Street Journal* ranked Tuck as the number one business school.

VG's area of expertise is strategy, with particular emphasis on strategic innovation, industry transformation, and global strategy and organization. VG was cited by *Management International Review* as one of the Top 20 North American Superstars for research in strategy and organization. One of his papers was recognized as "one of the ten most-often cited articles" in the entire 40-year history of the prestigious *Academy of Management Journal.*

VG works with CEOs and top management teams in Global Fortune 500 firms to discuss, challenge, and escalate their thinking about strategy. He is often called to be the keynote speaker at events, conferences, CEO forums, and leadership development programs. Professional credits include: Outstanding Faculty, named by *Business Week* in its *Guide to Best B-Schools*; Top Ten Business School Professors in Corporate Executive Education, named by *Business Week*; and Outstanding Teacher of the Year, voted by MBA students.

CONTENTS

CHAPTER 1

THE CHALLENGE OF GLOBALIZATION

The world is your oyster. Do you have the right fork?

—*Thomas A. Stewart*[1]

THE **TWIN** forces of ideological change and technology revolution are making every industry a global industry and every business a knowledge business. As worldwide presence increasingly becomes an imperative rather than a choice for most medium and large companies, an increasing number of managers must confront the essential question: How do we engineer and exploit the ongoing globalization of our industry? In this chapter, we begin peeling the onion by answering some fundamental questions: *What is globalization? What is driving globalization? What do these trends imply for companies and for managers?*

WHAT IS GLOBALIZATION?

At one extreme, imagine a world that is a collection of economic islands connected, if at all, by highly unreliable and expensive bridges or ferries. At the other extreme, imagine the world as an integrated system where the fortunes of the various peoples inhabiting the planet are highly intertwined. The sneakers that you wear were manufactured in Indonesia. Your mutual fund company invests a part of your savings in companies in Ireland. The software that you just downloaded from the Web was developed in India. And the company that you work for routinely exchanges technologies and management ideas with its subsidiary operations in Japan. If you agree that, over the past fifty years, the world around you has undergone a transformation from something like the first scenario to something like the second one, then we would say that the worldwide economy is indeed undergoing a process of globalization. More succinctly stated, *globalization refers to growing economic interdependence among countries as reflected in increasing cross-border flows of three types of entities: goods and services, capital, and know-how.* The term *globalization* can relate to any of several levels of aggregation: the entire world, a specific country, a specific industry, a specific company, or even a specific line of business or functional activity within the company.

At a worldwide level, globalization refers to the aggregate level of economic interdependence among the various countries. Is the world truly becoming more global? Yes. As evidence, consider the following trends. Trade in goods and services now stands at almost 25 percent of world GDP, up from under 10 percent about three decades ago. The stock of foreign direct investment has grown from less than 5 percent of world GDP in 1980 to almost 10 percent now. Trends in cross-border transactions in bonds and equities are even more dramatic. In 1970, such transactions as a ratio of GDP stood at less than 5 percent for the United States, Germany, and Japan. By 1996, the respective figures for the three countries had soared to nearly 150 percent, 200 percent, and 100 percent respectively.[2] The pace of globalization continues unabated—as evidenced by the fact that the total asset size of cross-border mergers and acquisitions grew by 15 percent in 1996, 45 percent in 1997, and nearly 75 percent in 1998.[3]

The fact that the worldwide economy is indeed becoming more global does not in the least imply that all countries, all industries, or all companies are becoming globally integrated at the same rate. For a variety of historical, political, sociological, and even geographic reasons, diversity is and will remain one of the defining characteristics of humanity. Thus it is important to examine what this concept means at the level of a specific country, a specific industry, or a specific company.

At the level of a specific country, globalization refers to the extent of the interlinkages between that particular country's economy and the rest of the world. Historical and political reasons have caused some countries, such as Cuba, to remain quite isolated. Others such as China, India, Mexico, and Brazil have made great strides toward global integration—albeit at different speeds. Some of the key outcome indicators that can be used to measure the globalization of any country's economy are exports and imports as a ratio of GDP, inward and outward flows of both foreign direct investment and portfolio investment, and inward and outward flows of royalty payments associated with technology transfer.

Table 1.1 compares the global integration of China and India along some of the indicators at two points in time: 1980 and 2001. As this table indicates, starting from a roughly similar degree of economic isolation in 1980, China's economy globalized at a much faster rate between 1980 and 2001 than did India's economy.

At the level of a specific industry, globalization refers to the degree to which, within that industry, a company's competitive position in one country is interdependent with its competitive position in another country. Alternatively stated, the more global an industry, the greater the competitive advantage that a player within that industry can derive from leveraging technology, manufacturing prowess, brand names, and capital across countries. The greater the degree of such interdependence, the greater will be the extent to which the industry is dominated by the same set of global players who face each other in almost every market and coordinate their strategic actions across countries. The wireless handset industry, so far dominated globally by Nokia, Motorola, and Ericsson, and the soft drinks industry,

TABLE 1.1   **Global Integration: China Versus India**

	China		India	
	1980	2001	1980	2001
Exports of goods and services as percentage of GDP*	6	23	7	9
External debt as percentage of GDP*	2.2	12.9	12.0	20.7
Inward flows of foreign direct investment as percentage of GDP*	1.7	3.3**	0.1	0.5**

*Abstracted from *World Development Report 2003*, World Bank.

**Data pertain to 2000.

dominated globally by Coca-Cola, Pepsi-Cola, and Cadbury-Schweppes, are two examples of highly global industries. In contrast, the construction and hospital industries, populated by hundreds of domestic companies all over the world, represent two good examples of industries still in the very early stages of globalization.

Some of the key outcome indicators of the globalization of an industry are the extent of cross-border trade within the industry as a ratio of total worldwide production, the extent of cross-border investment as a ratio of total capital invested in that industry, and the proportion of industry revenue accounted for by players competing in all major regions of the world. For illustrative purposes, consider the ratio of cross-border trade to worldwide production. On this measure, relative to an index of 1.0 for all manufacturing industries, the mid-1990s figures for the computer industry were 2.2, for the auto industry 1.6, and for the pharmaceutical industry 0.7.[4] These figures indicate that, in terms of cross-border flow of goods and services, the computer industry is more global than the auto industry, which is more global than the pharmaceutical industry.

WHAT IS A GLOBAL COMPANY?

Ask ten different executives "What is a global company?" and, more likely than not, you will get ten different answers. Some might argue that a global company is one that is pursuing customers in all major economies, in particular the Americas, Europe, and Asia. Others might argue that a global company puts down roots in every major market in the form of producing locally what it sells locally. Yet others might suggest that the real test of globalization lies instead in whether your business unit headquarters are globally dispersed, whether your top management team consists of individuals from different nationalities, and so forth.

There are two problems with each of these perspectives regarding the nature of a global company. First, each definition overlooks the fact that globality is a multidimensional phenomenon and, like the proverbial elephant, can never be understood fully from just one perspective—be it market presence, production bases, composition of the top management team, or any other. Second, each definition overlooks the fact that globality is a continuous variable along a spectrum from low to high rather than a categorical binary variable with only two extreme values (global and nonglobal).

As depicted in Figure 1.1, we believe that the concept of "corporate globality" should be viewed as a four-dimensional construct based on the premise that an enterprise can be more or less global along each of four major characteristics: globalization of market presence, globalization of supply chain, globalization of capital base, and globalization of corporate mindset.

The first dimension, globalization of market presence, refers to the extent to which the company is targeting customers in all major markets for its industry throughout the world. Even within the same industry, globalization of market presence can range from relatively low to very high. For illustrative purposes, Table 1.2 presents comparative data on the interregional dispersion of sales for selected firms in the information technology industry. As these data indicate, in 1993, NTT of Japan was the least globalized company on this one dimension. In comparison, IBM, Sun Microsystems, and Canon appeared to be among the most globalized companies.

The second dimension, globalization of supply chain, refers to the extent to which the company is accessing the most optimal locations for the performance of various activities in its supply chain. It is entirely possible for a company to have fairly local or regional market presence and yet a highly globalized value chain or vice versa. For example, in 1999, as a key element of the turnaround strategy for British retailer Marks & Spencer, CEO Peter Salsbury announced plans to set up a global supply chain for apparel goods with manufacturing hubs in Portugal, Morocco, and Sri Lanka.[5]

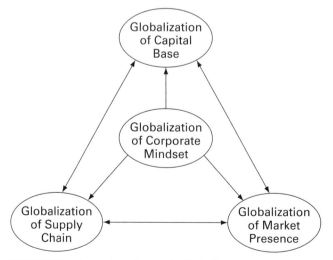

FIGURE 1.1 Assessing Corporate Globality

TABLE 1.2   Interregional Distribution of Information Technology Sales for Selected Companies, 1993 (Percentages)

	North America	Europe	Asia
IBM	41	33	16
Fujitsu	6	26	65
Hewlett-Packard	51	34	9
NEC	6	4	88
Compaq	45	38	5
Canon	30	29	37
Sun Microsystems	51	24	23
NTT	0	0	100
Microsoft	56	30	9

Abstracted from *Globalization of Industry: Overview and Sector Reports*, OECD 1996.

Toyota is another good example of a company with a global supply chain. At the end of 1995, Toyota produced about two-thirds of all its cars in Japan; the remaining one-third were produced in wholly or partially owned affiliates in 25 countries spread over the Americas, Europe, and Asia. Furthermore, the company exported 38 percent of its domestic production to foreign markets. Aside from this flow of capital, goods, and know-how between Japan and overseas affiliates, Toyota also engaged in significant intrafirm flows among the affiliates. For example, within its Southeast Asian regional network, it exported diesel engines from Thailand, transmissions from the Philippines, steering gears from Malaysia, and engines from Indonesia.[6]

The third dimension, globalization of capital base, refers to the extent to which the company is tapping into the most optimal sources of capital on a worldwide basis. The Hong Kong-based Internet service provider China.com represents a good example of how it is entirely possible for a company to be quite "local" along the dimensions of market presence and supply chain and yet have a highly globalized capital base. China.com's market base and operations are centered primarily around Hong Kong and China. Yet in early 1999 the company chose to get itself listed on the U.S.–based NASDAQ. A listing on the NASDAQ, where price-earnings ratios tend to be very high, can potentially yield many benefits for China.com: less expensive capital, enhanced ability to use stock options for attracting top talent, and enhanced ability to make stock-based acquisitions.

Last but not least, the fourth dimension, globalization of corporate mindset, refers to the extent to which the corporation as a collectivity reflects an understanding of diversity across cultures and markets coupled with an ability to integrate across this diversity. The state of any enterprise's corporate mindset depends on the mindsets of the individuals who lead the enterprise as well as the organization that determines how these individuals interact, what information is collected, how it is processed, and how decisions are made. General Electric serves as a good example of a company with an increasingly global mindset. All GE businesses are managed through a global line-of-business structure, investment opportunities are identified and assessed on a global basis, corporate leaders are pushing hard to globalize "the intellect of the company," and, while the company has a strong unified worldwide corporate culture, the composition of the leadership itself is becoming increasingly diverse in terms of nationalities.[7]

WHAT IS DRIVING GLOBALIZATION?

Irrespective of the level of aggregation—the entire world, an individual country, a specific industry, or a particular company—globalization occurs because specific managers in specific companies make decisions that result in increased cross-border flows of capital, goods, or know-how. Two intertwined considerations are driving managers to make such decisions on an increasing basis: one, globalization is becoming increasingly feasible; two, globalization is becoming increasingly desirable. The following trends explain why.

First, an ever-increasing number of countries are embracing the free-market ideology. The policy shift from a planning to a market mentality is well known and has been well documented.[8] Suffice it to say that, since the end of the Second World War, the gale winds of market forces have continued to gather momentum—starting from the developed economies (Table 1.3), moving on first to South Korea, Taiwan, Hong Kong, and Singapore, then to the other countries of Southeast Asia, and finally sweeping up other major economies such as China, India, Latin America, Central and Eastern Europe, and parts of Africa. Table 1.4 provides evidence of ongoing liberalization in investment regimes across a whole horde of countries.

As a consequence of economic liberalization, free trade already has become or is rapidly becoming a reality within regional blocks such as the EU, NAFTA, ASEAN, and Mercosur. Furthermore, the World Trade Organization continues to chip away at the remaining barriers to the free flow of capital, goods, services, and technology among countries and regional blocks. The financial crisis that engulfed much of East Asia and Latin America, as well as Russia during 1997–1999 has accelerated the pace of structural reforms and the further integration of many countries in these regions into the global economy. As illustrated dramatically by Renault's acquisition of a controlling stake in Nissan, countries such as Japan, South Korea, Thailand, Brazil, and Argentina have considerably eased the restrictions on foreign ownership of domestic assets and companies.[9] In terms of the globalization of currencies, the Euro is already here; in addition, there now is increasing talk of "dollarization" (adoption of the U.S. dollar as the official currency) in major Latin American countries such as Brazil and Argentina.[10] To sum up, barriers to trade and investment among countries continue to decline rapidly and are making globalization increasingly more feasible and less expensive.

Second, technological advances continue their onward march. Table 1.5 depicts the sharp decline in the costs of air transportation, telecommunication, and computers since 1950.

The decline in transportation costs has radically shrunk the cost of shipping goods across countries. In the case of computers and communications, the steep

TABLE 1.3 Average Tariff Rates on Manufactured Products (Weighted average; percentage of value)

Country	1913	1950	1990
France	21	18	5.9
Germany	20	26	5.9
United Kingdom	—	23	5.9
Italy	18	25	5.9
Japan	30	—	5.3
United States	44	14	4.8

Abstracted from: *World Investment Report 1994*, UNCTAD.

TABLE 1.4 Liberalization in Investment Regimes

	1991	1994	1998
Total number of countries that changed their investment regimes	35	49	60
Total number of changes	82	110	145
Changes in the direction of liberalization or promotion	80	108	136
Changes in the direction of control	2	2	9

Abstracted from *World Investment Report 1999*, UNCTAD.

TABLE 1.5 Declining Costs of Air Transportation, Telecommunications, and Computers (In 1990 U.S. dollars unless otherwise indicated)

Year	Average Air Transportation Revenue/ Passenger Mile	Cost of a Three-Minute Call from New York to London	U.S. Department of Commerce Computer Price Deflator (1990 = 1000)
1950	0.30	53.20	—
1960	0.24	45.86	125,000
1970	0.16	31.58	19,474
1980	0.10	4.80	3,620
1990	0.11	3.32	1,000

Abstracted from *World Economic Outlook 1997*, International Monetary Fund; and Richard J. Herring and Robert E. Litan, *Financial Regulation in the Global Economy*, Washington, D.C.: Brookings Institution, 1995, p. 14.

decline in costs has continued unabated since 1990. Aside from radical cost decline, the decade of the 1990s also witnessed the emergence and widespread adoption of technologies such as videoconferencing, mobile telephony, e-mail, groupware such as Lotus Notes, and the Internet. These developments in information technology have dramatically reduced the "operative distance" between companies, their customers, and their suppliers and made coordination of far-flung operations not only more feasible but also more reliable and efficient.

Third, the economic center of gravity is shifting from the developed to the developing countries. Assuming certain infrastructural conditions, economic liberalization promotes competition, increases efficiency, fuels innovation, attracts new capital investment, and generally bears fruit in the form of faster economic growth. Not surprisingly, the embrace of market mechanisms has allowed the developing economies of the world to start catching up with the advanced economies. International organizations such as the IMF already count Korea, Taiwan, Hong Kong, and Singapore—some of the world's poorest countries in the 1950s—among the advanced economies. Other, even larger, economies are on their way to advancement, the most notable cases being China and India. Table 1.6 provides comparative data on the growth rates of the advanced, developing, and transition economies since 1981, along with projections through 2004. Despite the financial crisis of 1997–1999, on an aggregate basis the developing economies are estimated and projected to have grown at a faster rate than the advanced economies during 1997–2000.

Indeed, the world's economic center of gravity is shifting. The advanced economies are relatively mature and, for most industries, offer modest prospects for growth. In contrast, many developing economies are experiencing much faster growth in virtually every industry ranging from toothpaste and lightbulbs to home appliances, cars, computers, Internet services, and, not surprisingly, even fine wine. Thus, any company today that seeks to grow—be it ABB, Samsung, Sony, Coca-Cola, General Electric, Microsoft, Wal-Mart, or Amazon.com—has little choice but to go where the growth is. For the vast majority of the world's leading corporations, such growth is rarely just in the home market.

Finally, the opening of borders to trade, investment, and technology transfers is rarely a one-way street. While opening borders opens up new and much larger market opportunities for companies, it also opens up their home markets to competition from abroad. In other words, economic liberalization brings about not only

TABLE 1.6   Comparative Data on Economic Growth Rates of Different Groups of Countries (Annual percentage change in real GDP)

	1981–1988	1989–1996	Estimated 1997–2000	Projected 2001–2004
Advanced economies[a]	3.0	2.5	2.4	2.8
Developing economies[b]	4.2	5.7	4.3	5.8
Transition economies[c]	2.9	−4.7	0.9	4.6
World total	3.0	3.2	3.1	4.1

[a]28 countries; for the complete list, see *World Economic Outlook 1999*, International Monetary Fund.

[b]128 countries; for the complete list, see *World Economic Outlook 1999*, International Monetary Fund.

[c]28 countries; for the complete list, see *World Economic Outlook 1999*, International Monetary Fund.

Abstracted from *World Economic Outlook 1999*, International Monetary Fund.

access to a much larger market but also more intense competition. As a consequence, it fuels the ongoing race among competitors to seek a first-mover advantage in serving globalizing customers, capturing economies of global scale, exploiting the cost-reducing or quality-enhancing potential of optimal locations, and tapping technological advancements wherever they may occur. The net result of this competitive dynamic is that the quest for economies of global scale and scope has now become a self-feeding frenzy—be it in automobiles, aluminum, pharmaceuticals, tires, retailing, or Internet commerce. As the business historian Louis Galambos has observed, "Global oligopolies are as inevitable as the sunrise."[11]

WHY GLOBALIZATION IS HERE TO STAY

It is important to remember that, notwithstanding the increasing obviousness of today's "global village," the early twenty-first century is not the first time that we have witnessed the emergence of globalization.[12] Relatively unfettered trade, capital flows, and migration of people across national borders were very much a reality in many parts of the world during the period from the mid-nineteenth century to World War I. Barriers around national borders began to go up in 1914 and it was only in 1970 that the ratio of exports to world output again caught up with the figure for 1913.

There are, however, major quantitative and qualitative differences between the globalization of today and that of a hundred years ago. Average tariff rates are much lower now than at any time in the past two hundred years. And, relative to world GDP, the volumes of international trade, foreign direct investment, portfolio investment, and technology flows are much greater than ever. In the late nineteenth century, the term *globalization* would have been interpreted largely in terms of international trade and the flows of private capital from a few rich families to finance the building of railroads and other infrastructure in the new world. It also would have referred to economic integration among a relatively small number of wealthy countries. In contrast, the globalization of today encompasses every corner of the earth, is financed by the savings and retirement funds of billions of people, and is far more multidimensional and deeper than ever before. The present-day global enterprise—with interlinked value chain activities dispersed across the world—was virtually unknown and might well have been unthinkable in the late nineteenth century.[13] Barring unforeseeable and catastrophic developments, it would appear that in the emerging digital era, globalization is here to stay.

When we say that we are now in the digital age, what we usually mean is the following set of trends:

- *Convergence between computing and communications technologies and the spread of the Internet:* The number of Internet users worldwide stood at 350 million in mid-2000 and is expected to exceed one billion well before the end of the decade.

- *Ongoing increase in the power of the computing and communications technologies coupled with an ongoing decline in the cost of these technologies:* Over the past twenty years, bandwidth capabilities have increased more than a thousand times while the cost of transmitting one million bits of data over one kilometer has declined by a similar factor.[14]

- *Emergence of ubiquitous point-and-click interfaces that are based on open standards, are cheap to set up and run, and are global:* You can now send an e-mail message, access your brokerage account, or place an order to buy chemicals or steel from almost any computer with almost any type of Internet browser in any corner of the world.

- *The anticipated roll-out of broadband communications technologies over the next five to ten years across major parts of the world:* Always-on Internet connections running at 2 megabits per second are expected to become a reality in more than 70 percent of the households in the developed countries over the next five to ten years.[15]

- *The ongoing explosive growth in mobile communications (for both voice telephony and Internet usage) in developed as well as developing regions of the world:* The number of mobile phone users is expected to have increased to one billion people—one sixth of the world's entire population—before the end of 2002.[16]

It is a certainty that digital technologies will continue to make ours an increasingly connected world. Nonetheless, the emerging digital era is likely to be at best a mixed blessing for the global enterprise and for those responsible for leading it. On one hand, in a digital world you will have radically enhanced access to a wider base of potential customers and resources worldwide. On the other hand, this will also be true for your current competitors—and a whole range of potential competitors as well. Moreover, in the digital age, corporations will operate in a more transparent environment that will enable and foster greater comparison shopping by customers, faster imitation by competitors, and demands for enhanced accountability by investors. As Daniel Yergin has observed, "The global shareholder is going to be an ever-tougher taskmaster. It's mathematically impossible for every company to be No. 1 or 2 in its market and for every fund manager to be in the upper quartile. As performance becomes more transparent, and information more accessible, the pressures [on companies] will only increase. There will be no rest, no matter how great the weariness."[17]

IMPLICATIONS FOR COMPANIES

By definition, all strategic action represents a dialog between the company and its environment. Every company must adapt to the changes in its environment that are inevitable. Yet there are choices. First, you can choose whether to be a first mover or a laggard in anticipating these changes and turning them into competitive advantage. Second, and perhaps more critically, you often have the power to shape the direction as well as the pace of environmental changes in ways that are more favorable to your own firm.

There are several fundamental changes in the global economic landscape that we regard as inevitable. *First, the economic map of the world will change more radically in the next twenty years than it has in the past twenty.* Given the commitment of the post-Deng Chinese leadership to a widening and deepening of economic reforms, China will likely remain a particularly interesting economic story. Notwithstanding its rapid growth since 1979, China's economy has begun to acquire bulk only during the past few years. Because of the magic of compounding, continuation of high growth rates over the next two decades would have significantly greater material effect on the world's economic topography with each new year. In any case, China will be just one of the many interesting economic stories. Major countries such as India, Brazil, and Mexico have embraced economic reforms and begun the process of global integration only within the past ten years. As these economies continue to gather momentum, they will increasingly become major contributors to the creation of new wealth on this planet. Thus it is a reasonable bet that in twenty years the economic center of gravity would not be merely shifting toward the developing countries, it may lie squarely in the middle of what we currently regard as the developing countries.

Second, the regional composition of the world's five hundred to one thousand largest corporations will be radically different in twenty years from what it is today. As a consequence, intraindustry competition will become significantly more intense. The *Financial Times* year 2000 list of the world's five hundred largest companies, based on market capitalization, included only three companies from India and (excluding seven companies based in Hong Kong) none from China.[18] Given the increasing bulk of these two economies (China and India), we deem it unthinkable that, in the year 2020, the composition of the world's largest five hundred to a thousand companies will look anything like what it does today. China has already started a process of massive consolidation coupled with privatization. The list of state-owned enterprises likely to become globally prominent giants includes Baoshan Iron & Steel (steelmaking), Haier Group (appliances), Sichuan Changhong (television), North China Pharmaceutical (drugs), Jiangnan Shipyard Group (shipbuilding), Peking University Founder Group (computer software), and Legend Holdings (personal computers).[19] As an illustration, consider Sichuan Changhong, China's largest television manufacturer, with a production volume of about 10 million sets annually in 1999–2000. Changhong has stated publicly that it fully intends to join the ranks of the Global 500 as soon as it can. There are similar companies in a multitude of other industries that are currently in their adolescence and that are likely to emerge as major global players early in the twenty-first century. As Ernst Behrens, president of Siemens China, observed: "Western companies have been downloading technology and know-how into China intensively in the last eight to ten years. Of course it has to bear fruit and it does. I am certain we will be confronted with Chinese competition in the same way as we are confronted with Japanese, Korean, and western competition today in five or ten years."[20]

As an illustration from India, consider Infosys Technologies, a software-services provider that in March 1999 became the first Indian company to be listed on NASDAQ. By late 2000, its market capitalization exceeded U.S. $16 billion. According to Narayana Murthy, chairman of Infosys, a NASDAQ listing makes "doors open much easier" and gives his company the muscle to hire top professionals and make acquisitions globally, particularly in the United States and Europe.[21] Other emerging software giants from India include TCS, Satyam Infoway, WIPRO, NIIT, and HCL Group. Software exports from India are currently growing at 50 percent a year and many observers expect the export figures to grow from $4 billion in 1999 to $50 billion in 2008.[22] Should these numbers materialize even halfway, in ten years' time, software giants from India might become as well known as Oracle or SAP are today.[23] The list of emerging global giants from India is not confined to the software sector only. In financial services, ICICI was listed on the NYSE in 1999. Some other giants include Ranbaxy in pharmaceuticals, Reliance Industries in petrochemicals, and the diversified Tata Group in a variety of manufacturing and service industries.

To this list of budding powerhouses from China and India, one must also add rapidly growing players from other big emerging economies such as Brazil and Mexico. In short, if you think that, having witnessed the emergence of global players from Japan, Korea, and Taiwan over the past twenty years, you understand what intense competition really means, watch out. Compared to the world of 2020, this may have been just a warm-up.

Third, the ongoing technology revolution will make real-time coordination of globally dispersed operations routine. International telecommunications prices have already fallen by more than 75 percent over the past ten years. According to many predictions, cost and price declines over the next ten years are likely to be even steeper—that is, we should expect to pay less than 10 percent of what we paid in 2000. Combine these trends with mobile and broadband telecommunications (voice, video, and Internet) and it is inevitable that real-time coordination with globally dispersed customers, suppliers, and across the company's own subsidiaries will become commonplace over the next twenty years. One major outcome of these trends will be a further increase in the intensity of global competition and an even more desperate search for the best locations for the execution of discrete activities in the company's value chain.

Assuming that these trends are inevitable, we believe that the following questions merit serious consideration for inclusion in the strategic agenda of any medium-sized or large company today:

• *What must be (versus is) the extent of your market presence in the world's major markets, particularly the major emerging markets, for your products and services? How should you build the necessary global presence?* Rapid economic growth around the world, particularly in the emerging economies, will continue to create huge demand for virtually everything—be it shoes, cement, fast food, refrigerators, computer software, insurance, or management consulting services. Explicitly or implicitly, your decisions and actions will help determine who will supply the products and services to meet this demand—your company, your current competitors, or new entrants. Given the largely borderless nature of the Internet, many start-ups in the high-technology sector are now realizing that they have little choice but to globalize at Internet speed—lest some other player pre-empt them, perhaps by imitating their business model, and occupy the global marketspace. For such companies, the evolutionary trajectory may well need to be something along the following lines: start up in year one, entry into another major region in year two, and full-scale globalization by year three or four.

• *What must be (versus is) the extent to which you capture the cost-reducing and quality-enhancing potential of optimal locations around the world for the execution of various activities in your company's value chain? How should you reduce the existing suboptimalities?* Countries differ in cost structures, in ways of looking at the world, and in the pool of talent and ideas being generated on an ongoing basis. Capturing the comparative advantages of countries effectively and efficiently can create significant competitive advantage for your company. Witness the case of Nike, which must constantly scout for the lowest-cost manufacturing locations, and Microsoft, which must constantly scout for the best software talent wherever it may reside. Similarly, you have no choice but to look at the world not merely as a market to exploit but also as a potential gold mine to reduce your cost structure, recruit needed talent, and tap for new ideas.

• *What must be (versus is) the effectiveness with which you are able to exploit global presence and turn it into true global competitive advantage, as opposed to global mediocrity or even global mess? How should you eliminate the existing shortcomings?* As we suggested earlier, global presence does not automatically translate into global competitive advantage. In fact, without systematic analysis, purposeful thinking, and careful orchestration, widespread global presence can easily degenerate into managerial distraction, resource duplication, and inefficiency. Thus you must constantly examine whether you are indeed doing the hard work needed to transform global presence into global competitive advantage.

• *Is the mindset of your company's top management, indeed every employee, sufficiently global? As the world around you changes and new opportunities open up in various corners of the world, is your company generally a leader or a laggard in identifying and exploiting these opportunities? How should you create the needed global mindset?* Managers, like all people, are the products of their origins and past experiences. It matters where you were born, what cultural environment you grew up in, where you live, who you interact with, what media you are exposed to, and what you see and hear with your eyes and ears as you go about your daily business. Being human, each one of us individually is and will remain at least somewhat parochial. However, collectively, in the form of an enterprise such as Cisco, IBM, Sony, or ABB, we do have the possibility of creating a truly global mindset that treats the entire world as its home, that is sensitive to important events in any corner of the world, and that has the wisdom to differentiate between value-creating, value-destroying, and value-neutral opportunities. You must constantly ask whether your company has that type of a global mindset today and take developmental action, as needed.

We conclude this chapter by focusing on the implications of globalization for individual managers. We predict that knowledge, skills, and experience regarding how to navigate the company in a global environment will become increasingly a core requirement for promotion to leadership positions. We also believe that the need for global knowledge and skills will rapidly become crucial not just at senior levels in the company but at all levels and in all units. A systems analyst in Stockholm may interact on a daily basis with software programmers in India. An R&D team may work on a collaborative development project spread across the United States, Japan, and Switzerland. A plant manager in Detroit may have crucial dependencies on auto parts suppliers in Mexico, Brazil, and Germany. A sales representative based in Atlanta may be an integral member of a global account management team serving the customers' needs across multiple locations on a coordinated basis.

Thus, aside from promotion to senior ranks, succeeding in one's job will depend increasingly on skills at managing across national and cultural borders. Look at the career of Douglas M. Daft, chairman and CEO of The Coca-Cola Company since February 2000. An Australian national, he joined Coca-Cola in the Sydney office in 1969. He then held various positions in diverse markets in the Asia-Pacific region. In 1988, he became president of Coca-Cola Japan as well as of the North Pacific Division. His subsequent responsibilities included presidencies of the Pacific Group (1991), the Middle and Far East Group (1995), and the Africa Group (1999). In 1999, he became president and chief operating officer of the company and, a few months later, was appointed chairman and CEO. It appears quite likely that such a career track will become the norm rather than the exception for the corporate leaders of tomorrow.

SUMMARY

Globalization refers to growing economic interdependence among countries as reflected in increasing cross-border flows of three types of entities: goods and services, capital, and know-how. Based on both logic and factual data, we believe that globalization is here to stay. As Thomas Friedman of The *New York Times* has observed recently: "While pampered college students and academics in the West continue to debate about whether countries should globalize, the two biggest countries in the world, India and China—who represent one-third of humanity—have long moved beyond that question. They have decided that opening their economies to trade in goods and services is the best way to lift their people out of abject poverty and are now focused simply on how to globalize in the most stable manner. Some prefer to go faster, and some prefer to phase out currency controls and subsidies gradually, but the debate about the direction they need to go is over."[24]

Notwithstanding the huge changes we have already witnessed in the past two decades, the extent and pace of change in the next two decades will almost certainly be much greater. In our view, the inevitability of such changes implies that companies and managers today face a relatively simple choice: Get on board or get left behind.

CHAPTER 2

DEVELOPING A GLOBAL EXPANSION STRATEGY

There is a race and a lot of people are qualified for the race. But to go global, you need to be early enough. Generally in new countries you need to be the first in for the first win. When you arrive as number three or four, it is too late.

—*Daniel Bernard, Chairman, Carrefour, 1998*[1]

THIS CHAPTER starts by answering the question *Why* do firms globalize? The next logical question is *How* do firms pursue global expansion? Becoming global is never exclusively the result of grand design. Nor is it simply a sequence of incremental, ad hoc, opportunistic, and random moves. The wisest approach is one of *directed opportunism*, an approach that maintains opportunism and flexibility within a broad path set by a systematic framework.

The framework and set of conceptual ideas presented in this chapter can guide firms in approaching the strategic challenge of casting their business lines overseas and establishing global presence. How should the firm choose which of its multiple product lines it should use as the initial launch vehicle for the global market? What factors make some markets more strategic than others? What should companies consider in determining the right mode of entry? How should the enterprise transplant the corporate DNA as it enters new markets? What approaches should the company use to win the local battle? And how rapidly should a company expand globally? Addressing these six issues—choice of products, choice of strategic markets, mode of entry, transplanting the corporate DNA, winning the local battle, and speed of global expansion—helps firms go about building global presence in a systematic manner.[2] This chapter provides frameworks and models for resolving the six issues.

THE IMPERATIVES TO GLOBALIZE

There are five imperatives that drive any firm to pursue global expansion. Because of differences in industry structure and the firm's strategic position, the intensity of these factors can be expected to differ across firms and, for the same firm, over time.

The growth imperative. For many industries, developed country markets are quite mature. Thus the growth imperative generally requires companies to look to emerging markets for fresh opportunities. Consider a supposedly mature industry such as paper. Per capita paper consumption in developed markets such as North America and Western Europe is around six hundred pounds. In contrast, per capita consumption of paper in China and India is around thirty pounds.[3] If you are a leading paper manufacturer today, can you really afford not to build market presence in places like China or India? We doubt it. If per capita paper consumption in both China and India increased by just one pound over the next five years, demand would increase by 2.2 billion pounds, an amount that can keep five state-of-the-art paper mills running at peak capacity.

The efficiency imperative. Whenever there are one or more activities in the value chain (research and development, production, and so on) where the minimum efficient scale exceeds the sales volume feasible within one country, a company with global presence will have the potential to create a cost advantage relative to a domestic player within that industry. Mercedes-Benz, now a unit of DaimlerChrysler, illustrates this principle. Historically, Mercedes-Benz concentrated its research and manufacturing operations in Germany but derived its revenues from the entire global market. Given the highly scale-sensitive nature of the auto industry, it is clear from the company's annual reports that Mercedes-Benz's ability to compete in Europe, or even Germany, has for long depended not just on its market position in Europe (or Germany) but also worldwide.

The knowledge imperative. No two countries, even close neighbors such as Canada and the United States, are completely alike. Therefore, when a company expands its presence to more than one country, it must adapt some features of its products and processes to the local environment. This adaptation requires the creation of local know-how. Some of this know-how may be too idiosyncratic to be relevant outside the particular local market. However, in many cases, local product or process innovations emerge as world-leading innovations and thus have the potential to generate global advantage. For instance, GE India's innovations in making CT scanners simpler, more transportable, and cheaper, like P&G Indonesia's innovations in reducing the cost structure for cough syrup, would appear to enjoy wide-ranging applicability.

Globalization of customers. The phrase "globalization of customers" refers to customers who are global corporations (such as soft drinks companies served by advertising agencies) as well as those who are globally mobile (corporate executives served by American Express or global travelers served by hotels such as Sheraton). When the customers of a domestic company start to globalize, the firm must keep pace with them. These customers may strongly prefer worldwide consistency and coordination in the sourcing of products and services or they may prefer to deal with a small number of supply partners on a long-term basis. Furthermore, allowing customers to deal with different suppliers in other countries puts a company at risk of losing them to one of these suppliers even in the domestic market. It is motivations such as these that have driven GE Plastics to become global. Whereas historically it supplied plastic pellets to largely U.S.–based telephone companies (such as AT&T and GTE), as these companies globalized, setting up manufacturing plants outside the United States, GE Plastics' annual reports show the company had no choice but to follow its customers abroad.

Globalization of competitors. If your competitors start to globalize and you do not, you become vulnerable to a two-pronged attack. First, they can develop a first-mover advantage in capturing market growth, pursuing global scale efficiencies, profiting from knowledge arbitrage, and providing a coordinated source of supply to global customers. Second, they can use multimarket presence to cross-subsidize and wage a more intense attack in your own home markets. Underestimating the rate at which competition can accelerate the pace of globalization is dangerous. Look at Fuji's inroads into the U.S. film market, historically dominated by Kodak.

CHOICE OF PRODUCTS FOR LAUNCHING GLOBALIZATION

When any multiproduct firm decides to go abroad, it must also decide whether it should globalize its entire portfolio simultaneously or whether it should use a subset of product lines as the launching pad for initial globalization. Consider the case of Marriott Corporation, which was essentially a domestic company in the late 1980s.[4] The company had two principal lines of business: lodging and contract services. Within the lodging sector, four of the major product lines were full-service hotels and resorts (Marriott brand), midprice hotels (Courtyard brand), budget price hotels (Fairfield Inn brand), and long-term stay hotels (Residence Inn brand). On the other hand, the contract services sector consisted of the following three product lines: Marriott Management Services, Host/Travel Plazas, and Marriott Senior Living Services (retirement communities). As the company embarked on its globalization venture, it had to confront the question of which one or more of these product lines should serve as the starting point for its globalization efforts. How should Marriott address this question?

Global expansion forces companies to develop at least three types of capabilities: knowledge about foreign markets, skills at managing people in foreign locations, and skills at managing foreign subsidiaries. Without these capabilities, firms are likely to remain strangers in a strange land, with global expansion posing a high risk. Globalizing the entire portfolio of products at once compounds these risks dramatically. Often it is wiser to choose only one or a small number of product lines as the initial launch vehicle for globalization. The choice of launch vehicle should adhere to the twin goals of maximizing the returns while minimizing the risks associated with early globalization moves. For the corporation, these initial moves represent experiments with high learning potential and it is important that these experiments succeed: success builds psychological confidence, credibility within the corporation, and last but not least, cash flow to fuel further rapid globalization.

Figure 2.1 presents a conceptual framework to identify those products, business units, or lines of business that might be preferred candidates for early globalization. Using this framework, each line of business in the company's portfolio should be evaluated along two dimensions: one pertaining to potential returns (that is, expected payoffs) and the other to potential risks (that is, required degree of local adaptation).

The first dimension focuses on the magnitude of globalization's payoffs. These payoffs tend to be higher when the globalization imperatives are stronger.[5] In the case of Marriott Corporation, these imperatives clearly are much stronger for full-service lodging, whose primary customers are globe-trotting executives, than they are for the retirement community business. In the full-service lodging business, a worldwide presence can create significant value by using a centralized reservation system, developing and diffusing globally consistent service concepts, and leveraging a well-known brand name on whose high quality and service customers can rely. In contrast, none of these factors is pivotal in the retirement community business—thereby rendering the imperatives for globalization much less urgent.

The second dimension in our framework concerns the extent to which different lines of business require local adaptation to succeed in foreign markets. The greater the extent of required adaptation, the greater the degree to which new

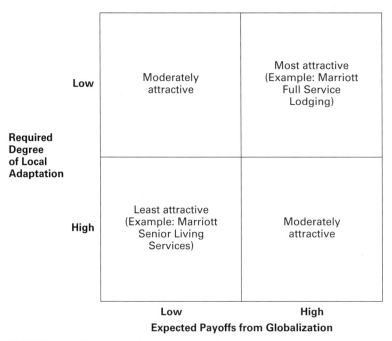

FIGURE 2.1 A Framework for Choice of Products

product or service features would need to be developed locally, as opposed to cloning proven and preexisting concepts and capabilities. Any new development involves risk, and the greater the need for local adaptation, the greater the risks— particularly when such development entails the already significant "liability of foreignness." Marriott Corporation exemplifies these principles. Compared to full-service lodging, the retirement community business is a very local business, and hence requires more local adaptation.

Combining both dimensions, as indicated in Figure 2.1, full-service lodging emerges as a particularly attractive candidate for early globalization. In fact, as the spearhead for globalization moves, full-service lodging provides Marriott with a high-return, low-risk laboratory for developing knowledge and skills pertaining to foreign market entry and managing foreign subsidiaries. Having overcome the liability of foreignness, Marriott would be much better positioned to exploit the globalization potential of its other lines of business.

In sum, almost no line of business today is devoid of potential for exploitation on a global scale. However, any multiproduct firm that is starting to globalize must remember that a logically sequenced, as opposed to random, approach is likely to serve as a higher-return, lower-risk path toward full-scale globalization.

CHOICE OF STRATEGIC MARKETS

Consider the case of Dell Computers, which until the early 1990s was a largely U.S.–based domestic company. When Dell embarked on building a global presence, it could choose among a wide array of options as to the regional or country markets that it could enter. In a situation such as this, how does a company decide which markets it should enter first and what its sequence of global expansion should be? Of course, one option is to pursue opportunities in an ad hoc, random fashion. In a dynamic environment, we accept the relevance of an opportunistic stance. However, we have observed that, rather than merely muddling through the opportunities as they emerge, effective globalizers engage instead in *directed opportunism,* that is, opportunism guided by a systematic and logical framework.

The sequence with which a globalizing company enters various markets should depend on two factors: the strategic importance of the market, and the firm's ability to exploit that market. Going after a strategic market without the ability to exploit it is generally a fast track to disaster.

The first factor, "strategic importance of a market," encompasses current and future market size as well as the learning opportunities offered by that market. Notwithstanding the importance of the size of a country's economy, potential market size does not always go hand-in-hand with the country's GDP. Some authors, overlooking this reality, have derived highly simplistic conclusions to the effect that companies are not global unless they are present in the triad of Europe, Japan, and United States. Such conclusions are often absolutely fallacious. If, for example, you are managing ABB's power plant business, the bulk of your market for new power plants lies outside the triad countries. The same is true for highrise elevators manufactured by companies such as Otis or Mitsubishi and for paper machines manufactured and sold by companies such as Valmet or Voith.

Let's look now at variations in learning opportunities offered by different markets. Such opportunities are likely to be high when the market is populated by sophisticated and demanding customers who would force the company to meet the world's toughest standards for quality, cost, cycle time, and a host of other attributes—thereby giving the company a head start in developing leading-edge innovations and in learning about the market needs of tomorrow. For example, France and Italy are leading-edge customer markets for the high-fashion clothing industry, a fact of significant importance to a company such as DuPont, which manufactures Lycra and other textile fibers.[6] Learning opportunities also depend on the pace at which relevant technologies are evolving in the particular market. This technology evolution can emerge from one or more of several sources: leading-edge customers, innovative competitors, universities and other local research centers, and firms in related industries.

The second factor, "ability to exploit a market," depends on the height of entry barriers and the intensity of competition within the market. Entry barriers are likely to be lowest when there are no regulatory constraints on trade and investment (as in the case of regional economic blocks) and when new markets are geographically, culturally, and linguistically proximate to the domestic market. However, even when such entry barriers are low, the intensity of competition can hinder a company's potential for exploiting a market. For example, the large U.S. market in the apparel retailing industry has often proved to be a graveyard for foreign entrants such as Marks & Spencer, precisely because of the intensity of local competition. Figure 2.2 presents a conceptual framework that combines the two key dimensions—"strategic importance of market" and "ability to exploit"—to offer guidelines to firms that want to engage in directed opportunism in their choice of markets.

A firm's stance toward markets that have high strategic importance and high ability to exploit should be "must enter rapidly." By comparison, the firm can afford to be much more opportunistic and ad hoc in markets that have low strategic importance but are easier to exploit. In the case of markets that have high strategic importance but are also very difficult to exploit, we recommend an incremental, phased approach where the development of needed capabilities precedes market entry. One way in which a company can develop such capabilities is to first enter a *beachhead market*: this would be a market that, while closely resembling the targeted strategic market, provides a lower-risk opportunity to learn how to enter and succeed in the chosen strategic market. Typical examples of beachhead markets are Switzerland or Austria for Germany, Canada for the United States, and Hong Kong or Taiwan for China. Finally, the firm should steer clear of those markets that are neither strategic nor easy to exploit.

The next box summarizes the global expansion of Ikea over the past two decades and illustrates our framework for choosing target markets.

As a final observation, we would like to emphasize that these frameworks should be applied not at the level of the firm as a whole but at the level of the individual business units within the firm.

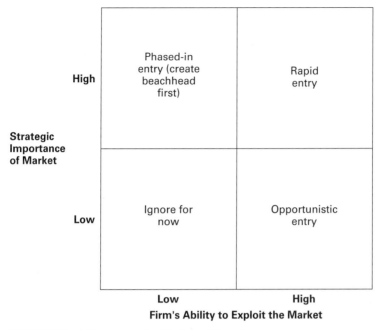

FIGURE 2.2   A Framework for Choice of Markets

MODE OF ENTRY

Once a company has selected the country or countries to enter and designated the product lines that will serve as the launch vehicles, it must determine the appropriate mode of entry. At this point, the company must look at two fundamental issues. The first is the extent to which it will rely on exports to versus local production within the target market. Figure 2.3 depicts some of the choices available to a firm. It can rely on 100 percent export of finished goods, export of components but localized assembly, 100 percent local production, and so forth. The second issue is the extent of ownership control over activities that will be performed locally in the target market. Here, companies' options range from 0 percent ownership modes (licensing, franchising, and the like) or partial ownership modes (such as joint ventures or affiliates) to 100 percent ownership modes (fully owned greenfield operations or acquisitions).

Choosing the right mode of entry is critical because this choice, once made, is often difficult and costly to alter. Inappropriate decisions can impose unwanted, unnecessary, and undesirable constraints on the options for future development.

Turning to the first issue, greater reliance on local production would be appropriate under the following conditions:

- *Size of local market is larger than minimum efficient scale of production.* The larger the local market, the more completely local production will translate into scale economies for the firm while minimizing tariff and

BOX *2-1*

TIME LINE OF IKEA EXPANSION

1958	First store in Sweden
1963	Enters Norway
1969	Enters Denmark
1973	Enters Switzerland
1974	Enters Germany
1975	Enters Australia
1976	Enters Canada
1976	Enters Austria
1978	Enters Singapore
1979	Enters Holland
1981	Enters France
1983	Enters Saudi Arabia
1984	Enters Belgium and Kuwait
1985	Enters United States
1987	Enters United Kingdom and Hong Kong
1989	Enters Italy
1990	Enters Hungary and Poland
1991	Enters Czech Republic and United Arab Emirates
1992	Enters Slovakia
1994	Enters Taiwan
1996	Enters Finland, Malaysia, and Spain
1998	Enters mainland China

Strategic Importance of Market	Ability to Exploit — Low	Ability to Exploit — High
High	United States (Beachhead: Canada) China (Beachhead: Taiwan and Hong Kong)	Germany France Italy United Kingdom
Low		Norway Denmark Finland Holland

transportation costs. Bridgestone's entry into the U.S. market by acquiring the local production base of Firestone instead of exporting tires from Japan illustrates this point.

- *Excessive shipping and tariff costs discourage exporting to the target market.* In some cases, shipping and tariff costs are so high as to neutralize any cost advantages associated with producing in any country other than the target market. This is the primary reason that cement companies such as Cemex and Lafarge Coppee rely heavily on local production in the countries that they have entered.

- *Need for local customization of product design is high.* Product customization requires two capabilities: a deep understanding of local market needs accompanied by an ability to incorporate this understanding in the company's design and production decisions. Localization of production in the target market greatly enhances the firm's ability to respond to local market needs accurately and efficiently.

- *Local content requirements are strong.* If the size of the local market is large and government regulations require significant local content, the globalizing

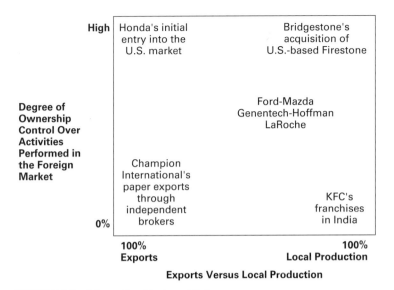

FIGURE 2.3 Alternative Modes of Entry

enterprise has little choice but to comply. This is one of the reasons why telecom equipment companies such as Nokia, Ericsson, Motorola, and Siemens rely on significant local production in order to serve the Chinese market. Along the same lines, constraints imposed on foreign auto companies to adhere to local content requirements have forced them to rely heavily on local production in markets such as the EU, China, and India.[7]

As noted earlier, the second issue pertains to the extent of ownership and control over the locally performed activities. Given their differing costs and benefits, neither alliances nor complete ownership are universally desirable in all situations. Unlike the complete ownership mode, alliance-based entry modes have several advantages: permitting the firm to share the costs and risks associated with market entry, allowing rapid access to local know-how, and giving managers the flexibility to respond more entrepreneurially and more quickly to dynamic global competition than is offered by the conquer-the-world-by-yourself approach. However, a major downside of alliances is their potential for various types of conflict stemming from differences in corporate goals and corporate cultures. To quote Judy Lewent, chief financial officer at Merck: "The beauty of a joint venture is the elimination of the risk and elimination of an acquisition premium. The downside is the complexity of managing the venture and having to share the pie."[8]

Taking into account both the pros and the cons, alliance-based entry modes often are more appropriate under the following conditions:

- *Physical, linguistic, and cultural distance between the host and the home country is high.* The more dissimilar and unfamiliar the target market, the greater the need for the firm to rely on a local partner to provide needed local know-how and networks. Conceivably, the firm could obtain the requisite local knowledge and competencies through an acquisition. However, if no suitable acquisition candidates are available or if the firm's ability to manage an acquired subsidiary in a highly dissimilar market is quite limited, then an alliance-based entry mode may be the best strategy to access local know-how and relationships. It is this set of reasons that explain AOL's decision to enter many European, Asian, and Latin American markets through the joint venture route.

- *The subsidiary's operational integration with the rest of the global operations would be minimal.* By definition, tighter integration between a subsidiary and the rest of the global network increases the degree of mutual interdependence between them. In this context of high interdependence, it becomes crucial that the subsidiary and the network pursue shared goals and that the firm be able to reshape the subsidiary according to the changing needs of the rest of the network. Shared ownership of the local subsidiary puts major constraints on the firm's ability to achieve such congruence in goals and on its freedom to reshape the subsidiary operations when needed, so such ownership is desirable mainly when it seems unlikely that the subsidiary's activities will affect the rest of the network.

- *The risk of asymmetric learning by the partner is (or can be kept) low.* In the typical joint venture, two partners pool different but complementary know-how into an alliance. Ongoing interaction between their core operations and the alliance gives each partner an opportunity to learn from the other and to appropriate the partner's complementary know-how. In effect, this dynamic implies that the alliance often is not just a cooperative relationship but also a learning race.[9] If Firm A has the ability to learn at a faster rate than Firm B, the outcome is likely to be asymmetric learning in favor of Firm A. Over time, Firm A may seek to dissolve the alliance in favor of going it alone in competition with a still-disadvantaged Firm B.

- *The company is short of capital.* Lack of capital underlay Xerox Corporation's decision in the 1950s to enter the European market through an alliance with the U.K.–based Rank Organization.[10]

- *Government regulations require local equity participation.* Historically, many countries with formidable market potential (such as China, India, and Brazil) have been successful in imposing the joint venture option on foreign entrants, even when all other considerations might have favored the choice of a complete ownership mode. Recently, however, it is noteworthy that the creation of regional economic blocks (such as the EU, NAFTA, and Mercosur) and the ongoing adoption of liberal trade and investment policies by most nations worldwide is lessening the impact of government regulations on the mode of entry decision in an increasing number of industries.

A firm that decides to enter the foreign market through local production rather than through exports faces a secondary decision: whether to set up greenfield operations or to use an existing production base through a cross-border acquisition. A greenfield operation gives the company tremendous freedom to impose its own unique management policies, culture, and mode of operations on the new subsidiary. In contrast, a cross-border acquisition poses the much tougher challenge of cultural transformation and post-merger integration. On the other hand, setting up greenfield operations also has two potential liabilities: lower speed of entry, and more intense local competition caused by the addition of new production capacity along with one more competitor. Taking into account both the pros and the cons, Figure 2.4 provides a conceptual framework to determine when greenfield operations or cross-border acquisitions are likely to be the more appropriate entry mode.

This framework has two dimensions. In terms of the first dimension—the uniqueness of the globalizing company's culture—Nucor Corporation is a good example of a newly globalizing firm with a very strong and unique culture. Nucor differs significantly from other steel producers in its human resource policies, egalitarian work environment, performance-based incentives, teamwork, decentralization, and business processes.[11] The more committed a company is to preserving its unique culture, the more necessary it becomes to set up greenfield operations in the foreign markets. Building and nurturing a unique culture from scratch (as would be feasible in the case of a greenfield operation) is almost always easier than transforming an entrenched culture (as would be necessary in the case of a cross-border acquisition).

Aside from corporate culture considerations, a firm must also consider the impact of entry mode on the resulting intensity of local competition. If the local

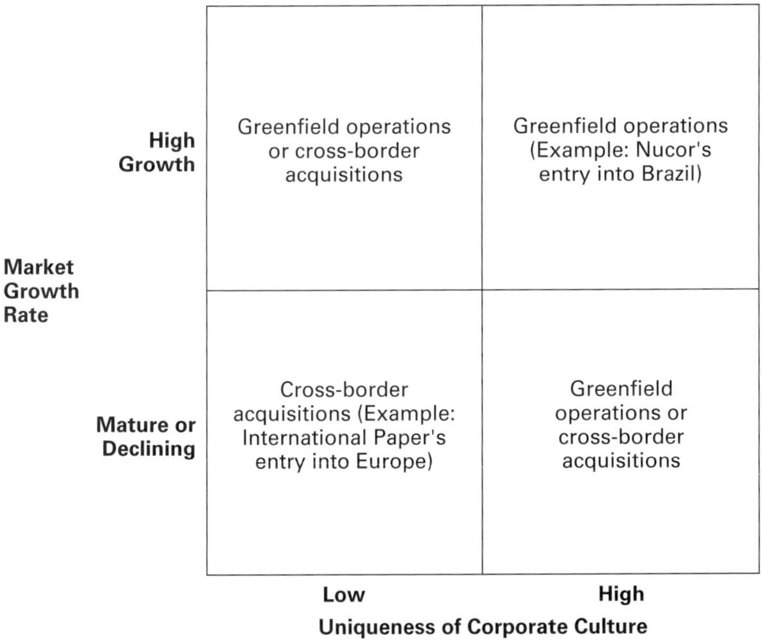

Market Growth Rate		Low	High
	High Growth	Greenfield operations or cross-border acquisitions	Greenfield operations (Example: Nucor's entry into Brazil)
	Mature or Declining	Cross-border acquisitions (Example: International Paper's entry into Europe)	Greenfield operations or cross-border acquisitions
		Uniqueness of Corporate Culture	

FIGURE 2.4 Greenfield Versus Cross-Border Acquisition

market is in the emerging or high-growth phase (as with the market for mobile phones in India and China), new capacity additions would have little downside effect on the intensity of competition. In contrast, when the local market is mature (as with the tire industry in the United States), new capacity additions will only intensify an already high degree of local competition. For example, in the forest products industry, Asia Pulp & Paper has chosen the greenfield mode for its expansion into other high-growth Asian markets. In contrast, in the same industry, the U.S.–based International Paper has pursued a different path, relying on the acquisition mode for its expansion into the mature European market.

In short, it follows that a company with a highly unique culture should have a clear preference for the greenfield mode when entering a high-growth market. At the other extreme, a company with a less unique culture should have a clear preference for the acquisition mode when entering a mature market. However, in the mixed case of a company with a highly unique culture entering a mature market or one with a less unique culture entering a high-growth market, the choice of mode should depend on the particular circumstances and nature of the opportunity.

TRANSPLANTING THE CORPORATE DNA

Having decided on the mode of entry for a particular product line into a particular target market, a company moves on to its next challenge: the implementation of actual entry. One of the most important things the globalizing company must figure out is how to transplant the core elements of its business model, its core practices, and its core beliefs—in short, its DNA—to the new subsidiary. The following examples illustrate the experience of two U.S. companies in their efforts to transplant their respective DNAs.

After acquiring two thousand employees from Yamaichi Securities, Merrill Lynch & Co. counted on its American-style investment adviser approach to establish a high-trust image in the securities brokerage industry in Japan. Historically, the brokerage industry in Japan has earned a poor reputation. "One well-known abuse ... is 'churning'—in which sales people persuade naive investors to buy and sell a lot of securities so the sales people can boost their commissions. Merrill Lynch promised that there would be no churning. Instead, its sales people were instructed to try to get an overall picture of customers' finances, ascertain their needs and then suggest investments. Something got lost in the translation, however. Japanese customers have complained that Merrill Lynch sales people are too nosy, asking questions about their investments instead of just telling them what stocks to buy."[12]

When the Walt Disney Company opened its Euro Disney theme park near Paris in the early 1990s, it faced considerable resistance from French applicants, employees, and labor leaders on the issue of grooming requirements. Following its core practices in the United States and their successful replication at Tokyo Disneyland in Japan, the company was strict in enforcing "a dress code, a ban on facial hair, a ban on colored stockings, standards for neat hair and fingernails, and a policy of appropriate undergarments."[13] These requirements were severely and publicly criticized by French labor leaders as well as the French media, which made recruitment and retention more difficult for the company, particularly in the beginning.

As these examples illustrate, obstacles to transplanting the corporate DNA can emerge from any of several sources: local employees, local customers, local regulations, and so forth. Given such obstacles, every company must be absolutely clear about exactly what its true core beliefs and practices are. Having achieved this clarity, the company would know where it should stay committed to its own beliefs and practices and where it should be willing be adapt. Then the company has to set to work constructing mechanisms to transfer core beliefs and practices to the new subsidiary. Finally, and most important, the company must be able to embed these beliefs and practices in the new subsidiary.

Clarifying and Defining Core Beliefs and Practices

Core beliefs and practices can be defined at several levels of abstraction. For instance, take Wal-Mart's historical practice of promoting "Made in America" goods in its U.S. stores. Assuming that promoting origin-of-manufacture is a core practice for Wal-Mart, the company can define this core practice in more or less abstract terms. A more abstract definition would be "Wherever we operate, we believe in promoting locally manufactured products." In contrast, a less abstract definition would be: "We promote products that are made in America." As this example points out, the more abstract definition of core beliefs and practices permits a higher degree of local adaptation. At the same time, the dilemma is that, if the core beliefs and practices become too abstract, they could lose much of their meaning and value.

As another example, consider the establishment of the Mercedes-Benz plant to manufacture M-Class sport utility vehicles in Alabama during the mid-1990s. In the words of Andreas Renschler, the leader of this project, "We wanted the M-Class project to be *more* than just another plant building another car. We wanted it to be a 'learning field'—the creation of a new product and a new plant, with new administrative systems in a new country."[14] In this case, the company held steadfast to the view that the M-Class car must preserve the look and feel of a Mercedes-Benz, but many other practices (for example, the degree of plant automation, the formality versus casualness of attire) were viewed as flexible and subject to adaptation.

The definition of what constitutes a company's core beliefs and practices is and must always be the result of learning through experimentation. These definitions will be different across industries and across firms within an industry—and even for the same firm, different at different times. As a senior executive of a major global retailer observed, "Cut your chains and you become free. Cut your roots and you die. Differentiating between the two requires good judgment, something that you acquire only through experience and over time."

Transplanting Core Beliefs and Practices to the New Subsidiary

Transplanting core beliefs and practices to a new subsidiary, whether a greenfield operation or an acquisition, is always a transformational event, with the challenge much greater in the case of acquisitions. The transplanted beliefs and practices are likely to be at best only partly understood and, in the case of acquisitions, often seen as alien and questionable. Transferring core beliefs and practices to a new subsidiary usually requires physically transferring a select group of committed believers (the DNA carriers) to the new operation. The size of this group depends largely on the scale of the desired transformation effort. If the goal is essentially to replace an entire set of preexisting beliefs and practices (as with ABB's acquisitions in Eastern Europe), it may be necessary to send in a veritable army of DNA carriers. On the other hand, if the goal is to create a new business model (as in the case of Mercedes-Benz's Alabama plant), then fewer, carefully selected transplants would be needed.

Obloj and Thomas[15] have described vividly how the invasion process worked in the case of ABB Poland:

> The transformation began with an influx and invasion of external and internal ABB consultants that signaled clearly the introductory stage of organizational change. Their behavior was guided by their perception of the stereotypical behavior of an inefficient state-owned firm typically managed by a cadre of administrators who do not understand how to manage a firm in a market economy. They did not initially perform any sophisticated diagnosis or analysis of local conditions or develop a strategic vision for the transformation process. Rather, they forcefully implemented market enterprise discipline in the acquired former state-owned firms by a series of high-speed actions. They implemented massive training efforts aimed at exposing employees and managers of acquired firms to the principles of the market economy, modern management principles, and the ABB management system. This was adopted in all acquired firms following Percy Barnevik's dictum that the key to competitiveness is education and re-education.

The contrast between ABB's approach in Poland and Mercedes-Benz's slower, more open, more learning-oriented approach in Alabama is interesting:

> Of the six top executives in charge of the plant, three are native Germans.... Two are Americans.... There is one Canadian.... In late 1993, after the management team was hired, they were sequestered in Stuttgart, Germany, Daimler's base, for a year. They gathered each Wednesday at 10 A.M. in a temporary trailer office on a Mercedes parking lot ... often meeting past midnight. The executives clashed repeatedly. They disagreed over whether the plant should be highly automated—as Mercedes officials believed—or revolve around streamlined manual techniques— which the American executives supported. In the end, automation was kept to a minimum, compared with industry standards now.[16]

Embedding the Core Beliefs and Practices

The process of transplanting the corporate DNA, which begins with transferring a select group of DNA carriers to the new subsidiary, can be judged successful only when the new beliefs and practices have become internalized in the mindsets and routines of employees at the new subsidiary. Achieving such internalization requires visibly explicit and credible commitment by the parent company to its core beliefs and practices, a systematic process of continuous education within the new organization right down to middle managers and the local workforce, and concrete demonstration that the new beliefs and practices yield individual as well as corporate success.

The approach taken by the Ritz-Carlton chain at its hotel in Shanghai, China, illustrates how a company can initiate the successful embedding of its core beliefs and practices in a new subsidiary. Ritz-Carlton acquired the rights to manage this hotel, with a staff of about a thousand people, under its own name as of January 1998. The company believed that, consistent with its image and its corporate DNA, the entire operation required significant upgrading. The company brought in a sizable contingent of about forty expatriates from other Ritz-Carlton units in Asia and around the world to transform and manage the new property. What is particularly noteworthy, however, is the approach taken by Ritz-Carlton managers to embed the company's own standards of quality and service in the hearts, minds, and behavior of their local associates. Among its first actions in the very first week the property was under its control, the company decided to begin the renovation process with the employees' entrance and changing and wash rooms rather than from more typical starting points such as the main lobby. The logic, as explained by a senior executive, was that, through this approach, every employee would personally see two radical changes in the very first week: one, that the new standards of quality and service would be dramatically higher, and two, that the employees were among the most valued stakeholders in the company. This approach served as a very successful start to embedding the company's basic beliefs in every associate's mind: "We Are Ladies and Gentlemen Serving Ladies and Gentlemen."

WINNING THE LOCAL BATTLE

Winning the local battle requires the global enterprise to anticipate, shape, and respond to the needs and actions of three sets of players in the host country: its customers, its competitors, and the host country government.

Winning Host Country Customers

One of the ingredients in establishing local presence is an understanding of the uniqueness of the local market and of which aspects of the company's business model require little change, which require local adaptation, and which need to be reinvented. If the targeted segment in the foreign market is similar to the one served in the home market, the company's business design will need little adaptation. However, if the firm wants to expand the served customer base in a foreign market, then adapting the business model to the local customers' unique demands becomes mandatory. The following cases illustrate the varied experiences of U.S. companies in their pursuit of host country customers.

When FedEx entered the Chinese market, it had to decide, as an element of its entry strategy, who its target customers should be: local Chinese companies or multinational corporations. FedEx chose to target multinational companies, a customer segment identical to the one it has historically served. Given this decision, FedEx was able to export the U.S. business model into China, including employing its own aircraft, building a huge network of trucks and distribution centers, and adopting the aggressive marketing and advertising typical in the U.S.[17] If, on the other hand, FedEx had selected local Chinese companies as its targeted customer segment, winning host country customers would have required a much greater degree of local adaptation of the business model.

Nike suffered an initial setback in Europe when it mistakenly transplanted the U.S. marketing approach to the continent. In the United States, Nike became a huge success by projecting the image of an irreverent rebel who glorifies the lowly sneaker, worships athletes, and rebels against the establishment. Initially, Nike took the same approach in Europe. Two of the company's commercials in Europe were a team of Nike endorsers playing soccer against Satan and his demons and a French bad boy explaining how he had won a Nike contract by insulting his coach and spitting at a fan. Though these commercials might have done well in the United States, they backfired in the more tradition-bound European culture. Learning from this setback, Nike decided that it must "Europeanize" its approach and become more of a diplomat than a rebel. As Phil Knight, chairman of Nike, remarked: "The fine line is gone from being a rebel to being a bully. Nike is now making an effort to get along [in Europe]. Ten years ago, we would have never thought of doing that, because we were the antiestablishment."[18]

Winning the Battle Against Host Country Competitors

Whenever a company enters a new country, it can expect retaliation from local competitors as well as from other multinationals already operating in that market. Successfully establishing local presence requires anticipating and responding to these competitive threats. Established local competitors enjoy several advantages—knowledge of the local market, working relationships with local customers, understanding of local distribution channels, and so on. In contrast, the global firm suffers from the liability of newness. When a global firm enters their market, local competitors are likely to feel threatened and their retaliation in defense of their position will act as a barrier to entry. The new invader has four possible options to overcome these barriers.

Acquire a dominant local competitor. This option will succeed if there is significant potential for synergies between the global firm and acquisition target, the acquirer has the capability to create and capture such synergies, and the acquirer does not give away the synergies through a huge up-front acquisition premium.

An example of successful entry through acquisition of a dominant local competitor is Accor, the French hospitality company, which entered the U.S. low-priced lodging market by acquiring Motel 6, the best-managed market leader in this category. On the other hand, Sony Corporation paid a huge premium to acquire Columbia Pictures and to date has had great difficulty in justifying this premium, despite significant potential synergies between Sony's hardware competencies and Columbia's content expertise and assets.

Acquire a weak player. This option is attractive when the global firm has the ability to transplant its corporate DNA into the acquired firm quickly so as to transform the weak player into a dominant one. The sheer act of acquiring a weak player signals to other local competitors that they will soon be under attack. It is therefore to be expected that local competitors will retaliate. If the global firm is unable to transform the acquired operations in a very short time, these operations are likely to become even weaker due to more intense attack from local competitors.

Consider Whirlpool's entry into Europe in 1989 by acquiring the problem-ridden appliance division of Philips. Unfortunately, Whirlpool could not quickly embed the capabilities needed to turn Philips's struggling appliance business around. In the meantime, Whirlpool's entry gave two European rivals—Sweden's Electrolux and Germany's Bosch-Siemens—a wake-up call. Not surprisingly, both these companies invested very heavily in plant modernization, process improvements, new product introductions, and restructuring—all with the intent of improving their competitiveness to repel the new invader. The net result was a disappointment for Whirlpool, which had hoped to consolidate the white goods industry in Europe. By 1998, Whirlpool had only 12 percent market share in Europe, half of its expected position, and was also underachieving in profitability. To quote Jeff Fettig, Whirlpool's head of European operations: "We underestimated the competition."[19]

Enter a poorly defended niche. If acquisition candidates are either unavailable or too expensive, the global firm has no choice but to enter on its own. Under these circumstances, it should find a poorly defended niche for market entry and, assuming such a niche exists, use that niche as a platform for subsequent expansion into the mainstream segments of the local market. Often the mobility barriers to move from the niche market to the mainstream segments are much lower than the barriers to direct entry in the mainstream segments.

In the early 1970s, Japanese automobile manufacturers entered the U.S. market at the low end, a segment that was being ignored by U.S. car companies and hence a "loose brick" in their fortress. In time, the Japanese companies used their dominance of the lower-end segment to migrate to the middle and upper ends very effectively.

Financial Times's entry into the U.S. market in 1997 also illustrates the wisdom of avoiding a frontal attack. To quote Richard Lambert, editor of *Financial Times*:

> *When we started our expansion here [in the U.S.], some existing readers*
> *told us they were worried we might be seeking to replicate the* Wall Street

Journal. *This was the last thing on our minds: 800-pound gorillas are usually best left well alone. Instead, our aim has been to develop a paper that would be uniquely positioned for the new global market place. Here is what you can expect from* Financial Times*: a much broader and more consistent coverage of international business, economic, and political news than is available in any other publication, a global perspective on the comment and analysis pages, [and] strong coverage of the world's biggest and most dynamic economy. We seek to put U.S. business, economic, and political news into an international context.*[20]

Stage a frontal attack. The global firm can choose a head-on attack on the dominant and entrenched incumbents provided its competitive advantage is sufficiently large that it can be leveraged outside its domestic market. If this were not true, taking on an 800-pound gorilla with all the liability of newness could prove suicidal. Lexus's frontal attack on Mercedes and BMW in the U.S. market succeeded mainly as a result of its overwhelming advantage in areas such as product quality and cost structure. For instance, Lexus enjoyed a 30 percent cost advantage. Given the high labor cost Mercedes and BMW faced in Germany, where they manufactured their automobiles, they could not neutralize the Lexus cost advantage quickly.

Managing Relationships with the Host Government

Local government can often be a key external stakeholder, particularly in emerging markets. Two points are worth noting in this context. First, the global firm can ill afford to ignore nonmarket stakeholders such as the local government. For instance, in the late 1990s, the Chinese government's ban on all door-to-door selling had a negative impact on companies (such as Mary Kay Cosmetics and Avon) who depend on a highly personalized direct marketing approach. Second, managing nonmarket stakeholders should be seen as a dynamic process. Simply reacting to existing government regulations is not enough. Firms must anticipate likely future changes in the regulatory framework and even explore the possibility of helping to shape the emerging regulatory framework. Persistence and constructive dialogue with the local government, instead of appeasement or confrontation, are often critical elements of winning the local battle.

SPEED OF GLOBAL EXPANSION

Having commenced the journey to globalization, a company has yet another major issue to address, namely, How fast should it expand globally? Microsoft's worldwide launch of Windows 95 *on the same day* epitomizes using globalization for aggressive growth. By moving quickly, a company can solidify its market position very rapidly. However, rapid global expansion can also deplete managerial, organizational, and financial resources, thereby jeopardizing the company's ability to defend and profit from its newly created global presence. Consider, for example, the Japanese retailer Yaohan. In the early 1990s, Yaohan set about aggressive expansion into many countries in Asia. In 1992, it was the first foreign retailer to enter China and spent $350 million to construct Asia's largest department store in Shanghai. Yet by 1996 the company's plans had gone astray. It was forced to close a store in Singapore, divest some of its operations in Hong Kong, and put further expansion into China on hold.[21] Accelerated global expansion is more appropriate under certain conditions:

It is easy for competitors to replicate your recipe for success. Particularly vulnerable are fast food and retailing companies, such as KFC and Starbucks, where competitors can take a proven concept from one market and easily replicate it in another unoccupied market with relatively low investment. This phenomenon is also observable in other, very different industries such as personal computers, software, and e-commerce. The rapid globalization of companies like Dell, Microsoft, and Yahoo! reflects their determination to prevent replication or pirating of their product concepts and business models in markets worldwide.

Scale economies are extremely important. Very high scale economies afford the early and rapid globalizer considerable first-mover advantages and handicap slower globalizers for long periods of time. For this reason, expeditious globalizers in the tire industry, such as Goodyear, Michelin, and Bridgestone, now hold a sizable advantage over tardy globalizers, such as Pirelli and Continental.

Management's capacity to manage (or learn how to manage) global operations is high. Consider, for example, the case of experienced global players such as Coca-Cola, Citicorp, Unilever, or ABB. Should these companies successfully introduce a new product line in one country, it would be logical and relatively easy for them to roll out this product line rapidly to all potential markets worldwide. In addition to the company's ability to manage global operations, the rate of globalization also depends on its ability to leverage its experience from one market to another. The faster an organization can recycle its knowledge about market entry and market defense from one country to another, the lower the risk of depleting its managerial and organizational capacity.

Box 2.2 identifies a set of questions that managers can use to assess their firm's global presence at any given point in time and design a course of action to expand this global presence in the future.

SUMMARY

The central idea underlying the framework developed and elaborated upon in this chapter has been that when a company embarks on the road to globalization, six major issues need to be sorted out: choice of products, choice of markets, mode of entry, transplantation of the corporate DNA, winning the local battle, and speed of global expansion.

BOX 2-2

BUILDING GLOBAL PRESENCE: A MANAGER'S GUIDE TO ACTION

Using Marriott as an illustrative example, the following is a list of questions that a firm should ask in its attempt to assess its globalization efforts to date and direct actions needed to secure its global presence in the future. As mentioned earlier in the chapter, until the early 1990s, Marriott Corporation was essentially a domestic company. In the fast decade, the company has established a major global presence by using full-service lodging as its initial launch vehicle.

The Globalization Imperatives

- What goals have motivated our globalization efforts to date?
- What benefits have accrued from globalization so far?
- Are we ahead of, at par with, or behind the extent of globalization demanded by our target customers?
- Are we ahead of, at par with, or behind the extent of globalization of our actual (or benchmark) competitors?
- Would more proactive globalization give us an edge over our competitors?
- What goals should drive our globalization strategy over the next three to five years? The next five to ten years?

Choice of Products

- Why did we pick full-service lodging as the first launch vehicle for globalization?
- To what extent was full-service lodging a good or not-so-good choice? What have we learned?
- What logic should guide us in the selection of the next launch vehicle?
- What should the next launch vehicle be? Why?

Choice of Strategic Markets

- How have we picked the target markets for globalization so far? What logic, if any, have we followed?
- Based on our experience, what have we learned about the factors that differentiate good from not-so-good markets?
- Taking into account emerging market opportunities, push from customers, and the actual or expected market presence of our competitors, what should our goals regarding market presence be three to five years from now for full-service lodging? For the next product line to be globalized?

Choice of Entry Mode

- What logic has guided our choices between own-management versus franchise approaches to entering target markets?

BOX 2-2

(CONTINUED)

- Based on our experience to date, what have we learned about the characteristics that differentiate good from not-so-good franchisees, negotiating terms and conditions with franchisees, and ongoing oversight and management of franchise operations?
- Over the next three to five years, what logic should guide us in the selection of entry mode? Should we have any preference between the various modes? If so, what and why?

Transplanting the Corporate DNA

- Are we clear about what our core (as distinct from peripheral) beliefs and practices are? What have we learned in our experiments in the past on what constitutes core versus non-core?
- What mechanisms have we used so far to transfer these beliefs and practices in the new subsidiary? How efficient and effective are these mechanisms?
- What processes have we used to embed these beliefs and practices in the new subsidiary? What have we learned from our successful as well as unsuccessful attempts?

Winning the Local Battle

- Which customer segments have we targeted in our foreign market entries to date? What have we learned regarding tailored versus standardized formats? How can we use this knowledge in the future?
- What logic has guided our choices between a loose-bricks approach versus a frontal attack in entering target markets? What have we learned?

Speed of Expansion

- What factors have determined the speed of our global expansion to date? What have been the (internally or externally imposed) constraints on faster expansion? What have been the facilitators?
- Based on our experience to date, what have we learned about how to maintain a high rate of global expansion or to increase it even further?
- For the next three to five years, what should be the pace of our global expansion efforts?

CHAPTER 3

ANALYSIS OF WAL-MART'S GLOBAL EXPANSION

The entire world is our marketplace. Just think of all the people in the world who haven't had the opportunity to shop at Wal-Mart.
—*David D. Glass, CEO, Wal-Mart, 1999*[1]

IN **2002,** Wal-Mart was the largest retailer in the world. With its headquarters in Bentonville, Arkansas, the company achieved sales revenues of $218 billion for the year ending January 31, 2002. Wal-Mart operated three types of retailing outlets: discount stores, which marketed soft goods such as clothing and linen, hard goods such as small appliances and hardware, sporting goods, and other items at everyday low prices; Sam's Clubs, large wholesale warehouse clubs, which marketed merchandise displayed in bulk and required customers to purchase memberships; and supercenters, which offered the combined inventories of a Wal-Mart discount store and a full-line supermarket.

Why did Wal-Mart go global? What moves did it make to transform itself globally? What alternative moves could it have made? What was the sequence of its entry into the global market? What modes of entry did the company choose for each market? How well did it establish local presence after entering a foreign market? Has its global expansion happened quickly enough? What choices did Wal-Mart have in mounting its globalization efforts? Did it make optimal decisions? We will explore these questions using the framework for building global presence developed in Chapter 2.[2]

WAL-MART'S GLOBAL EXPANSION

Since its first move outside the United States in 1991, Wal-Mart has pursued globalization aggressively (see Table 3.1). Whereas in 1993, just 1 percent of all Wal-Mart stores were located outside the United States, by 2002, that figure had grown to 27 percent. Between 1996 and 2000, 27 percent of the company's growth in sales came from international operations. By January 2002, of a total

TABLE 3.1 Wal-Mart's Globalization

Financial Statistics ($ millions)

Year (ending January 31)		2000	2001	2002
Sales	Wal-Mart Stores and Supercenters	$108,721	$121,889	$139,131
	Sam's Club	24,801	26,798	29,395
	Domestic Total*	142,285	159,229	182,314
	International	22,728	32,100	35,485
	International as percentage of Total Sales	13.8	16.8	16.3
Operating Income	Wal-Mart Stores and Supercenters	$8,419	$9,700	$10,300
	Sam's Club	759	942	1028
	Domestic Total*	9288	10,354	10,614
	International	817	1,112	1,458
	International as percentage of Total Operating Profit	8.09	9.70	12.08
Operating Return on Total Assets	Total Assets: Domestic*	$45,019	$52,388	$57,127
	Total Assets: International	25,330	25,742	26,324
	Operating Return on Assets: Domestic (percentage)*	21	20	19
	Operating Return on Assets: International (percentage)	3	4	6

Breakdown in Number of Stores

Year (ending January 31)	1996	1997	1998	1999	2000	2001	2002
Wal-Mart Stores	1,995	1,960	1,921	1,869	1,801	1,736	1,647
Supercenters	239	344	441	564	721	888	1,066
Sam's Club	433	436	443	451	463	475	500
Neighborhood Markets	–	–	–	–	–	19	31
Domestic Total	2,667	2,740	2,805	2,884	2,985	3,118	3,244
International	276	314	601	715	1,004	1,071	1,170
Total stores	2,943	3,054	3,406	3,599	3,989	4,189	4,414
International as percentage of Total Stores	9	10	18	20	25	26	27

(continues)

37

TABLE 3.1 *(Continued)*

Distribution of Stores by Country (January 31, 2002)

Type of Store	Canada	Argentina	Brazil	Mexico	Puerto Rico	China	Korea	Germany	U.K.	Total
Discount	196	0	0	443	9	0	0	0	0	648
Supercenters	0	11	12	62	1	15	9	95	250	455
Sam's Club	0	3	8	46	7	3	0	0	0	64
Neighborhood Markets	0	0	2	0	0	1	0	0	0	3
TOTAL	196	11	22	551	17	19	9	95	250	1,170

*including McLane, a distribution subsidiary.

**Return on Assets is defined as Operating Profit Before Tax divided by Total Assets.

Source: Company annual reports.

workforce exceeding 1,380,000, more than 300,000 Wal-Mart employees were working outside the United States. For fiscal year 2002, the company recorded $35.5 billion in sales and $1,458 million in operating profit from stores outside the United States. Box 3.1 presents a time line tracking Wal-Mart's global expansion.

The company's return on assets within its international operations did not yet match the figures for its U.S. operations. There are two likely explanations for this relative underperformance of international operations. First, Wal-Mart lacked the critical mass of stores to realize scale economies in its transportation and distribution infrastructure. Second, Wal-Mart had to make heavy up-front investments in building up its brand. Higher profitability from international operations was anticipated as Wal-Mart ramped up to peak turnover in each foreign market.[3]

BOX 3-1

TIME LINE OF WAL-MART'S GLOBALIZATION MOVES

Wal-Mart in Mexico
1991   50–50 joint venture with Cifra, Mexico's largest retailer
1994   Enters agreement with Cifra that all new Cifra stores will be through joint venture
1997   Buys a controlling stake in Cifra

Wal-Mart in Brazil
1994   60–40 joint venture with Lojas Americana, Brazil's largest retailer
1997   Acquired the 40 percent minority interest in the joint venture

Wal-Mart in Argentina
1995   Entered without a local partner (100 percent Wal-Mart ownership)

Wal-Mart in Canada
1994   100 percent acquisition of 122 Woolco stores from Woolworth; rapidly converted into Wal-Mart stores

Wal-Mart in Japan
1992   Entered agreement to supply 100 Wal-Mart items to Ito-Yokado
1993   Entered agreement to supply Wal-Mart products to Yaohan

Wal-Mart in China
1994   Partnership with Thailand-based conglomerate C.P. Pokphand Co. to open Value Clubs (mini-warehouse clubs) in Hong Kong
1995   Partnership with C.P. Pokphand Co. dissolved
1996   Opened one Wal-Mart Supercenter and one Sam's Club in China through joint ventures with Hong Kong Pearl River Investment Co. and Shenzhen International Co.

BOX

(CONTINUED)

Wal-Mart in Indonesia
1996   Opened a Supercenter through a joint venture

Wal-Mart in Germany
1997   Acquired the Wertkauf hypermarket chain of 21 stores, a German company owned by the Mann Family
1999   Acquired 74 stores from Spar Handels AG, a German company that owned multiple retail formats and wholesale operations throughout Germany

Wal-Mart in Korea
1999   Acquired a majority interest in four units operated by Korea Makro

Wal-Mart in United Kingdom
1999   Acquired Britain's third-largest food retailer, the supermarket chain Asda Group PLC (229 stores), for $10.8 billion

GLOBALIZATION IMPERATIVES

Did Wal-Mart need to go global at all? In view of its highly successful business model for competing in the U.S. market (shown in Box 3.2), couldn't it have continued to prosper as a purely American retailer? The answer is simple: The company needed to grow to survive, and only in the international arena was significant growth possible.

Why was growth so important to Wal-Mart? The company needed to show increases in both sales and profits to satisfy capital market expectations. It also needed to grow so as to satisfy the expectations of its own employees. One of the key factors in Wal-Mart's historical success has been its dedicated and committed workforce. Because of its stock purchase plan, the wealth of Wal-Mart employees was directly tied to the market value of the company's stock, strongly linking growth to its positive effect on stock price and to company morale.

Given the necessity for growth, Wal-Mart could not afford to confine its operations to the United States for several reasons. First, it had already saturated most of the domestic markets, both large and small; obviously, it is not easy for a $165 billion company with more than a 50 percent market share to sustain an annual growth rate of more than 20 percent while staying within the United States! Second, the United States accounts for just over 4 percent of the world's population; the remaining 96 percent of the world's potential customers are outside this market. Finally, emerging markets, with their lower levels of disposable

BOX *3-2*

WAL-MART'S COMPETITIVE ADVANTAGE IN ACTION

As of 2000, the winning strategy for Wal-Mart in the United States was based on selling branded products at low cost.

Purchasing

Wal-Mart enjoyed scale economies in purchasing as a result of its more than 50 percent market share position in the discount retailing industry. Though Wal-Mart may have been the top customer for consumer product manufacturers, it deliberately ensured that it did not become too dependent on any one vendor (no single vendor constituted more than 4 percent of its overall purchase volume). Further, Wal-Mart had persuaded its nearly 3,000 vendors to have electronic "hook-ups" with its stores so as to reduce overall order entry and processing costs for Wal-Mart as well as its vendors.

In-Bound Logistics

About 85 percent of all the merchandise sold by Wal-Mart was shipped through its distribution system to the stores (competitors supplied to their retail outlets, on an average, less than 50 percent of the merchandise through their own distribution centers). Wal-Mart used a "saturation" strategy for store expansion. The standard was to be able to drive to a store within a day from a distribution center. A distribution center was strategically placed so that it could eventually serve between 150 and 200 Wal-Mart stores within a day. Stores were first built as far away as possible but still within a day's drive of the distribution center; then the area was filled back (or saturated back) to the distribution center. The distribution centers operated twenty-four hours a day using laser-guided conveyer belts and cross-docking techniques that received goods on one side while simultaneously filling orders on the other. The company owned a fleet of more than 3,000 trucks and 12,000 trailers (most Wal-Mart competitors outsourced trucking). Wal-Mart had implemented a satellite network system that was used daily to share information between the company's wide network of stores, distribution centers, and suppliers—so that orders for goods could be consolidated enabling the company to buy full truckloads without incurring the inventory costs. Wal-Mart's distribution and logistics infrastructure saved transportation costs (2 percent to 3 percent cost advantage relative to competitors), increased flexibility, ensured 100 percent in-stock position on its merchandise at all times (critical for customer service), and increased the selling space at stores (by reducing the space required in stores for back-room inventory storage).

Store Operations

As a result of better management of stores, Wal-Mart enjoyed a cost advantage and a sales per square foot advantage vis-à-vis competitors. These advantages were derived from several sources.

> *Store Location*: In the early years, Wal-Mart's strategy was to build large discount stores in small rural towns, which yielded three benefits: (1) These rural locations resulted in lower operating expenses, especially for payroll and rental expenses; (2) Competitors, such as Kmart, who were focused on

BOX 3-2

(CONTINUED)

large towns with more than 50,000 population, ignored Wal-Mart; and (3) This built effective entry barriers as it became highly uneconomical for competitors to enter regions Wal-Mart had already saturated.

Human Resource Management: Wal-Mart had created a dedicated and committed workforce (with the attendant benefits in terms of higher labor productivity, lower employee turnover, and excellent customer service) through several policies and programs: profit sharing, incentive bonus, and discount stock purchase plans available to the workforce; promotion from within; promotion and pay raises based on performance, not seniority; and an open-door policy.

Management Information and Control Systems: Wal-Mart's management information and control systems had helped the company manage its more than 3,000 stores located in remote places thousands of miles away from headquarters. Store-level data on sales, expenses, and profit and loss were collected, analyzed, and transmitted electronically on a real-time basis to see how a particular region, district, store, department within a store, or even an item was performing. This information enabled the company to eliminate the likelihood of stock-outs, reduce the need for markdown on slow-moving stock, and maximize inventory turnover. The benchmark information across stores was also a valuable tool to help "problem" stores.

Control over Shoplifting: One of the areas of particular concern for retailers was shoplifting or pilferage. Wal-Mart was able to cut its pilferage-related losses by instituting a policy where 50 percent of the savings due to decrease in pilferage in a particular store versus the industry standard would be shared among the employees of the store via store incentive plans.

Marketing

Wal-Mart's marketing strategy was to guarantee "everyday low prices" as a way to pull customers in. The traditional discount retailer, who relied on "sales," not only had to do more advertising and promotions but also had to rely more on catalog mailing, buildup of inventory before a sale, markdown on the unsold inventory, etc. Wal-Mart was able to save these costs.

Abstracted from "Wal-Mart Inc.," a case and an analysis of the case prepared by Rob Lynch, 1996, and used here with permission from the author.

income, offered huge platforms for growth in discount retailing. Other firms had already capitalized on such growth thanks to the rapid expansion of information technology, increase in cultural homogenization, and lower trade barriers.[4] Wal-Mart could meet this competition only through aggressive global expansion.

Fortunately, Wal-Mart had the capacity to leverage two key resources originally developed in the United States. First, it could exploit its mammoth buying power with giant suppliers, such as Procter & Gamble, Campbell Soup, Clorox, Colgate, General Electric, Hallmark, Kellogg, Nestlé, Coca-Cola, Pfizer, Revlon, 3M, Sara Lee, and Wrigley, to procure cost-effectively for its non–U.S. stores. Imagine the formidable clout that Wal-Mart would enjoy when it could buy Tide detergent from Procter & Gamble for its nearly four thousand stores worldwide! Wal-Mart could convert these tremendous economies of scale into a cost advantage. Second, it could use domestically developed knowledge bases and competencies in such areas as efficient store management, merchandising skills, logistics, and the deployment of information technology to benefit its foreign outlets. Moreover, an unforeseen but positive byproduct of this process was that Wal-Mart was also able to take advantage of sales-generating or cost-reduction ideas learned in its international outlets (such as speedy checkouts and gravity walls) to benefit its three thousand U.S. stores.

For instance, Wal-Mart was able to borrow several worthwhile practices from the British chain Asda, which it acquired in 1999: "The U.S. stores and distribution centers are now adopting Asda's system for replenishing fresh food more quickly and in the right quantities. And Asda's popular line of George brand clothing is being rolled out in the women's department of all U.S. stores this Christmas season. Thomas M. Coughlin, president of the Wal-Mart Stores Div., even removed all the chairs from the room where his managers hold their weekly meeting after he saw Asda's 'air-traffic controllers' room in Leeds. There, managers meet every morning around a high table with no chairs—to keep meetings short and to encourage action—as they pore over figures charted on the walls...."[5]

CHOICE OF MARKETS: ROADS TAKEN VERSUS ROADS NOT TAKEN

Which market was optimal as Wal-Mart's initial launching pad: Europe, Asia, or other countries in the western hemisphere? It could not afford to enter them all at once in 1991, because at that time Wal-Mart lacked the competencies and resources (financial, organizational, and managerial) to launch a simultaneous penetration all over the globe. Further, for any company, a logically sequenced approach to market entry (as opposed to a do-it-all-at-once scheme) enables the company to apply the learning gained from its initial market entries to its subsequent entries. For example, for Wal-Mart, the experience of managing operations in the high-inflation climate that characterized the Mexican economy in the 1990s was potentially applicable to other markets experiencing high inflation rates. This type of learning and adaptation is vital for first-time globalizers.

Nonetheless, the choice regarding which market a company should target for its initial foray is not always obvious. As shown in Box 3.1, during the first five years of its globalization campaign (1991–1995), Wal-Mart concentrated heavily on establishing presence in the Americas—Mexico, Brazil, Argentina, and Canada. What was the rationale behind this decision? Should Wal-Mart instead have focused first on Europe or Asia?

The European market had certain characteristics that made it less attractive to Wal-Mart as the initial point of entry. First, the European retail industry is mature, so that a new entrant would have to take market share away from an existing player—a very difficult task. Second, there were well-entrenched competitors on the scene (such as Carrefour in France and Metro AG in Germany) who would be likely to retaliate vigorously against any new player. Third, the business models of European retailers are similar to Wal-Mart's, thereby reducing the size of the potential competitive advantage Wal-Mart might have expected had its format been entirely new to this market. Further, as with most newcomers, Wal-Mart's relatively small size in these markets and lack of strong local customer relationships would be severe handicaps in the intense competitive battles its entry into the Europe arena would be likely to provoke.

Wal-Mart might have overcome these difficulties by entering Europe through an acquisition, but given the higher growth rates of Latin American and Asian markets, a delayed entry into the latter markets would have been extremely costly in terms of lost opportunities. In contrast, the opportunity costs of delaying acquisition-based entries into European markets appeared to be relatively small.

Looking at Asia, it is undoubtedly true that Asian markets appeared to have huge potential in 1991 when Wal-Mart launched its globalization effort. But this market is the most geographically distant and culturally and logistically distinct from the U.S. market—customer needs are different, the labor market is complex, the regulatory environment is volatile, and information technology and distribution networks are inadequate. It would have taken considerable financial resources to establish a presence in Asia, and even greater managerial resources to oversee stores thousands of miles away.

The question is not whether Europe or Asia would have been the wrong choices as launching pads but rather, given limited resources, where could Wal-Mart gain maximum leverage? In the end, Wal-Mart chose Mexico (1991), Brazil (1994), Canada (1994), and Argentina (1995) as its initial points of entry. In addition to being relatively close to the United States compared to Europe or Asia, these countries constitute the four largest economies in the Americas (other than the United States) and thus offer huge potential for retail business.

In 1996, Wal-Mart felt ready to take on the Asian challenge more directly, targeting China as the growth vehicle. This choice made abundant sense in that the lower purchasing power of the Chinese consumer offered huge potential to discount retailers like Wal-Mart. Still, given China's other high entry barriers (cultural, linguistic, and geographical distance), Wal-Mart decided to use two beachhead markets as learning vehicles for establishing an Asian presence.

First, in 1992 and in 1993, Wal-Mart made initial moves toward the Asian market by entering into agreements to sell low-priced products to two Japanese retailers, Ito-Yokado and Yaohan; these companies would, in turn, market these products in Japan, Singapore, Hong Kong, Malaysia, Thailand, Indonesia, and the Philippines. Then, in 1994, Wal-Mart entered Hong Kong through a joint venture with C.P. Pokphand Co., a Thailand-based conglomerate, to open three Value Club membership discount stores in Hong Kong.

In 1997, Wal-Mart finally entered Europe, acquiring the Wertkauf hyper-market chain of 21 stores in Germany. Wal-Mart expanded its presence in Germany in 1999 by acquiring 74 stores from Star Handels AG, which owned multiple retail formats and wholesale operations throughout Germany. Germany provided a secure foothold on the continent because of the stability of the deutsche mark, the affluence of German consumers, the relatively large size of the consumer base (Germany has a population of greater than 80 million), and the country's central location.

Wal-Mart consolidated its position in Western Europe in 1999 by acquiring Britain's third-largest food retailer, the supermarket chain Asda Group PLC, with 229 stores, for $10.8 billion. Eastern Europe, on the other hand, was becoming the most promising area for the future growth. Wal-Mart could potentially lever-age its knowledge and the distribution competencies established in Western Europe to pursue greenfield development in Eastern Europe.

MODE OF ENTRY: ROADS TAKEN VERSUS ROADS NOT TAKEN

Once Wal-Mart had chosen which markets to enter, its next decision was the appropriate mode of entry. Every company making this decision faces an array of choices: It can acquire an existing player, build an alliance with an existing player, start greenfield operations, or use some combination of the three approaches. As Wal-Mart's experience in entering different markets illustrates, the optimal choice—whether acquisition, strategic alliance, or green-field opera-tion—varies from one context to another.

In 1994, Wal-Mart entered Canada through a straight 100 percent acquisi-tion. This was a logical move for three reasons. First, Canada is a mature market, which makes greenfield operations an unattractive option—adding new stores (that is, new capacity) will only intensify an already high degree of local compe-tition. Second, given the many income and cultural similarities between the U.S. and Canadian markets, Wal-Mart would have relatively little need for new learn-ing. Thus entering through a strategic alliance and sharing profits with an alliance partner was unnecessary. Third, a poorly performing player, Woolco, was avail-able for purchase at an economical price. Furthermore, Woolco was a good fit for another reason: Wal-Mart's business model was precisely what Woolco needed to transform itself into a viable and healthy organization.

For its entry into Mexico, Wal-Mart took a different route since significant income and cultural differences exist between the United States and Mexican markets. This move was to be Wal-Mart's first globalization effort. The company needed to learn much about the local market and how to tailor its operations to the local environment, requirements that would have made a 100 percent-owned greenfield start-up very problematic. Even if the necessary local knowledge and competencies could have been obtained through an acquisition, Wal-Mart's ability to manage an acquired subsidiary in unfamiliar and highly dissimilar markets was likely to be quite limited. Instead, the company chose to form a 50–50 joint venture with Cifra, Mexico's largest retailer, counting on Cifra to provide operational expertise in the volatile Mexican environment.

For further expansion in Latin America, Wal-Mart targeted the region's two next-largest markets, Brazil and Argentina. The entry into Brazil was also accomplished through a joint venture, in 1994, with Lojas Americana, a local retailer. But Wal-Mart was now able to leverage its Mexican experience, and chose to establish a 60–40 joint venture in which it had the controlling stake. Whether it should have gone with 100 percent ownership instead is debatable. It is worth noting that Lojas was able to provide Wal-Mart with many competencies required for success in Brazil, including local expertise in acquiring real estate, operating in a turbulent, high-inflation environment, and even doing business in the unique Brazilian culture. Three years later, in 1997, Wal-Mart acquired the remaining 40 percent minority interest in the joint venture.

Wal-Mart's entry into Brazil provided even greater experience in Latin America, which may explain why Wal-Mart chose to enter Argentina through a wholly owned subsidiary. The 1995 decision to undertake 100 percent ownership of greenfield operations was bolstered by the fact that there are only two markets in Argentina of significant size.

CLONING THE CORPORATE DNA

Wal-Mart had developed several major capabilities in the United States (as Box 3.2 shows). If these capabilities could be successfully transferred to non–U.S. locations, the company would gain a significant advantage over local competitors. The company's ability to clone its domestically grown DNA and implant it into its global operations would advance its position, as illustrated by its entry into Canada.[6]

Wal-Mart acquired Woolco Canada in 1994 at a time when a combination of high costs and low productivity had driven the Canadian company into the red. Wal-Mart turned the situation around by reconfiguring Woolco along the lines of its successful U.S. model, a strategy facilitated by the similarity between the U.S. and Canadian markets. This transformation occurred in four central arenas: the workforce, the stores, the customers, and the business model.

- *Workforce.* More than any other element, Woolco employees were in need of a cultural transformation. Once the purchase was finalized, Wal-Mart sent its transition team to Canada to familiarize Woolco's 15,000 employees with (indeed, to indoctrinate them in) the Wal-Mart way of doing business, especially the concept of total dedication to the customer. The transition team succeeded in clarifying and defining Wal-Mart's core beliefs and practices to its new "associates."

- *Stores.* At the time of the sale, many of Woolco's 122 stores were in very poor shape. Wal-Mart undertook the hefty task of bringing every single outlet up to its own standards in record time. Renovations of each physical plant were completed within three to four months on average. It took an additional three to four months to restock each store.

- *Customers.* Although the Woolco acquisition was Wal-Mart's first entry into Canada, the company had a head start in building a consumer franchise since many Canadians living near the U.S. border were already familiar with the Wal-Mart image. Wal-Mart leveraged this high brand recognition into customer acceptance and loyalty by introducing its "everyday low prices" approach to a market accustomed to high/low retail pricing.

- *Business model.* A broad merchandise mix, excellent customer service, a high in-stock position, and a policy of rewarding employees for diminished pilferage were among the U.S. core practices that were successfully transplanted and embedded into Wal-Mart's Canadian operation.

The transfer of Wal-Mart's corporate DNA to Canada produced dramatic results. Between 1994 (the time of acquisition) and 1997, sales per square foot almost tripled (from C$100 to C$292) and market share doubled (from 22 percent to 45 percent). During the same period, expenses as a percentage of sales in Canada declined by 3.3 percent. Wal-Mart's Canadian operation turned profitable in 1996, only two years after acquisition. By 1997, it had outpaced Zellers and Sears to become the leading discount retailer in Canada.

Wal-Mart also effectively transferred some of its capabilities to benefit Asda: "Wal-Mart acquired a strong chain (Asda) and gave local managers the freedom to run the business. While Asda is still No. 3 in the grocery market, its share grew from 7.4 percent in 1995 to 9.6 percent last year. Wal-Mart gave Asda better technology for tracking store sales and inventories. And it pulled Asda into its global buying effort, led by a 40-person unit in Bentonville that helps negotiate prices for products that can be sold in different markets. This enabled Asda to cut prices on fans and air conditioners, for example, by 50 percent, boosting sales threefold."[7]

WINNING THE LOCAL BATTLE

For Wal-Mart, winning the local battle involved two steps: understanding the local landscape to determine the degree and nature of required local adaptation, and responding to the moves and countermoves of local competitors.

Local Adaptation

To establish local presence, a company must first understand the uniqueness of the local market so as to decide which aspects of its business model require little change, which require local adaptation, and which need to be wholly reinvented. Wal-Mart's entry into China provides insights into this process.[8]

On one hand, as the most populous country in the world, China is obviously an immense potential market for retailers. Retail sales in China grew at an annual rate of 11 percent between 1990 and 1995, propelled by economic liberalization and a large pent-up demand for consumer goods. On the other hand, several unique characteristics make the Chinese market particularly challenging. First, regulations and government policies can change and have often been unpredictable. Second, China's information, communication, distribution, and transportation infrastructure—critical to Wal-Mart's strategy—are not yet well developed. Third, the disposable income of the middle class is dramatically lower in China than in the United States, so that even a company like Wal-Mart, whose retailing concept is targeted to price-conscious customers, must modify its business model to operate within the reach of China's key population groups. Finally, China's unique culture imposed additional hurdles. Most Chinese tend to buy in small quantities due to space constraints in their homes. Further, language differences require local tailoring of marketing approaches in areas such as product labeling and brand names.

Wal-Mart responded to the uncertainties and the uniqueness of the Chinese environment by conducting a number of experiments designed to help it understand the local market and incorporate the lessons learned in a subsequent rollout. For example, it experimented with different store formats to see which had the greatest customer appeal. One such format was the Shenzen supercenter, a hybrid store combining a supercenter and a warehouse club where memberships were sold but nonmembers could also shop at "everyday low prices" (plus a 5 percent premium). In a bow to local demographics, the Shenzen operation also experimented with stocking merchandise targeted at a predominantly male market. Wal-Mart also began testing smaller satellite stores that were tailored to the buying habits as well as transportation and shopping trends in China.

In addition to varied formats, Wal-Mart tested different merchandise items to determine what would have the greatest consumer appeal and fit best with the Chinese culture. As a result of these experiments, Wal-Mart stores in China began to carry a wide range of products, particularly in the area of perishable goods that appealed to Chinese palates.

Product sourcing was another area requiring adaptation. Wal-Mart had three sourcing options: products obtained from global suppliers anywhere in the world, products manufactured in China by global suppliers (such as Procter & Gamble), and products from local suppliers. Wal-Mart elected to purchase 85 percent of its merchandise for the Chinese market in China (combining the second and third options) in an effort to balance local customers' desire for high-status U.S.–made consumer goods and pressure from local governments to purchase goods produced domestically.

Battles with Local Competitors

Any company entering a new country can expect retaliation not only from local competitors but also from other multinationals already operating in that market. Anticipating and responding to these competitive threats is essential to establishing local presence successfully. Wal-Mart's approaches to neutralizing local competitors have differed in different markets, ranging from acquiring a weak player (such as Woolco in Canada) to acquiring an established successful player (such as Asda in the United Kingdom) to launching a frontal attack on the incumbent (such as the company's entry into Brazil).

Acquiring a successful established player. Wal-Mart used this approach in its entry into Germany as well as the United Kingdom.[9] Having determined that building new hypermarkets in Germany would be ill-advised due to the mature European market, and that strict zoning laws limited greenfield operations, Wal-Mart spent more than two years exploring potential acquisitions, including Britain's Tesco, Germany's Metro, and the Dutch firm Makro. In December 1997, it acquired the Wertkauf hypermarket chain from the German Mann family. Wal-Mart had several strong reasons to choose Wertkauf. It was one of the most profitable hypermarket chains in Germany. Wertkauf's hypermarkets were one-stop shopping centers that offered a broad assortment of high-quality general merchandise and food and were, therefore, similar to and compatible with Wal-Mart's supercenter format. The quality of Wertkauf's personnel, its store locations, and its relationships with local customers were also attractive to Wal-Mart. And Wertkauf's stores had an average space of 110,000 square feet, larger than the average German hypermarket.

As in Germany, the British retail market was also mature, necessitating entry through acquisition rather than a greenfield start-up. In 1999, Wal-Mart acquired the Asda Group PLC, a financially strong, well-managed supermarket chain and one of the major players in the U.K. retail sector. Asda's fit with Wal-Mart was particularly good. In fact, the Asda Group had, for a long time, emulated and copied Wal-Mart's core practices and business formula, which meant that it would not require the kind of substantial cultural transformation needed in Wal-Mart's acquisitions in Canada and Germany. Several of Asda's operating philosophies resembled Wal-Mart's: everyday low prices, no sales promotions, merchandising strong private-label brands, heavy emphasis on customer service, placing the trademark Wal-Mart type "people greeters" at the entrance, calling employees "colleagues" (equivalent to Wal-Mart's "associates"), and outfitting them with "Happy to Help" badges similar to Wal-Mart's "Who's Number One? The Customer" badges).[10]

Transplanting and embedding core beliefs and practices into a new subsidiary is difficult in general but is especially problematic in acquisitions, where the acquired partner typically views the new parent's beliefs and practices as alien and of questionable value. Acquiring the Asda Group meant that Wal-Mart could circumvent the daunting task of having to transplant its beliefs and practices into the new subsidiary.

Launching a frontal attack on the incumbent. Attacking dominant and entrenched local competitors head-on is feasible only when the global firm can bring significant competitive advantage into the host country. Wal-Mart's entry into Brazil illustrates the potential—and the limitations—of a frontal attack.[11] Carrefour, the French retailer, had been operating in Brazil since 1975. When Wal-Mart entered Brazil in 1994, its approach was to overtake competitors by aggressively pricing its products. This strategy backfired, as Carrefour and other local competitors also cut prices, leading to a price war and initial losses for Wal-Mart. The company quickly realized that its global sourcing did not provide any built-in price advantage because the leading sales category in Brazilian super-centers was food items, whose sourcing tended to be local. Competitors such as Carrefour had leverage in local sourcing because of their long relationships with local vendors.

Rather than continue trying to undercut Brazilian competitors on price, Wal-Mart chose to focus on the two areas in which it could differentiate itself. The first, customer service, was targeted at neutralizing Carrefour. As an industry observer remarked:

> While small shops in Brazil have a strong customer service component, most large stores, including Carrefour, have adopted the European ethic that the customer is fortunate enough to have them available and if they are unhappy about something, they are welcome to go next door. To entice shoppers away from these large but user-unfriendly stores, Wal-Mart stressed its customer service, an asset enhanced by its open door policy for hiring and promotion. With college education widely available at nominal or no cost, Brazil has more skilled workers than high-skill jobs. Wal-Mart's willingness to give decision-making power to young, entry-level associates attracted able and enthusiastic workers, many of whom might have had to serve coffee to their elders for years before other employers would allow them a more responsible role.[12]

Wal-Mart's second point of differentiation, especially vis-à-vis smaller local vendors, resulted from its decisions to improve the selection, breadth, depth, and presentation of merchandise—improvements developed locally rather than imported from the United States.

After recovering from an initial setback at the hands of its competitors in Brazil, Wal-Mart identified areas in which it could differentiate itself. By emphasizing its strengths, the company was able to successfully counterattack both Carrefour and smaller local vendors, and solidify its market presence in Brazil.

SPEED OF GLOBAL EXPANSION: HOW RAPID IS "RAPID"?

Did Wal-Mart globalize quickly enough? A comparison with its competitors, other retailers both within the United States and in Europe, is informative. We look at three United States retailers—J.C. Penny, Kmart, and Sears—along with two large non–U.S. retailers—Carrefour of France and Metro AG, the German retailer.

As of 1999, J.C. Penny was in the very early stages of venturing abroad. It entered Brazil that year through an acquisition; in addition, the company also had three stores in Mexico. As of 2000, Kmart was a wholly domestic company, deriving 100 percent of its sales revenues from its U.S. stores. As for Sears, its non–U.S. outlets (located only in Canada) were responsible for 10 percent, or $4.1 billion, of the company's total 1999 sales revenues of $41 billion. Sears's global presence appeared to have shrunk in recent years; in 1997, the company divested a controlling stake in its Mexican operations. As these comparisons indicate, Wal-Mart's global presence clearly exceeded that of its three large U.S. competitors in terms of the number of countries entered, number of stores operated outside the United States, and growth in international stores as well as international sales.

Table 3.2 contains a summarized business profile of Carrefour, headquartered in France. Carrefour's first international move occurred in 1973 in Spain. It took Carrefour almost a quarter of a century to achieve 79 billion FFr ($15 billion) in international sales. In contrast, in only seven years, Wal-Mart surpassed $12 billion in international sales. However, a comparison of Table 3.1 with Table 3.2 indicates that Carrefour's financial performance in its international operations outpaced Wal-Mart's.

In August 1999, Carrefour merged with another French retailer, Promodes SA, in a $16 billion deal to create the second-largest retailer in the world, with a combined sales revenue of $49 billion.[13] This merger was motivated in part as a defense against Wal-Mart's strong entry into Europe. Also, Promodes was a good

TABLE 3.2 Carrefour's Globalization

Financial Statistics (FFr in million)

Year		1995	1996	1997	1998
Sales	Domestic total (France)	89,677	92,193	96,328	99,702
	International	54,935	62,712	72,941	78,781
	International as percentage of Total Sales	38.0	40.5	43.1	44.1
Profit after tax*	Domestic total (France)	979	1,141	1,495	1,696
	International	1,904	2,447	2,492	2,775
	International as percentage of Total Profit	66.0	68.2	62.5	62.1

Breakdown in Number of Stores—December 31,1999

Store Type	France	Outside France	Worldwide
Hypermarkets	227	453	680
Supermarkets	1,078	1,182	2,260
Hard discount stores	418	2,702	3,120
Other	2,243	697	2,940
Total	3,966	5,034	9,000

*Average Tax Rate (37.5 percent).

Source: CSFB, 28 April 1998, pp. 3–4, and company annual reports.

fit as it had strong presence in markets where Carrefour was weak (Southern Europe) and vice versa (Carrefour had established a strong presence in Asia and Latin America). This move clearly accelerated the pace of globalization for Carrefour in 1999. During fiscal year 1999, Carrefour derived 38 percent of its revenues and 38 percent of its profits from stores outside France.

In 1999, Metro AG (which operates a cash-and-carry business, department stores, hypermarkets, discount food stores, and specialty outlets) was the third-largest retailer in the world, following Wal-Mart and Carrefour. In 1997, 7 percent of its total sales revenues were generated outside Germany (compared to 4 percent in 1995, and 5 percent in 1996). As of that year, its degree of globalization was on a par with Wal-Mart's. The next year, in 1998, Metro acquired SHV Makro of The Netherlands, making Metro AG's consolidated sales revenues for 1998 about 108 billion DM, of which foreign sales constituted 37 percent.

How does Wal-Mart's rate of globalization rate on an absolute scale? Based on Tables 3.1 and 3.2, it could be argued that the company is entering emerging markets at a slow and conservative pace. Keep in mind, however, that major penetration of an emerging growth market, such as China or India, requires a different approach. In India, for example, only a relatively small number of consumers have incomes greater than $20,000, but these customers prefer and can afford global brands. To serve these customers, Wal-Mart could exploit its buying power with global suppliers. But what about the several million potential Indian customers with income levels between $5,000 and $20,000, who remain loyal to local customs, local habits, and often to local brands? And then there is the biggest segment of the Indian population, whose per capita income level is well below $5,000. Members of this group are unlikely to become active Wal-Mart customers any time soon. China presents a similar profile.[14]

To make a significant dent in the mid-level consumer groups in these vast markets—those in which incomes range from $5,000 to $20,000—it will not be enough for Wal-Mart simply to export its business model from the United States, making local adjustments as needed. An entirely new business model may be needed. Any company embarking on such an enterprise must have a global mindset. But, as of 1999, not only was Wal-Mart's International Division headed by an American but its board of directors and top fifteen executives were all Americans. Thus one of Wal-Mart's greatest needs in the near future will be to diversify its senior management ranks.

GLOBALIZATION OF TOYS "Я" US

This section presents a condensed view of the globalization of another well-known retailer, Toys "Я" Us—one whose choices were different from Wal-Mart's—to emphasize that optimal choices are specific to each company's situation. As can be seen in Box 3.3 (key events in the globalization of Toys "Я" Us), of its two product lines—toys (Toys "Я" Us) and clothing (Kids "Я" Us)—the company chose to globalize its toy store chain. This decision appears logical in light of the wide range of tastes in children's clothing compared to the similarity in preferences for toys from country to country; globalization of the toy store chain would be more likely to have higher payoffs and lower risks than would globalization of the clothing store chain.

As also indicated in Box 3.3, Toys "Я" Us has until recently relied exclusively on greenfield start-ups and not sought cross-border acquisitions. This, too, seems logical since Toys "Я" Us invented the toy superstore concept and therefore historically could find few—if any—foreign acquisition targets that would not require radical transformation.

Note too that Toys "Я" Us has almost always shied away from strategic alliances, relying instead on complete ownership of its foreign operations. Its independent approach contrasts sharply with that of Wal-Mart, which has been much more open to strategic alliances. This difference reflects the difference in product offerings: Toys require very little customization, unlike the merchandise carried by Wal-Mart. As a leading business magazine phrased it, "toys need no translation,"[15] which means that Toys "Я" Us has considerably less need for local learning than does Wal-Mart. Also worth noting is that the only country in which Toys "Я" Us has engaged in a strategic alliance is Japan, where there is a high

BOX 3-3

TIME LINE OF GLOBALIZATION MOVES OF TOYS "Я" US

Sequence of Market Entry		*Salient Features of Globalization*
1948	Founded	• All stores are greenfield operations
1984	First move outside United States. Enters Canada and Singapore.	• In Europe, approximately 80 percent of items are the
1980s	Enters Hong Kong, Taiwan, and Malaysia	same as in the United States; the rest cater to local tastes.
1985	Enters United Kingdom	• In Japan, 65 percent of the toys are Japanese; the rest are imports.
1987	Enters Germany	
1988	Enters France and Spain	
1989	Forms 80–20 joint venture with McDonald's Japan for entry into Japan. First store opens in 1991.	
1992	Enters Austria	Portfolio: January 29, 1994
1993	Enters Australia, Belgium, Holland, Portugal, Switzerland	581 Toys "Я" Us stores in the United States
1994	Enters Scandinavia	217 Kids "Я" Us stores in the United States
		234 Toys "Я" Us stores outside the United States

demand for local products. In Japan, the proportion of local toys sold by Toys "Я" Us is 65 percent, considerably higher than in any other market. In Europe, for example, approximately 80 percent of the items sold by Toys "Я" Us are the same as those sold in the United States, and only 20 percent cater to local tastes.

SUMMARY

To sum up, every company embarking on global expansion must make wise decisions in each of six areas: choice of products, choice of markets, mode of entry, transplanting core beliefs and practices, winning the local battle, and speed of global expansion. The content of these decisions depends very heavily on the industry and strategic context of the particular firm.

CHAPTER 4

BUILDING GLOBAL COMPETITIVE ADVANTAGE

The question is not whether the global company adds value. It is whether it adds more than it simultaneously subtracts.[1]

—Tony Jackson

SECURING GLOBAL presence is anything but synonymous with possessing global competitive advantage. Presence in strategically important markets is certainly a precondition for creating global competitive advantage. However, it says little about whether and how you will actually create such advantage. To use a sports analogy, once you have assembled a team (that is, created global presence), you must get the players geared up for battle, harmonize and coordinate their actions, plan your offensive and defensive strategies, and anticipate and respond to opponents' moves. Furthermore, winning one game doesn't ensure that you will win the next one. In short, transforming global presence into solid competitive advantage requires systematic analysis, purposeful thinking, and careful orchestration and is a never-ending process. Without a rigorously disciplined approach, global presence can easily degenerate into a liability that distracts management and wastes resources. The end result can even be a loss of competitive advantage in the domestic market. A company's overall performance will generally worsen rather than improve if it does not effectively harness global presence.

In this chapter, we address the following questions: *What are the unique value creation opportunities resulting from global expansion? How does effective exploitation of these opportunities yield competitive advantage for a firm? What challenges is a firm likely to face in exploiting these opportunities? Finally, what type of analysis must managers undertake in order to learn how to transform global presence into global competitive advantage?*

SOURCES OF GLOBAL COMPETITIVE ADVANTAGE

To convert global presence into global competitive advantage, a company must pursue six value creation opportunities, each of which encounters specific strategic and organizational obstacles:[2]

- Adapting to local market differences
- Exploiting economies of global scale
- Exploiting economies of global scope
- Tapping the most optimal locations for activities and resources
- Maximizing knowledge transfer across locations
- Playing the global chess game

Adapting to Local Market Differences

A direct implication of being present in multiple countries is that the company must respond to the inevitable heterogeneity it will encounter in these markets. Differences in language, culture, income levels, customer preferences, and distribution systems are only some of the factors to be considered. Even in the case of apparently standard products, at least some degree of local adaptation is often necessary—or at least advisable; for example, in the case of cellular phones, it matters whether companies adapt their products to differences in language, magnitude of background noise on the street, affordability, and so forth. By responding to country-level heterogeneity through local adaptation of products, services, and processes, a company can reap benefits in three fundamental areas: market share, price realization, and competitive position.

Increased Market Share By definition, offering standard products and services across countries constricts the boundaries of the served market to only those customers whose needs are uniform across countries. Local adaptation of products and services has the opposite effect, expanding the boundaries to include those customers within a country who value different features and attributes. One of McGraw-Hill's products, *BusinessWeek*, provides a good illustration of how local adaptation of products and services can enlarge the customer base. As *BusinessWeek*'s editor-in-chief explained: "Each week, we produce three editions. For example, this week's North American cover story is 'The New Hucksterism.' The Asian edition cover is 'Acer, Taiwan's Global Powerhouse.' And the European-edition cover is 'Central Europe.' In addition, our writers create an additional 10 to 12 pages of stories customized for readers in Europe, Asia, and Latin America. They also turn out four pages of international-finance coverage, international editorials, and economic analysis, and a regional feature column called SPOTLIGHT."[3] Similarly, anyone who travels abroad (or just about anywhere) knows that McDonald's has adapted the Big Mac to local tastes, ranging from lamb-based patties in India to teriyaki burgers in Tokyo and the "McDeluxe," a salty and spicy hamburger, in France.

Improved Price Realization   Tailoring products and services to local preferences enhances the value delivered to local customers. As a corollary, a portion of this increased value should translate into higher price realization for the firm. Consider, for instance, the case of Yahoo! portals in various countries. The more tailored the portal is to local market needs (in terms of content, commerce, and community), the greater would be the number of users and the amount of time they spend with Yahoo! These advantages can be monetized by Yahoo! directly in the form of higher advertising rates and merchant commissions accruing to the company from its various commercial partners.

Neutralizing Local Competitors   One of the natural advantages enjoyed by most local competitors stems from their deep understanding of and single-minded responsiveness to the needs of the local market. For example, in the Japanese soft drinks market, Suntory Ltd. and Asahi Soft Drinks Co. have been among the first movers in offering new concepts such as Asian teas and fermented-milk drinks. When a global player also customizes its products and services to local needs and preferences, this move is essentially a frontal attack on the local competitors in their market niche. In its efforts to neutralize Suntory's and Asahi's moves and attack them on their home turf, Coca-Cola has introduced several new products in Japan that are not offered by the company in other markets, including an Asian tea called Sokenbicha, an English tea called Kochakaden, and a coffee drink called Georgia.[4]

Challenges.   While seeking the benefits of local adaptation, however, companies must be prepared to face a number of challenges and obstacles.

In most cases, local adaptation of products and services will increase the company's cost structure. Given the inexorable intensity of competition in most industries, companies can ill afford any competitive disadvantage on the cost dimension. *Thus managers have to find the right equilibrium in the trade-off between localization and cost structure.* For example, cost considerations initially led Proctor & Gamble to standardize diaper design across European markets, despite market research data indicating that Italian mothers, unlike those in other countries, preferred diapers covering the baby's navel. After some time, however, recognizing that this particular feature was critical to Italian mothers, the company incorporated this design feature for the Italian market, despite its adverse cost implications.[5]

In many instances, local adaptation, even when well intentioned, may prove to be misguided. For example, when the American restaurant chain TGI Friday's entered the South Korean market, it deliberately incorporated many local dishes, such as kimchi, in its menu. This responsiveness, however, backfired. Company analysis of the tepid market performance revealed that Korean customers anticipated a visit to TGI Friday's as "a visit to America." They found the same old local dishes on the menu inconsistent with their expectations. *Thus companies must take the pulse of their market continually to detect if and when local adaptation becomes misguided.*

As with many other aspects of global marketing, the necessary degree of local adaptation will usually shift over time. In many cases, the shifts tend toward less need for local adaptation. A variety of factors, such as the influence of global media, greater international travel, and declining income disparities across countries, are paving the way toward increasing global standardization. Back to the example of *BusinessWeek,* we foresee a diminished need over time for geography-based customization. *Thus companies must recalibrate the need for local adaptation on an ongoing basis; overadaptation extracts a price just as surely as does underadaptation.*

Exploiting Economies of Global Scale

Building global presence automatically expands a company's scale of operations (larger revenues, larger asset base, and so on). However, larger scale will create competitive advantage if and only if the company systematically undertakes the tough actions needed to convert "scale" into "economies of scale." The potential benefits of economies of scale can appear in various ways—spreading fixed costs, reducing capital and operating costs, pooling purchasing power, and creating critical mass—as we describe next.

Spreading Fixed Costs over Larger Volume   This benefit is most salient in areas such as research and development, operations, and advertising. For instance, Merck can spread R&D costs over its global sales volume, thereby reducing its per-unit costs of development. Similarly, financial services companies enjoy economies of scale in credit card processing where unit costs fall sharply with an increase in activity.

Reducing Capital and Operating Costs per Unit   This type of benefit is often a consequence of the fact that doubling the capacity of a production facility typically increases the cost of building and operating the facility by a factor of less than two.

Pooling Global Purchasing Power over Suppliers   Concentrating global purchasing power over any specific supplier generally leads to volume discounts and lower transaction costs. For example, as Marriott has raised its stakes in the global lodging business, its purchase of goods such as furnishings, linen, beverages, and so on has stepped up dramatically. Exercising its global purchasing power over a few vendors (as with PepsiCo for soft drinks) is part of Marriott's efforts to convert its global presence into global competitive advantage. Similarly, in the early 1990s, General Motors consolidated 27 largely autonomous purchasing operations under one global purchasing division. In 1998 alone, this division purchased a total volume of parts and raw materials worth between $70 and $80 billion, with a net cost savings of $2 billion.[6] The creation of Internet-based procurement hubs (such as Covisint, a joint venture between General Motors, Ford, and DaimlerChrysler) represents the ongoing pursuit of such scale economies through new enabling technologies.

Creating Requisite Critical Mass in Selected Activities   A larger scale gives the global player the opportunity to build centers of excellence for the development of specific technologies and products. To develop a center of excellence, a company generally needs to focus a critical mass of talent in one location. In view of the potential to leverage the output of such a center on a global scale, a global player will be more willing and able to make the necessary resource commitments required for such a center.

Challenges.   Few if any of these potential strategic benefits of scale materialize automatically. The following challenges await firms in their efforts to secure these benefits.

Scale economies can be realized only by concentrating scale-sensitive resources and activities in one or a few locations. Concentration is a two-edged sword, however. For example, with manufacturing activities, concentration means that firms must export centrally manufactured goods (components, subsystems, or the finished product) to various markets. *Thus, in making decisions about the choice of location for any activity, firms must weigh the potential benefits from concentration against increased transportation and tariff costs.*

One unintended result of the geographic concentration of any activity is to isolate that activity from the targeted markets. Such isolation can be risky since it may cause delayed or inadequate response to market needs. *Thus another management challenge is to minimize the costs of isolation.*

Concentrating an activity in a designated location also makes the rest of the company dependent on that location. This "sole source" dependence implies that, unless that location has world-class competencies, you may wind up with global mess instead of global competitive advantage. As underscored by a European executive of Ford Motor Company reflecting on the company's concentration of activities as part of a global integration program in the mid-1990s: "Now if you misjudge the market, you are wrong in fifteen countries rather than only one." *Thus the pursuit of global scale economies raises the added challenge of building world-class competencies at those locations in which the activities will be concentrated.*

In situations where global presence stems from cross-border acquisitions, as with British Petroleum's acquisition of Amoco, realizing economies of scale requires massive restructuring. Firms must scale up at locations at which activities are to be concentrated and scale down or even close shop at the other locations. This restructuring demands large financial investment, incurs huge one-time transition costs, and always results in organizational and psychological trauma. Furthermore, scale-downs or closures may damage the company's image and relations with local governments, local customers, and local communities. On top of all this, erroneous decisions in choosing locations are usually very difficult, expensive, and time-consuming to reverse. Nonetheless, firms cannot realize the advantageous economies of scale without making tough decisions. *Thus management must be willing to undertake a comprehensive and logical analysis and then have the courage to carry out timely and decisive action.*

Exploiting Economies of Global Scope

Global scope, as distinct from global scale, refers to the multiplicity of regions and countries in which a company markets its products and services. By way of example, consider the case of two hypothetical advertising agencies, Alpha and Beta, whose sales revenues are roughly comparable. Assume that Alpha offers its services in only 5 countries whereas Beta offers its services in 25 countries. In this instance, we would consider the global scope of Beta to be broader than that of Alpha. Global scope is rarely a strategic imperative when vendors are serving customers who operate in just one country or customers who are global but who engage in centralized sourcing from one location and do their own internal distribution. In contrast, the economic value of global scope can be enormous when vendors are serving customers who, despite being global, need local delivery of identical or similar products and services across many markets. In fulfilling the needs of such multilocation global customers, companies have two potential avenues through which to turn global scope into global competitive advantage: providing coordinated services, and leveraging their market power.

Providing Coordinated Services to Global Customers   Consider three scenarios: the case of Microsoft, as it launches a new software product in more than 50 countries on the same day and needs to source advertising services in every one of the targeted markets; the case of McDonald's, which must source virtually identical ketchup and mustard pouches for its operations in every market; and the case of Shell Oil, which needs to source similar process control equipment for its many refineries around the world. In all of these examples, a global customer needs to purchase a bundle of identical or similar products and services across a number of countries. The global customer could source these products and services from a host of local suppliers or from a single global supplier that is present in all of its markets. In comparison to local suppliers, a single global supplier can provide value for the global customer through greater consistency in the quality and features of products and services across countries, faster and smoother coordination across countries, and lower transaction costs.

Market Power Vis-à-Vis Competitors   A global supplier has the opportunity to understand the unique strategic requirements and culture of its global customer. Since it takes time to build this type of customer-specific proprietary knowledge, particularly in the case of multilocation global customers, potential competitors are initially handicapped and can more easily be kept at bay.

Federal Express, a major supplier of logistics and distribution services to Laura Ashley, enjoys this advantage. As a global logistics provider, FedEx has had the chance to deepen its understanding of its role in Laura Ashley's value chain in every one of its served markets. By definition, this understanding is customer-specific and takes time to build. As long as FedEx continues to provide effective and efficient logistics services to Laura Ashley, this knowledge will serve as a major entry barrier for other local or global logistics suppliers.

Challenges.   Notwithstanding the twin benefits outlined in this section, securing economies of global scope is not without its own specific challenges.

The case of a multilocation global vendor serving the needs of a multilocation global customer is conceptually analogous to one global network serving the needs of another global network. Every global network, however effectively managed, typically has a plethora of power centers, accompanied by competing perspectives on the optimal course of action. *Thus one of the management challenges for a global vendor is to understand the ongoing tug-of-war that shapes the needs and buying decisions of the customer network.*

Even for global customer accounts, the actual delivery of goods and services must be executed at the local level. Yet local country managers cannot be given total freedom in their operations vis-à-vis global customer accounts. They must orient their actions around their global customers' need for consistency both in product and service features and in marketing terms and conditions. *Thus another challenge in capturing the economies of global scope lies in being responsive to the tension between two conflicting needs: the need for central coordination of most elements of the marketing mix and the need for local autonomy in the actual delivery of products and services.*

Tapping the Most Optimal Locations for Activities and Resources

Even as global economies have become increasingly integrated and influenced by the global media so that cultures take on many of each other's aspects, most countries are and will continue to be largely heterogeneous for many years to come. As discussed earlier, intercountry heterogeneity has an impact on the need for local adaptation in a company's products and services. But differences across countries also reveal themselves in the form of differences in cost structures, skill levels, and resource endowments. If it can exploit these intercountry differences better than its competitors, a firm has the potential to create significant proprietary advantage.

In performing the various activities along its value chain (for example, research and development, procurement, manufacturing, assembly, marketing, sales, distribution, and service), every firm has to make a number of crucial decisions, among them where the activity will take place. Several factors influence this decision. Box 4.1 elaborates on some of these factors and suggests that tapping the optimal locations for each activity can yield one or more of three strategic benefits: performance enhancement, cost reduction, and risk reduction.

BOX *4-1*

CRITERIA FOR LOCATION DECISIONS

Performance Enhancement

- *Criticality of customer proximity in the execution of the activity:* For example, for an aircraft manufacturer such as Boeing, the preflight checkup and maintenance activity must be performed at the various airport locations around the world.

- *Availability of needed talent:* For example, in 1997 Microsoft decided to establish a major corporate research center in Cambridge, England. This decision was driven predominantly by the availability of outstanding graduates from Oxford and Cambridge universities, and by the desire to build stronger alliances with the leading-edge software research labs of these universities.

- *Impact on the company's speed at improving critical competencies:* Locating an activity in a country or region that is the home base of particularly demanding customers or leading-edge competitors exposes the company's operations to the highest standards of excellence at close range, thereby pushing the speed at which the competencies underlying this activity are upgraded.

- *Impact on the quality of internal coordination:* To the extent that the successful performance of two or more activities depends on intense coordination on an ongoing basis, the choice of locations for these activities must take into account the ease with which frictionless coordination across locations can be achieved. In such situations, location decisions would also be guided by factors such as the quality of travel and communication links between locations as well as the extent to which the locations are separated by time and language.

- *Ability to work around the clock:* Distribution of certain activities (such as development projects) to three different time zones can dramatically accelerate the pace at which the activities can be completed.

Cost Reduction

- *Impact of location on the cost of activity execution:* Relative to other alternatives, any particular location will generally reduce some cost elements (say, labor costs) but increase some other cost elements (for example, infrastructure-related costs such as power, transportation, and so on). In cost terms, an optimal location would be one that yields the lowest cost structure on a net basis.

- *Government incentives and tax structure:* In many instances, local governments give sizable direct or indirect incentives to specifically targeted companies as a means to boost capital investment and technology inflows into that location. Some examples of this phenomenon would be the incentives provided by the state of Alabama to Mercedes-Benz and the government of Italy to Texas Instruments. For any value-chain activity, such incentives (or disincentives in the form of higher taxes and tariffs) can also have a significant impact on the cost optimality of various locations.

BOX 4-1

(CONTINUED)

Risk Reduction
- *Currency risks:* Given the unpredictable nature of exchange rate movements, companies can protect themselves against currency risk exposure by performing the particular activity in a small number of very carefully chosen countries. For obvious reasons, guarding against currency risks through locational decisions would be most critical in the case of activities that account for a significant fraction of the firm's total cost structure.
- *Political risks:* Notwithstanding the presence of other advantages, a location can become unattractive if the political uncertainties associated with it are particularly high.

Performance Enhancement Fiat's decision to choose Brazil rather than its native Italy to design and launch Palio (its "third-world" car), and Microsoft's decision to establish a corporate research laboratory in England are good examples of location decisions that were guided predominantly by the goal of building and sustaining world-class excellence in the selected activities.

Cost Reduction Two illustrative examples of location decisions founded predominantly on cost reduction considerations are Nike's decision to source the manufacture of athletic shoes in Asian countries such as China, Vietnam, and Indonesia, and Texas Instruments' decision to set up a software development unit in India.

Risk Reduction Given the wild swings in exchange rates between the U.S. dollar and the Japanese yen (against each other as well as against other major currencies), a critical basis for cost competition between Ford and Toyota has been their relative ingenuity at managing currency risks. For these competitors, one of the ways to manage currency risks has been to spread the high cost elements of their manufacturing operations across a few select, carefully chosen locations around the world.

Challenges. We examine now the challenges associated with using geographical differences to create global competitive advantage.

The way in which activities are performed depends not only on the characteristics of the factor inputs but also on the management skills with which these inputs are converted into value-added outputs. The choice of a seemingly optimal location cannot guarantee that the quality and cost of factor inputs will be optimal. *It is up to managers to ensure that the comparative advantage of a location is captured and internalized rather than squandered because of weaknesses in productivity and the quality of internal operations.* Ford Motor Company illustrates how the company's efforts have amplified the magnitude of proprietary advantage derived from locating some of its manufacturing operations in Mexico. Ford has benefited not just from lower labor costs in Mexico but also from superior management of its Mexican operations, leading to productivity levels that have been even higher than in the United States. People often assume that in countries such as Mexico, lower wage rates come side-by-side with lower productivity. Although this may be true statistically at the level of the country as a whole, it does not have to be so for a specific firm such as Ford. Unemployment levels in Mexico are higher than in the United States. Thus in its Mexican operations, Ford can be more selective about whom it hires. Also, given lower turnover of employees, the company can invest more in training and development. Thus the net result can easily be not just lower wage rates but also higher productivity than in the United States. It goes without saying that, without conscious efforts of this type, the reverse can just as easily occur.

Furthermore, the optimality of any location hinges on the cost and quality of factor inputs at this location relative to all other locations. This fact is important because countries not only evolve over time but do so at different rates and in different directions. Thus, for any particular activity, today's choice location may no longer be optimal three years down the road. A relentless pursuit of optimal locations requires the global company to remain somewhat footloose. Nike's example is illustrative. Nike continuously assesses the relative attractiveness of various manufacturing locations and has demonstrated a willingness and ability to shift locations over time. *Thus managers should not let today's location decisions diminish the firm's flexibility in shifting locations as needed.*

Optimal locations will generally be different for different resources and activities. *Thus yet another challenge in fully capturing the strategic benefits of optimal locations is to excel at coordination across dispersed locations.* This is illustrated by the case of Texas Instruments' high-speed telecommunications chip, TCM9055. This sophisticated chip was conceived in collaboration with engineers from Sweden, designed in France using software tools developed in Houston, produced in Japan and Dallas, and tested in Taiwan.[7]

Maximizing Knowledge Transfer Across Locations

Foreign subsidiaries can be viewed from several perspectives. For instance, one way to view Nokia's subsidiary in China would be in terms of its market position within China's mobile telecommunications industry. An alternate view would be to see Nokia China as a bundle of tangible assets such as buildings, equipment, capital, and so on. Yet another view would be to see Nokia China as a reservoir of knowledge in areas such as wireless technology, the creation of world-class manufacturing operations in a developing country, market penetration, revenue and cost management, and dealing with local governments. Building on this last perspective, we can view every global company not only as a portfolio of subsidiaries with tangible assets but also as a portfolio of knowledge centers.

Given the heterogeneity of countries, every subsidiary has to create some degree of unique knowledge so as to exploit the resource and market opportunities of the local environment. Of course, not all locally created knowledge is relevant outside the local environment (for example, advertising execution in the Japanese language lacks pertinence outside Japan). However, other types of locally created knowledge may be relevant across multiple countries and, if leveraged effectively, can yield various strategic benefits to the global enterprise ranging from faster product and process innovation to lower cost of innovation and reduced risk of competitive preemption.

Faster Product and Process Innovation All innovation requires the incorporation of new ideas, whether they are developed internally on a de novo basis or acquired and absorbed from others. A global company's skill at transferring knowledge across subsidiaries gives these subsidiaries the added benefit of innovations created by their peers. And by minimizing, if not altogether eliminating, counterproductive reinvention of the wheel, product and process innovations get accelerated across the entire global network. For example, Yahoo! introduced a new service—Yahoo! Photos—in its U.S. portal in March 2000. Within just three months after the U.S. launch, the company had made this service available on its portals in 18 other markets. P&G's highly successful launch of Liquid Tide in the late 1980s provides a different yet equally interesting example. This product incorporated technologies pioneered in Cincinnati (a new ingredient to help suspend dirt in washwater), Japan (cleaning agents), and Brussels (ingredients that fight the mineral salts present in hard water).[8]

Lower Cost of Innovation A second byproduct of not reinventing the wheel is considerable savings in the costs of innovation. For example, the efficient "stockist-based" distribution system developed by Richardson Vicks's Indian operations, now a part of Procter & Gamble India, found ready applicability in the company's Indonesian and Chinese operations.[9] Such cross-border replication of an innovation from one country to another can eliminate or significantly reduce the costs associated with from-the-ground-up experimentation in that country.

Reduced Risk of Competitive Preemption A global company that demands constant innovations from its subsidiaries but does not leverage these innovations effectively across subsidiaries risks becoming a fount of new ideas for competitors. Procter & Gamble is one company that is keenly aware of these risks. Several of P&G's subsidiaries are dedicated to improving the fit, the performance, and the looks of the disposable diaper. Over the past decade, P&G's ability to systematically identify the successful innovations and expedite a global roll-out of these innovations has thwarted competitors' efforts to steal its new ideas and replicate them in other markets. Effective and efficient transfer of knowledge across its subsidiaries has helped P&G safeguard its innovations and enabled it to significantly reduce the risk of competitive preemption.

Challenges.   Most companies tap only a fraction of the full potential for enormous economic value inherent in the transfer and leveraging of knowledge across borders. The rest of this section presents some of the primary reasons why (Chapter 6 details these and other pathologies in greater detail).

Knowledge transfer from one subsidiary to another cannot occur unless the source and the target units (or an intermediary such as regional or corporate headquarters) recognize both the existence of unique know-how in the source unit and the potential value of this know-how in the target unit. Since significant geographic, linguistic, and cultural distances often separate subsidiaries, the potential for knowledge transfer can easily remain lost in a sea of ignorance. *Thus companies face the management challenge of creating mechanisms that would systematically and routinely uncover the opportunities for knowledge transfer.*

A subsidiary with uniquely valuable know-how is likely to enjoy a knowledge monopoly within the global enterprise. Also, power struggles are both normal and ubiquitous in any organization. Taken together, these two facts imply that at least some subsidiaries will succumb to the "knowledge is power" syndrome, viewing uniquely valuable know-how as the currency through which they acquire and retain political power within the corporation. The symptoms of this pathology are most obvious in the case of manufacturing facilities where relative superiority on an internal basis often serves as survival insurance in a footloose corporation. *Thus another management challenge in making knowledge transfers happen is to ensure that subsidiaries are eager rather than reluctant to share what they know.*

Like the "knowledge is power" syndrome, the "not invented here" (NIH) syndrome is also a chronic malady in many organizations. Two of the engines of the NIH syndrome are ego-defense mechanisms that induce some managers to block information suggesting the greater competence of others, and power struggles within organizations that lead some managers to pretend that the know-how of peer units is neither unique nor valuable. *Thus global enterprises committed to knowledge transfer must also address the management challenge of making subsidiaries eager rather than reluctant to learn from peer units.*

Only a subset of an organization's knowledge exists in the form of codified knowledge—a chemical formula, an engineering blueprint, or an operations manual. Such codified knowledge readily lends itself to transfer and distribution across subsidiaries through electronic or other mechanisms for document exchange. However, much valuable know-how often exists in the form of *tacit knowledge,* knowledge that is embedded in the minds, behavior patterns, and skills of individuals or teams—for example, a vision of a particular technology's future or a particular competency at managing global customer accounts. With effort and investment, it might be possible to articulate and codify some fraction of the tacit knowledge. Nonetheless, its embedded and elusive nature often makes tacit knowledge impossible to codify and thus difficult to transfer. *Thus another challenge for the global enterprise is to design and erect effective and efficient bridges for the transfer of knowledge (especially noncodifiable tacit knowledge) across subsidiaries.*

Playing the Global Chess Game

In the global competition between Kodak and Fuji or Coke and Pepsi, each side can adopt one of two different approaches. The first option would be to view this as a war where your subsidiaries slug it out with your opponent's subsidiaries on a country-by-country basis. The other option would be to view the global war as analogous to a chess game; as in chess, you would continually identify specific target markets for attack and, when you do attack, you would do so through coordinated action of all your available resources. The latter is nearly always the smarter of the two approaches.

In playing the global chess game, one goal should be to weaken the competitor in its current strongholds. When launching such an attack, it is crucial to ensure a coordinated leveraging of worldwide resources (cash flow, scale economies, technological breakthroughs, and so forth). Otherwise, an attack on the competitor's strongholds could well prove to be very costly, riskladen, even suicidal. Only through skillful coordination can a company minimize both the cost and the risk of an assault on potentially high payoff markets. Fuji Photo provides a salient example of how leveraging resources across countries can check a competitor in its stronghold. In early 1997, Fuji cut prices on multiple-roll packs of film in the U.S. market by as much as 50 percent. These and other moves against Kodak narrowed the global market share gap between them (37 percent versus 39 percent) as compared to the previous year (35 percent versus 40 percent). Analysts attributed Fuji's aggressiveness to the presence of a profit sanctuary in Japan where it had 70 percent market share and apparently greater control over film distribution and pricing.[10]

A second goal should be to preempt the competitor from building a strong presence in future strategic markets. Procter & Gamble's early and aggressive entry into China shows how this course of action offers a major opportunity for the company to expand its future resource base more rapidly than competitors.

A central challenge in playing the global chess game and capturing the consequent benefits is to ensure strategic coordination across countries. It may make sense to sacrifice profits in one market in order to reap even greater benefits in another. In the absence of suitable organizational mechanisms, local managers are unlikely to be willing to sacrifice their own profits for the greater good.

The magnitude of the economic value underlying each of the six value creation opportunities discussed here varies across industries, and even across different segments within the same industry. For instance, take a company such as Unilever, which competes in cosmetics, detergents, and foods. The relative importance of a specific value creation opportunity (for example, economies of scale) varies greatly from cosmetics to detergents to foods. Even within the same business, such as foods, the sources of global value differ dramatically across individual product lines (for example, ice cream, frozen prepared meals, and cooking oil). Given these differences, analysis of how to exploit global presence must be undertaken not merely at the overall corporate level, but more important, also at the level of each individual business.

Focusing on the individual business as the unit of analysis, Box 4.2 summarizes the key issues that must be addressed so as to clarify the scope of each value creation opportunity and to uncover the underlying challenges.

BOX *4-2*

ISSUES TO CONSIDER IN EXPLOITING GLOBAL PRESENCE

1. Adapting to Local Market Differences
   a. Have we accurately drawn a distinction between those attributes where the customer truly values adaptation and those other attributes where the customer is either neutral or averse to adaptation?
   b. For those attributes where adaptation adds value, how much is the customer willing to pay for this value?
   c. Do we manage our product design and manufacturing activities in such a manner that we can offer the needed intercountry variety at the lowest possible cost?
   d. Do we have sensing mechanisms (such as market research and experimental marketing) that would give us early warning about increases or decreases in customers' preferences for local adaptation?
2. Exploiting Economies of Global Scale
   a. In designing our products, have we exhausted all possibilities to employ concepts such as modularization and standardization of subsystems and components?
   b. Have we accurately drawn a distinction between activities that are scale-sensitive and those that are not?
   c. Have we fully assessed the benefits from economies of scale against any resulting increases in other costs—transportation, tariffs, and so forth?
   d. Have we established effective and efficient coordination mechanisms so that we do not squander the benefits from scale economies?
   e. Have we built world-class competencies in the locations where we have chosen to concentrate the scale-sensitive activities?
3. Exploiting Economies of Global Scope
   a. Is our internal coordination of marketing activities across locations at least on par with (and preferably ahead of) the extent to which our customers have integrated their own purchasing activities?
   b. How well do we understand the various pulls and pushes shaping the needs and buying decisions of our customers' global networks?
4. Tapping the Optimal Locations for Activities and Resources
   a. Have we ensured that our location-based advantages are neither squandered by our own staff nor neutralized by competitors because of any weaknesses in the quality and productivity of our internal operations at these locations?
   b. Do we have the organizational and resource flexibility to shift locations over time as some other locations begin to become preferable to our current locations?

BOX *4-2*

(CONTINUED)

---

      c. How frictionless is the degree of our coordination across the various locations?

5. Maximizing Knowledge Transfer Across Locations
      a. How good are we at routinely and systematically uncovering the opportunities for knowledge transfer?
      b. How enthusiastic are our subsidiaries about sharing knowledge with peer units?
      c. How eager are our subsidiaries to learn from any and all sources, including peer subsidiaries?
      d. How good are we at codifying the product and process innovations generated by our subsidiaries? Have we built efficient communication mechanisms for the sharing of codified know-how across locations? How good are we at keeping codified knowledge proprietary to our company?
      e. Have we built effective mechanisms (people transfer, face-to-face interchange, and so forth) for the transfer of tacit knowledge across locations?

6. Playing the Global Chess Game
      a. Do we attack our competitors in a targeted or a random manner?
      b. When we launch an attack on a competitor's current or potential stronghold, do we have the organizational ability to bring together, if needed, our worldwide resources in support of such attack?

CREATING GLOBAL COMPETITIVE ADVANTAGE: ACTION IMPLICATIONS

Exploiting any opportunity requires action. All action occurs at the level of activities in the firm's value chain. Therefore, capturing the six sources of value requires the firm to optimize on a global basis the organization and management of each value chain activity—R&D, manufacturing, selling, customer service, and so forth. A look at Hewlett-Packard's PC business illustrates why disaggregated analysis is needed at the level of individual value chain activities. Somewhat simplified, a list of the value chain activities in this business would include the following:

- Technology development
- Product development
- Purchasing
- Manufacturing
- Selling
- Distribution

- After-sales service
- Human resource management
- Cash management

For each of these activities in the value chain, H-P must figure out how that specific activity can be managed in a way that unleashes its maximum value. Technology development, for example, might require centralization in just one or two locations. In contrast, selling might demand a high degree of operational decentralization in a context of a globally coordinated sales strategy. In other words, for any given business, exploiting global presence requires taking actions to create an optimal R&D network, an optimal purchasing network, an optimal manufacturing network, and so forth.

As depicted in the Star Framework (see Figure 4.1), creating and managing an optimal network for each value chain activity requires optimizing three elements of the network: network architecture, competencies at the nodes of the network, and coordination among the nodes.

Designing an Optimal Architecture

For any activity, network architecture refers to the number of locations in which that activity is performed, the actual identity of the locations, and the specific charter of

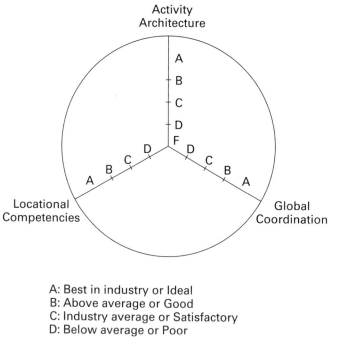

A: Best in industry or Ideal
B: Above average or Good
C: Industry average or Satisfactory
D: Below average or Poor
F: Worst in industry or Totally unsatisfactory

FIGURE 4.1 Drivers of Global Value: The Star Framework

each location. Although an infinite number of choices exist for the design of activity architecture, three of the most common options are

- Concentration in one location (for example, the development of one-click check-out technology at Amazon.com)
- Differentiated centers of excellence (for example, dedicated vehicle program centers in Ford)
- Dispersion to regional or local units (for example, the development of merchant alliances at Yahoo!)

It is worth noting that although activity architecture will shape organizational structure decisions, it is not the same thing as organizational structure. Take, for example, Honda's decision to build a design center in Italy, which is an activity architecture decision. On the other hand, organizational structure deals with questions such as who should report to whom (for example, who should have direct control over the Italian design center: the country manager for Honda Italy, the president of Honda Europe, or the corporate design chief). Because they require commitment of investment on the ground, architectural choices are less reversible than structural ones. Consequently, getting the activity architecture right is far more important than getting the organizational structure right.

The issues that must be addressed in designing an optimal global architecture are as follows: Does the number of locations where this activity will be performed ensure critical mass at each location and full exploitation of economies of scale? For each activity, does the choice of locations optimize both the quality with which this activity will be performed and its cost competitiveness, while minimizing the political, economic, and currency risks associated with it? Is the charter of each location defined in a way that eliminates unneeded duplication across locations?

It is essential to reassess the optimality of activity architecture on a periodic basis. Some of the important factors that can render today's optimal architecture less than desirable tomorrow are shifts in factor cost differences across countries, changes in tariff regimes, trends in demand patterns across countries, variations in product design, and adoption of new manufacturing technologies. In 1997, ABB's declaration that it would shift thousands of jobs from Western Europe to the emerging economies over the next five years illustrates the need for such ongoing reassessment. The company believed rightly that this shift in manufacturing architecture would increase efficiency, take greater advantage of lower labor costs in the emerging economies, and heighten the company's responsiveness to customers in its largest growth markets.[11]

Building World-Class Competencies

Once you have chosen the locations at which a particular activity will be performed, the next step is to build the requisite competencies at those locations. Otherwise, you could easily lose all the gains from creating a seemingly optimal architecture. As a hypothetical example, suppose you lead an American equipment manufacturer that has significant European presence and two production centers, one in Germany and the other in France, each supplying about 50 percent of your European market needs. With labor costs a significant portion, say 21 percent, of your total cost structure, you are weighing the option of consolidating your European production resources into one new facility in Spain. You anticipate about a 12 percent net reduction in the total cost structure: a 5 percent saving due to consolidating the two factories, and a 7 percent saving due to the one-third reduction in labor costs that would result from lower manufacturing wages in Spain. Is this change in the architecture of your European manufacturing operations the right move?

Despite the attraction of the projected reduction, you should not make this change unless you are confident that you can build the following competencies at the new Spanish location: the labor productivity in your Spanish plant will be greater than 67 percent of the average labor productivity in your existing German and French plants, the indirect effect of labor on other costs (for example, raw material usage and machine utilization) will be either neutral or positive, and the quality and performance of your products will remain world-class.

Objectively speaking, many countries with relatively lower wage rates also suffer from lower levels of productivity. Notwithstanding this generalization, companies should resist becoming prisoners of the aggregate statistics. For some very systematic reasons, it is often possible for a company to locate production in a low labor cost country and still achieve world-class productivity and quality levels. Both Motorola and Siemens have done this in China. This combination of low labor costs and world-class operations is particularly feasible under the following conditions:

- The developing economy, despite its relative poverty, has a large pool of highly educated workers, as in India, China, and the Philippines, for example.
- High unemployment levels in the economy furnish the multinational firm with a very talented and motivated pool of employees.
- The company is setting up greenfield operations, where it is possible to establish world-class processes from day one, a task that often is far easier than shaking up the status quo in a well-entrenched organization.

As you would expect, the greater a business's dependence on a particular location, the greater the need to have world-class competencies in the relevant activities there. The importance of any particular location is likely to be very high when it is the sole location or one of only a few locations where the particular activity is concentrated (as is often true in the case of upstream activities such as R&D and manufacturing). But even in the case of downstream activities such as sales, which often are dispersed across many locations, the need for world-class market-sensing and selling competencies is critical, especially in the major markets. For example, any weakness in Ikea's market-sensing competencies in a moderately sized market such as Spain would be far less costly for the company than in megamarkets such as the United States or China. Ikea's initial setbacks in the U.S. market can be attributed in part to major blind spots in its market-sensing capabilities.[12]

Ensuring Frictionless Coordination

In addition to creating an optimal architecture and ensuring requisite competencies at the different locations, the final component in creating an optimal global network is to develop and maintain smooth, indeed seamless, coordination across the various locations. The worldwide business team needs to foster this coordination along several dimensions: operational coordination between units performing similar activities (for example, two R&D labs or two production centers) as well as those performing complementary activities (for example, manufacturing vis-à-vis procurement and manufacturing vis-à-vis marketing). It also needs to promote the transfer of knowledge and skills across locations. The pursuit of seamless coordination along these dimensions requires two types of concrete actions: *creating motivation, indeed eagerness, among those managers whose cooperation is essential, and setting up mechanisms that will put the desired cooperation into practice.*

Some of the high-leverage organizational mechanisms to create eagerness for cooperation among managers working in different subsidiaries are as follows:

- *Using an incentive system that links at least part of the subsidiary managers' rewards to the business's regional or global performance.* For instance, Procter & Gamble gives explicit weight to both country- and region-level performance in computing annual incentive payments to its country managers.[13]

- *Instituting a benchmarking system that routinely compares the performance of relevant subsidiaries along key indicators and makes these comparisons visible to the subsidiaries and their corporate superiors.* A system of this kind puts the desired spotlight and pressure on the weak performers, making them eager to learn from peers. For example, the typical business area headquarters within Asea Brown Boweri (ABB) distributes internally detailed monthly information on critical parameters such as failure rates, throughput times, inventory turns, and days' receivables for each factory belonging to the business area. ABB management believes that these reports put even more intense pressure on the managers than does external marketplace competition.[14]

- *Giving high visibility to individuals who achieve excellent business results through collaboration with peers in other subsidiaries.* For instance, Procter & Gamble regularly publicizes as "success models" those managers who demonstrate a zest for and ability to succeed at cross-border coordination.[15]

Focusing now on the creation of organizational mechanisms that make cooperation feasible, some of the high-leverage mechanisms are as follows:

- *Formal rules and procedures that enhance communication.* Examples would include the use of a standard format for reports, use of common terminology and language, and the routine distribution of the reports to the relevant managers. Asea Brown Boweri's ABACUS system is an outstanding example of a formal communication system that works.[16]

- *The creation of global or regional business teams, functional councils, and similar standing committees that routinely bring key managers from various subsidiaries into face-to-face communication with each other.* IBM's Global Software Team[17] and Ford's Capstone Project Team[18] are examples of effective coordination forums.

- *Corporate investment in cultivating interpersonal familiarity and trust among the key managers of various subsidiaries.* Examples of mechanisms that promote interpersonal familiarity and trust are bringing managers from different subsidiaries together in executive development programs, rotating managers across locations, and building language skills among these managers so that these "get to know each other" encounters have high leverage. Motorola's Global Organizational Leadership Development (GOLD) program, which brings together 30 executives at a time from various subsidiaries within the Paging Group, is an outstanding example.

Box 4.3 summarizes the criteria by which a firm can systematically assess the optimal management of the three drivers—network architecture, nodal competencies, and network coordination—in the process of converting global presence into global competitive advantage.

BOX *4-3*

CRITERIA FOR ASSESSMENT OF THE FIRM'S GLOBAL NETWORK

Basis for Global Advantage	Typical Criteria for Assessment
Optimal Architecture (for each value chain activity)	• What is the size of asset and employment base? • Have we captured economies of scale and scope in manufacturing, subcontracting, and raw material purchases? Are there any diseconomies of scale? • Do we have the needed sales and distribution strength in all key markets? Are our distribution systems too concentrated or too dispersed? • Do we have the needed critical mass in each key technology area? Is there unneeded duplication across technology centers? • Do locational choices automatically create push for excellence in the particular activity (as with miniaturization in Japan)?

BOX 4-3

(CONTINUED)

Basis for Global Advantage	Typical Criteria for Assessment
	• Do we have critical talent available?
	• What will be the total impact on overall cost structure?
	• What will be the impact of government inducements and tax considerations?
	• What are the currency and political risks?
World-Class Competencies (by function, each facility)	• Do we define quality from our customers' point of view?
	• Do we define quality narrowly (product durability only) or broadly (quality of products, services, and overall management)?
	• Do we use measurable indicators of quality or operate on gut feel?
	• Do we constantly compare ourselves with external benchmarks?
	• How do we compare to competitors on key attributes of quality- and time-based competition?
	• In delivering quality and speed, are we improving at a slower or faster rate than the competition?
Frictionless Coordination (between similar activities, between complementary activities)	• How direct and frictionless are the communication channels for customers' priorities and concerns to be heard not just by marketing but also by production and R&D personnel?
	• How direct and frictionless are the communication channels between units performing complementary activities? Between units performing similar activities?
	• Do reward systems encourage or discourage needed coordination?
	• Has the company created a frictionless internal market for ideas that rewards both the producers and the buyers of a great idea? Is the head office active or sleepy in carrying out its "knowledge broker" responsibilities?

Applying the Star Framework—An Example

Every global business should use the Star Framework to assess the optimality of each activity in its value chain. Further, companies should undertake this evaluation separately for two different time frames—today and three to five years from now. The Star Framework is a diagnostic tool that can highlight the major problem areas and alert companies to the need to address these areas.

The global battle between ScanStar and GamMech[19] in a specific segment of the heavy machinery industry illustrates how a company can systematically improve its position along one or more dimensions of the Star Framework in order to launch an attack on a competitor or to strengthen a weak position. Both companies are headquartered in Europe, albeit in different countries. GamMech was founded a few decades ago and, in 1994, was the market leader at 36 percent market share. ScanStar was founded more recently by a former licensee of Gam-Mech; with a 22 percent market share in 1994, it was the number two player in the industry.

Figure 4.2 depicts a comparative assessment of the two companies' production bases in 1994. At that time, ScanStar suffered a nearly 15 percent cost disadvantage vis-à-vis its arch rival, which, as indicated in Figure 4.2, resulted from relative weaknesses in its activity architecture and locational competencies. In 1994, both GamMech and ScanStar had production activities concentrated in single locations and exported to sales companies and distributors based in most major markets around the world. However, ScanStar's location placed it at a significant disadvantage in that wage rates there were, on average, 10 percent higher than GamMech's. In terms of its locational competencies, ScanStar suffered from a competitive disadvantage as well. Given its shorter history, it had less cumulative

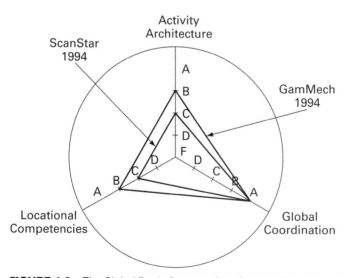

FIGURE 4.2 The Global Battle Between ScanStar and GamMech: Analysis of Production Activities (1994)

experience relative to GamMech. ScanStar's cost structure was also affected negatively by its lower market share, which reduced its potential to capture economies of scale.

In 1994, ScanStar's founder retired and a new CEO was recruited from outside to bring fresh ideas and a more aggressive mindset to the company. The new management team concluded that continuing to play the historical game would only result in ScanStar continuing to be second-best in its industry. A thorough reexamination of the competitive situation via the Star Framework resulted in a turnaround plan that sought to remedy the two disadvantages. By 1998, ScanStar had established six new regional assembly centers in the heart of major markets around the world. The original home-base location was now a much smaller factory that manufactured only the core components—that is, components that were technology- and capital-intensive rather than labor-intensive and where ScanStar possessed a competitive advantage. The new regional assembly centers were located in lower-labor-cost markets and set up to obtain other (so-called non-core) components locally or from global suppliers under centralized sourcing agreements. This new production architecture led to lower production costs, sharply lower shipping costs, and a smaller finished goods inventory in the supply pipeline.

Furthermore, the new assembly centers were located much closer to final customers and were managed by a mix of expatriates and newly recruited local professionals. A byproduct of these new market-specific competencies (largely nonexistent at GamMech) was that ScanStar gained much more knowledge about the unique needs of different markets and now was able to develop customized products for them.

As Figure 4.3 indicates, by 1998, ScanStar held the competitive edge. During the period from 1994 to 1998, it had closed the market share gap, transforming a 22 percent versus 36 percent situation into a 30 percent versus 30 percent dead heat. With a lower cost structure than GamMech's and more customized products, it now appeared set to capture the global leadership of this industry.

Figures 4.2 and 4.3 are only synopses of the ongoing multifaceted battle between ScanStar and GamMech. A more complete analysis would require a separate evaluation of each major subactivity within manufacturing as well as of other value-chain activities such as R&D, sales and distribution, after-sales service, and so forth.

SUMMARY

Managers should never assume that global presence by itself is the same as global competitive advantage. Having presence in multiple markets implies that the firm now has available to it six distinct opportunities for the creation of global competitive advantage: adapting to local markets, capturing economies of global scale, capturing economies of global scope, optimizing the choice of locations for

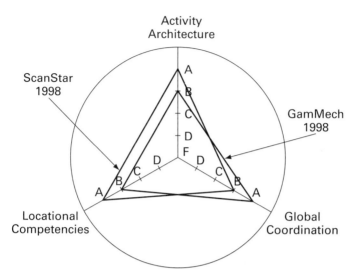

FIGURE 4.3 The Global Battle Between ScanStar and GamMech: Analysis of Production Activities (1998)

activities and resources, leveraging knowledge across subsidiaries, and playing the global chess game. Realizing these opportunities requires the firm to adopt a two-step approach for analysis and action. The firm should first evaluate the optimality of the global network for each activity in the value chain along the following three dimensions: activity architecture, locational competencies, and global coordination. Based on this evaluation, the firm should then design and execute actions to eliminate or at least to reduce the suboptimalities.

CHAPTER 5

CULTIVATING A GLOBAL MINDSET

There are no German or American companies. There are only successful or unsuccessful companies.

—Thomas Middlehoff, Chairman, Bertelsman AG, 1998[1]

INDIVIDUALS **DIFFER** in how they sense and interpret the world around them. So do organizations. And these differences matter. They matter because it is how we perceive our environment as well as ourselves that determines which of the multitude of opportunities and problems we go after and how we do so.[2] Consider, for example, this seemingly simple question: "What is Marriott's market share in the lodging business?" The answer, or answers, would depend on your perception of the company's relevant opportunity space: the North American hotel market, the global hotel market, or the global lodging market including not only hotels but also other forms of lodging such as apartments, college dormitories, and even prisons.

Recently, as part of our ongoing research on the global corporation, we posed the following question to the CEO of one of the world's largest pharmaceutical corporations: "What are the three things that might keep you awake at night?" His response: "First, people development. Second, setting business priorities to make sure that the short-term doesn't drive out the long-term. And, third, setting the tone for creating a global mindset." Although their words may differ, other CEOs and senior executives echo this viewpoint.

In this chapter, we address the following issues: why mindset matters, what a global mindset is, the value of a global mindset, and finally, what companies can do to cultivate a global mindset.[3]

WHY MINDSET MATTERS

Any company that wants to emerge as the global leader in its industry has to lead in three tasks: discovering new market opportunities, establishing presence in key markets, and converting such presence into global competitive advantage. Rooted in the premise that managers pursue only those opportunities they discern, we would contend that a deeply embedded global mindset is a prerequisite for global industry dominance. As Jacques Nasser, former CEO of Ford Motor Company, observed:

> *Ford can't build the company if it holds on to a mindset that doesn't respond swiftly to consumers' needs or pay attention to the capital markets. So that's why we are in the process of reinventing Ford as a global organization with a single strategic focus on consumers and shareholder value. That's not to say you wipe out national cultures or eliminate the idea that it makes sense to have people with expertise in one function or another, but it does mean you strive for some sort of Ford-wide corporate DNA that drives how we do things everywhere. That DNA has a couple of key components: a global mindset, as I've said, an intuitive knowledge of Ford's customers, a relentless focus on growth, and the strong belief that leaders are teachers.[4]*

Straightforward as these words sound, developing a global mindset is far from easy. In a survey of 1,500 executives from 12 large multinational companies, the International Consortium for Executive Development Research asked executives to rank their performance along various dimensions deemed vital to sustaining competitiveness. "The respondents rated their ability to cultivate a global mindset in their organization dead last—34th out of 34 dimensions."[5]

The concept of mindset, also referred to as *cognitive schema, mental map,* or *paradigm,* can be traced back to the research of cognitive psychologists who have addressed the question of how people make sense of the world with which they interact.[6] The central finding of this stream of research is that we, as human beings, are limited in our ability to absorb and process information. However, our information environment is not only abundantly rich in content but also complex, often ambiguous, and ever-changing. Thus we are constantly challenged by the problem of how to avoid becoming paralyzed by the complexity and ambiguity surrounding us. We address this challenge through a process of filtration. Without much if any conscious thought, we are selective in what we absorb and biased in how we interpret that which we absorb.[7]

For each of us, at any one time, these cognitive schemas are a product of our own peculiar and at least partially unique histories. Every mindset represents a theory of what the world is like. And like every theory, a mindset exists in the form of a "knowledge structure," that is, it consists of components as well as linkages among the components.[8] Suppose, for instance, that you are the European marketing manager for Hewlett-Packard's Home Products Division and are responsible for devising the company's strategy for the European home PC market. How would we uncover your mental map of the European PC market? The logical way would be to ask questions such as the following: What are your beliefs about the PC market in each country? And, what are your beliefs about the similarities, differences, and interlinkages among the PC markets across various countries?

Not unlike theories, mindsets evolve through an iterative process. The current mindset guides the collection and interpretation of new information. To the extent that this new information is consistent with the current mindset, it reinforces that mindset. From time to time, however, some elements of the new information appear to be truly novel and inconsistent with the existing paradigm. In this event, we either reject the new information or forge a change in our mindset. The likelihood that our mindsets will undergo a change depends largely on how explicitly self-conscious we are of our current mindsets: the more hidden and subconscious the cognitive schema, the greater the likelihood of rigidity.[9]

Furthermore, mindsets serve as doubled-edged swords. On one hand, they allow us to avoid becoming paralyzed by the richness and complexity of the information environment around us; on the other hand, they can blind us to alternate views of reality. In short, we operate in a paradox, viewing the world through cognitive schemas, yet being at the mercy of schema-driven information processing "can be at once enabling and crippling."[10]

The view that mindsets can differ and that they can have a powerful impact on corporate strategies is illustrated well by the case of Kenneth Olsen, founder and then-CEO of Digital Equipment (DEC). In the mid-1970s, DEC was the world's second-largest computer company and the market leader in the minicomputer segment. In 1977, Olsen observed that "There is no reason for any individuals to have a computer in their home."[11] This was the same year in which Steve Jobs and Steve Wozniak incorporated Apple Computer and launched the PC revolution. Olsen's mindset and his power over the company he had founded caused DEC to become a late entrant in the PC market, a delay that never allowed the company to recover its footing. By the mid-1990s, DEC ceased to exist as an independent company. It was acquired by Compaq, a personal computer manufacturer, and the rest is history.

The following question-and-answer excerpt from Coca-Cola's 1995 annual report is another illustration of the power of mindsets to drive strategies:

Q: What's our most underdeveloped market?

A: The human body. People can do without most things for an entire day. But every day, every one of the 5.7 billion people on this planet must consume roughly 64 ounces of fluid to live. We currently account for less than 2 of those ounces.

It is important to remember that mindset is not synonymous with behavior. Behavior is an outcome—a product of both what you consider worth doing (a derivative of your mindset) and what you are capable of doing (your competencies). Although having a less powerful theory of your industry is likely to constrain your efforts and imagination (probably channeling them in sub-optimal directions) having a more powerful theory is no guarantee that you will emerge as the dominant and the most successful player in your industry. For that to happen, you also need to assemble the competencies required to convert your vision into reality.

Although the concept of mindset applies to individuals as well as organizations, it is useful to draw a distinction between the two. When we talk about an individual's mindset, we are referring to how one human brain observes and interprets the signals it receives. But, given that organizations do not have an equivalent brain, what does it mean when we talk about an organization's mindset?

The question of whether it makes sense to conceptualize an organization as having the capability to think has long been debated.[12] The emerging and widely held view is that "when a group of individuals is brought together, each with their own knowledge structure about a particular information environment, some kind of emergent collective knowledge structure is likely to exist. This group-level representation of an information environment would act just like an individual's knowledge structure. It too functions as a mental template that when imposed on an information environment gives it form and meaning, and in doing so serves as a cognitive foundation for action."[13] Common experience—confirmed by scientific research—tells us that, although organizations cannot be said to have a brain as such, they do behave as if there exists a collective cognitive paradigm, a paradigm that transcends that of any signle individual—including the CEO.

In making sense of the concept of organizational mindset, it is helpful to keep several points in mind. First, every organization is a collectivity of individuals. Each individual has a personal mindset that continuously shapes and is shaped by the mindsets of others in the collectivity. How this shaping and reshaping of mindsets occurs depends crucially on who interacts with whom, in what context, for what purpose, and so forth. Hence, how the firm is organized plays a decisive role in the emergence of a collective mindset. Furthermore, depending on both the type of decision and how the firm is organized to make various types of decisions, different individuals in the collectivity have differing degrees of influence on the decision-making process. Building on these dynamics, *we would define an organization's mindset as the aggregated mindset of individuals adjusted for the distribution of power and mutual influence among the group.* In this light, unless the CEO is exceptionally powerful or has played a major role in shaping the organization's history and culture (like Bill Gates at Microsoft), it would be incorrect to view the CEO's own personal mindset as synonymous with the organization's mindset.

From these observations, it follows that there are three primary ways in which organizational mindsets can undergo change:[14]

- *A change in the relative power of different individuals in the various decision-making processes.* In such an event, even without any change in the mix of individuals belonging to the collectivity, we would observe a change in how the firm as a whole appears to "think" and behave.

- *A change in the social processes through which individuals meet and interact with each other.* Such a change would alter the process through which individual mindsets bounce off and reshape each other.

- *A change in the mix of individuals composing the firm such that the mindsets of incoming individuals differ from those of outgoing ones.* As is well known, the need for a fresh mental template is one of the most common reasons for involuntary changes in CEO positions.

WHAT IS A GLOBAL MINDSET?

To use the terminology of cognitive psychology, every mindset represents a *knowledge structure*, and the two primary attributes of any knowledge structure are differentiation (the number of elements in the person or organization's knowledge base) and integration (the person or organization's ability to synthesize the various elements).

Differentiation in knowledge structures refers to the narrowness versus breadth of perspective that the individual or organization brings to the particular context. For instance, think of the proverbial functional expert with almost no exposure outside one functional area. In colloquial terms, we would say that this person has "tunnel vision"—a classic case of low differentiation in knowledge structure. In contrast, a manager with significant experience in multiple functional areas has a more highly differentiated knowledge structure and is unlikely to exhibit the tunnel vision syndrome.

On the other hand, integration in knowledge structures refers to the extent to which the person or organization is able to rise above and integrate the various perspectives or knowledge elements. For those with low differentiation (that is, the person or organization with tunnel vision), integration is not an issue; multiple perspectives simply do not exist in the mental template so there is no need to integrate. However, integration becomes a critical attribute of mental templates in those contexts where differentiation is high.

Each of us, at one time or another, probably has met someone who appeared to swing from one position to another as a result of being swayed heavily by the opinions they encountered last. Using our terminology, such a person would be seen as exhibiting a combination of high differentiation coupled with low integration (High D–Low I). In contrast, an individual who seeks and values multiple opinions but then is able to develop and hold an integrative perspective is someone we would say has a combination of high differentiation and high integration (High D–High I).

At the organizational level, consider a new product development team that consists solely of technical experts. The mindset of such a team, operating in its own silo, would be Low D–High I. Compare this team to another whose composition includes experts from several functional areas such as R&D, manufacturing, marketing, after-sales service, and accounting but that has no strong leadership; the mindset of such a diffused and unfocused team would be High D–Low I. Finally, consider another team that in addition to being multifunctional has a strong leader who helps the team synthesize the diverse perspectives; the mindset of such a team would be High D–High I.

Borrowing from the language of differentiation and integration, we would define *global mindset* as a High D–High I mindset in the context of different cultures and markets.[15] More concretely, as depicted in Figure 5.1, *we would define a global mindset as one that combines an openness to and awareness of diversity across cultures and markets with a propensity and ability to synthesize across this diversity.*[16] As Percy Barnevik, the architect of ABB and its first CEO, aptly observed: "Global managers have exceptionally open minds. They respect how different countries do things, and they have the imagination to appreciate why they do them that way. But, they are also incisive, they push the limits of the culture. Global managers don't passively accept it when someone says, 'You can't do that in Italy or Spain because of the unions,' or 'You can't do that in Japan because of the Ministry of Finance.' They sort through the debris of cultural excuses and find opportunities to innovate."[17]

The simultaneous focus on developing a deep understanding of diversity and an ability to synthesize across diversity is illustrated well by Home Décor Inc. (disguised name), a U.S.–based household accessories company. Founded barely four years ago, the company is one of the fastest-growing manufacturers of household accessories, with a five-star customer base that includes some of the most prestigious retail chains in the United States. According to the CEO, an immigrant from China, the company's strategy can be summarized succinctly as "combining Chinese costs with Japanese quality, European design, and American marketing. There are other Chinese competitors in the market, but along with Chinese costs, what they bring is Chinese quality. On the other hand, our American competitors have excellent product quality but their costs are too high. We can and do beat both of them."

It is useful to compare and contrast a "global mindset" (High D–High I situation) with two alternative mindsets regarding the global economic environment

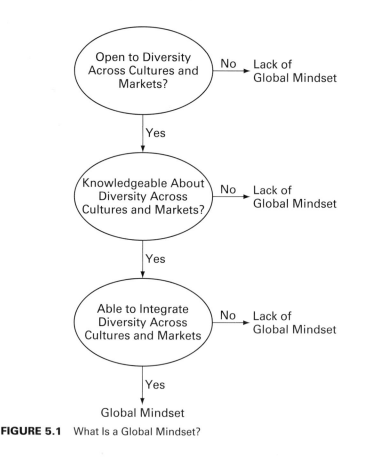

FIGURE 5.1   What Is a Global Mindset?

(see Figure 5.2): a "parochial mindset" (Low D–High I situation), and a "diffused mindset" (High D–Low I situation).[18]

As an illustration of a parochial mindset, consider the situation at Ikea, the world's largest furniture retailer. Until as recently as a decade ago, Swedish nationals constituted virtually the entire top management team of the company. Fluency in the Swedish language was considered essential at the senior levels. And when the company entered foreign markets, for example, the United States, it replicated traditional Swedish concepts: no home delivery, a Swedish cafeteria, beds that required sheets conforming to Swedish rather than U.S. standards, and so forth. In short, Ikea saw the world through a Swedish filter. It was almost blind to alternative views of market reality, and not surprisingly, the outcome was a very disappointing performance and unambiguous feedback that this mindset would be a major barrier to success in the U.S. market. As Ikea reexamined its format for U.S. operations, it faced two challenges: first, to develop a better understanding of how the needs and buying behavior of American customers differ from those of the customers it had served in the past, and second, to synthesize this understanding with its beliefs and competencies pertaining to the furniture business. Without the former, the company would continue to suffer from a misalignment between its product and service offerings and market needs; without the latter, it would be

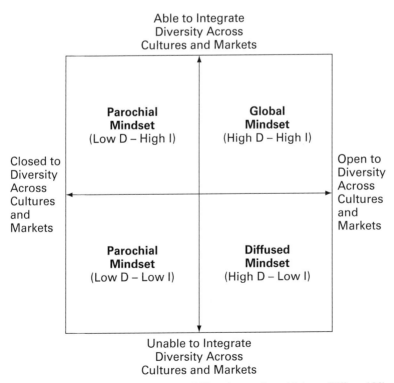

FIGURE 5.2   How a Global Mindset Differs from a Parochial or a Diffused Mindset

unable to develop competitive advantage over incumbent players. For Ikea, the shift from a parochial to a more global mindset required an understanding of differences between Europe and the United States and, equally important, a commitment to synthesize these differences and develop a more integrative perspective on the global retailing industry.

In contrast to a parochial mindset, we have observed a diffused mindset most often in the case of professional service firms (for example, in accounting and management consulting). Often, such firms are structured as networks of local partner-owned organizations. In such contexts, the power of the CEO and even the senior management team is severely constrained. While certain individual executives at the top may have highly developed global mindsets, the firm as a whole behaves as if it has a diffused mindset. The appreciation for and understanding of local issues and local differences is great, but often the ability to see the bigger global picture is inadequate.

Boxes 5.1 through 5.3 present sets of diagnostic questions that individual managers or organizations can use to assess the extent to which they have a global mindset, along with the results of global mindset audits conducted by the authors with senior executives in three Global 500 corporations.

As the results in Box 5.3 indicate, significant differences do exist in the extent to which different firms possess global mindsets. As we would expect by looking at the mindset of Gamma, this firm has been one of the slowest globalizers in its industry. The differences between Alpha and Beta are also instructive. Both firms, although headquartered in the United States, derive more than half their revenues from non–U.S. markets. Yet Alpha's global mindset is more highly

---

BOX 5-1

DO YOU AS AN INDIVIDUAL HAVE A GLOBAL MINDSET?

A Set of Diagnostic Questions

1. In interacting with others, does national origin have an impact on whether you assign equal status to them?
2. Do you consider yourself as equally open to ideas from other countries and cultures as you are to ideas from your own country and culture of origin?
3. Does finding yourself in a new cultural setting cause excitement or fear and anxiety?
4. When visiting or living in another culture, are you sensitive to the cultural differences without becoming a prisoner of these differences?
5. When you interact with people from other cultures, what do you regard as more important: understanding them as individuals or viewing them as representatives of their national cultures?
6. Do you regard your values to be a hybrid of values acquired from multiple cultures as opposed to just one culture?

BOX 5-2

DOES YOUR ORGANIZATION HAVE A GLOBAL MINDSET?

A Set of Diagnostic Questions

1. Is your company a leader (rather than a laggard) in your industry in discovering and pursuing emerging market opportunities in all corners of the world?
2. Do you regard each and every customer wherever he or she lives in the world as being as important as a customer in your own domestic market?
3. Do you draw your employees from the worldwide talent pool?
4. Do employees of every nationality have the same opportunity to move up the career ladder all the way to the top?
5. In scanning the horizon for potential competitors, do you examine all economic regions of the world?
6. In selecting a location for any activity, do you seek to optimize the choice on a truly global basis?
7. Do you view the global arena not just as a playground (that is, a market to exploit) but also as a school (that is, a source of new ideas and technology)?
8. Do you perceive your company as having a universal identity and as a company with many homes or do you perceive your company as having a strong national identity?

developed than Beta's, which would suggest that Beta is likely to be less effective than Alpha at exploiting global presence. Interviews with executives in these two companies appear to support this expectation. Box 5.3 also illustrates that the concept of global mindset is a multidimensional construct. A firm's mindset regarding different cultures and markets can be and often is more (or less) global along different dimensions.

THE VALUE OF A GLOBAL MINDSET

A look at Microsoft's entry into the Chinese market attests to the value, indeed centrality, of a global mindset. It is obvious that China presents a huge market for software today and promises an even larger market tomorrow. However, the promise of the Chinese market is accompanied by perils. Software piracy has historically been rampant. Public policy tends to be unpredictable and often favors local over foreign enterprises. The sophistication level of the market lags a few years behind the more economically developed countries, though this gap is closing. And the use of Chinese characters requires, at the very least, a major adaptation of the software's user interface and possibly even the internal code. We would contend that, when Microsoft formulates and reformulates its strategy for China, it would not be successful if its mindset vis-à-vis China were wanting along either of

BOX **5-3**

SURVEY RESULTS FROM GLOBAL MINDSET AUDITS IN THREE MAJOR CORPORATIONS

Mindset Assessment Questions	*On a 5-Point Scale (ranging from "Strongly Disagree" to "Strongly Agree"), percentage of executives who responded with "Agree" or "Strongly Agree"*		
	Alpha	Beta	Gamma
1. My company is a leader in discovering and pursuing emerging market opportunities in all corners of the world.	70	47	5
2. My company regards each and every customer wherever they live in the world as being as important as a customer in our own domestic market.	46	27	5
3. My company draws employees from the worldwide talent pool.	67	27	5
4. Employees of every nationality have the same opportunity to move up the career ladder all the way to the top.	27	33	30
5. We examine all economic regions of the world when we scan the horizon for potential competitors.	55	40	36
6. In selecting a location for any activity, my company seeks to optimize the choice on a truly global basis.	58	47	30
7. We view the global arena not just as a playground (that is, a market to exploit) but also as a school (that is, a source of new ideas and technology).	46	57	48
8. My company has a universal identity with many homes (as contrasted with having a strong national identity).	36	33	5

Note: "Alpha" is a major electronics company (data from 33 senior executives), "Beta" is a major heavy equipment company (data from 30 senior executives), and "Gamma" is a major forest products company (data from 21 senior executives).

the two dimensions: if it was shallow in its understanding of what is happening in China, or it was not sufficiently able to see events in China from a more integrative global perspective. China is not the only country where Microsoft faces dedicated pirates, nor is it the only one with a nationalistic public policy regime. Can Microsoft bring to bear lessons from other markets as it analyzes China? Alternatively, might lessons from China be relevant in other markets? What does

Microsoft's experience in other countries say about the rate at which the sophistication of the Chinese market might evolve and about how quickly the company should bring leading-edge products and services to China? Might China be one of the best global centers for Microsoft's research into voice and character recognition technologies? Given a global mindset, these are just some of the fundamental questions that would get raised in the process of developing the company's China strategy. In the absence of a global mindset, on the other hand, few if any of these questions would be identified or addressed.

As the discussion of Microsoft illustrates, what a global mindset does is enable the company to outpace its rivals in assessing various market opportunities, in establishing the necessary market presence to pursue the worthwhile opportunities, and in converting its presence across multiple markets into global competitive advantage. *The central value of a global mindset lies in enabling the company to combine speed with accurate response.* It is easy to be fast, simplistic, and wrong. It also is easy to become a prisoner of diversity, get intimidated by enormous differences across markets, and stay back—or, if the company does venture abroad, to end up reinventing things in every market. The benefit of a global mindset derives from the fact that, while the company has a grasp of and insight into the needs of the local market, it is also able to build cognitive bridges across and between these needs and the company's own global experience and capabilities. It is instructive to compare the mindsets of the CEOs of two of America's largest retailers, Sears Roebuck and Wal-Mart, both of whom are looking at the same global reality. Their views on the globalization potential of the retailing industry, as illustrated in the following quotes, are as starkly different as were those of DEC's Kenneth Olsen and Apple Computer's Steve Jobs on the future of personal computers.

- *Arthur C. Martinez, CEO (1995–2000), Sears Roebuck & Co.:*

    I think the order of difficulty is geometric because you are dealing not only with the translation of your format, you're dealing with different business practices. You're dealing with different sourcing strategies. The degree of difficulty in a global strategy is very very great.... It's tough. You have to understand distribution patterns. You have to understand how goods are advertised, the role of promotions in driving your business. The whole dynamics are different. So, it's not simply a matter of picking up your store and dropping it in a new environment. The degree of complexity represents a major challenge. I know it looks tempting because of all those consumers over there, and because we have too many stores in America. But a lot of people are going to stub their toes.[19]

- *David D. Glass, President & CEO, Wal-Mart Stores:*

    We are confident that the Wal-Mart concept is "exportable."[20]... If Wal-Mart had been content to be just an Arkansas retailer in the early days, we probably would not be where we are today. State borders were not barriers, and people and ideas moved freely from one area to another.... We believe the successful retailers of the future will be those that bring the best of each nation to today's consumer. We call it "global learning." We are committed to being a successful global retailer and we believe the attributes that made us successful in the United States will also lead to success internationally.[21]

Indeed, the corporate behavior of Sears Roebuck and Wal-Mart has mirrored their CEOs' perspectives. During the 1990s, Sears chose to remain confined inside North American borders; even within this region, it has been reducing its equity commitments in Canada and Mexico. In contrast, Wal-Mart has charged ahead aggressively, systematically, and successfully into a wide range of international markets spanning North and South America, Asia, and Europe.

There are several concrete ways in which a global mindset can yield beneficial outcomes:

An early mover advantage in identifying emerging opportunities: Consider, for example, the aggressiveness of GE Capital in Asia. In the late 1990s, one of the byproducts of the Asian financial crisis was that market valuations of industrial as well as financial services companies in the region dropped dramatically and appeared to offer knock-down bargains. Yet, according to a recent report in the business press, "Few giant multinationals have swooped down to pick up the pieces.... Only a handful of deals have been consummated, and those mostly between existing partners. There is one company, however, that looks set to break the deadlock in a rather grand fashion ... GE Capital.... 'They're everywhere,' groans the head of one competing bank."[22] Why did GE Capital see tremendous opportunities in a region when most other competitors saw only tremendous risks? We believe that the answer lies in the fact that, under Jack Welch, GE Capital has been much more successful in developing a global mindset.

Similarly, think about airport authorities. Most airport authorities see themselves simply as local (indeed, one-location) organizations. Yet, given a global mindset, the strategic charter of even an airport authority can undergo radical change. This is illustrated by the case of NV Luchthaven Schiphol, the organization that manages Amsterdam's Schiphol airport, which in 1997 signed a 30-year lease with the Port Authority of New York and New Jersey to operate the Arrivals Building at New York's John F. Kennedy Airport.[23]

Greater sophistication and more fine-grained analysis regarding the trade-off between local adaptation and global standardization: Ford Motor Company's "Ford 2000" program, launched in 1995, was designed explicitly to capture the scale economies from standardization of components and platforms while creating cars that remained tailored to the differing needs of customers in various markets. As Jacques Nasser, then Ford's group vice president for product development, observed, "If you start with a vision of the world as being divided up into different regional markets with extremely different attribute requirements, then you'll never get to a position where you think a global organization is the right direction. We're not in the business of geography; we're in the business of producing products for our customers wherever they may be."[24]

Smoother coordination across complementary functional activities distributed across borders: Liberalization of trade and investment barriers, coupled with the technology revolution, has added and continues to add significant fuel to the engine driving firms to achieve global scale and scope. We view the ongoing spate of megamergers (for example, DaimlerChrysler, BP and Amoco, Vodaphone and Airtouch) as a logical outcome of these forces. However, as illustrated by the travails of Marks & Spencer in its North American operations during the 1980s and 1990s, building or buying into global presence is anything but synonymous with having global competitive advantage. A company's ability to capture cross-border synergies (for example, in the form of lower costs, faster product development, or faster market development) more effectively and more efficiently than competitors lies at the heart of what distinguishes global presence from global competitive advantage. Without doubt, information technology plays a major role in the quest for effective and high-velocity coordination and communication. Yet, as every executive knows from experience, effective coordination among people depends on more than technology. It depends also, and crucially, on factors such as how well the people know each other, understand each other, like each other, and—most important—trust each other. A global mindset has the potential to serve as the foundation for the development of the necessary interpersonal glue.

Faster roll-out of new product concepts and technologies: It took Procter & Gamble 28 years to get Pampers, one of its diaper brands, into 27 countries. It took the company only 7 years to get Pert and Rejoice shampoos into 60 countries. Even more recently, it took the company only 2 years to get Vidal Sassoon, another shampoo, into 40 countries. How do we explain the increasing velocity with which P&G is able to roll out new products on a global scale? In part, the company's mindset clearly has become increasingly global over time.

More rapid and efficient sharing of best practices across subsidiaries: Take a company such as Marriott International, with several thousand properties spread across virtually all continents. Let's say that one of the properties in Asia has experimented and succeeded with a new service concept whereby a frequent-stay customer is greeted and assisted at the airport. How rapidly can the company first discover this innovation and then roll it out wisely to its other properties? The answer would depend heavily on the extent to which individual hotel general managers and their superiors have developed a global mindset.

Lower failure rate in expatriate assignments: Expatriate failure (that is, early return or below expected performance) is a very costly experience for any company: On average, expatriates cost three times as much as local nationals. Yet failure rates among expatriates tend to be alarmingly high, ranging anywhere from one-third to one-half of all expatriates.[25] In addition to the direct costs of failure, the company also must contend with the indirect costs that any failure imposes on the individuals in question, on their families, on other colleagues, as well as on the company's market position. Screening for and cultivating a global mindset among expatriates ready to embark on foreign assignments can have a huge impact in several pivotal areas; for example, the quality of the communication and social ties that they are likely to build with their hosts and on the depth of understanding they develop regarding the local culture and market, and thus, ultimately, on their effectiveness.

Cultivating a global mindset among local nationals based in their respective countries can also reduce the need for a company to rely on expatriates for global coordination. The resulting benefits, in terms of cost savings as well as cultural closeness to local customers, can be substantial. For example, during the 1990s, Standard Chartered, a London-based international bank employing about 25,000 people, has parlayed its investment in cultivating a global mindset into a nearly 50 percent reduction in the number of expatriates—from about 800 to about 420 people.[26]

Does Every Company Need a Global Mindset?

By now, the value of a global mindset is obvious for any company that already operates in multiple countries, or that is currently local but is about to embark on building a presence outside its domestic boundaries. But is a global mindset likely to have value for a company that is local and has no plans to venture outside domestic borders in the foreseeable future? This is often the situation of companies in industries where the most effective and efficient size of an operating unit is very small relative to the global size of the industry, as is true of many industries (often, but not always, in the service sector), such as nursing homes, hospitals, radio stations, TV stations, commercial cleaning services, and so forth.

Even assuming that the organization's decision to stay local is wise, having a global mindset—and looking at the local market as a fragment of the global market—can yield at least two benefits. One, a global mindset should make the organization much more proactive in benchmarking and learning from product and process innovations outside its domestic borders. This is illustrated well by the case of Nucor Steel, which—from its inception as a steel manufacturer in the late 1960s until the mid-1990s—was a purely domestic steel producer. Yet right from the beginning, Nucor benchmarked itself against the most efficient steel manufacturers worldwide and was often the steel industry's first mover in sourcing the latest steel-making technology wherever it was available. It was the first American company to adopt the minimill technology, to commercialize thin-slab casting and make flat rolled steel in a minimill, and to commercially produce iron carbide; all of these technologies originated outside the United States, especially in Germany and Japan. Two, a global mindset should make the organization much more alert to the entry of nontraditional (that is, foreign) competitors in its local market. In today's globalized market, it is always possible (and increasingly likely) that, whether you are a local TV station, a local supermarket, or a local commercial cleaning service, a global consolidator will acquire one of your local competitors and change the rules of what you viewed as just a local game. This is a lesson being learned by U.S.–based supermarket chains, for example, Safeway, as foreign players such as The Netherlands-headquartered Ahold begin to acquire Safeway's local competitors such as Giant Food.

Does Every Employee Need a Global Mindset?

Let us assume that you are persuaded that, as an organization, your company needs to cultivate a global mindset. Does this mean that every employee needs to develop a global mindset, or is it sufficient for just a few people to focus on cultivating a global mindset?

The imperative of cultivating a global mindset is most obvious in the case of those individuals responsible for managing activities that span borders (for example, a global product manager, a Europe region marketing manager). It also is obvious for those individuals who interface routinely with customers, suppliers, or peers from other countries (for example, scientists on global product development teams, sales managers on global customer account management teams, and so forth). However, what about those individuals who not only have purely local responsibilities (for example, a production supervisor or a machine operator) but who also have little if any routine interaction with customers, suppliers, or peers in other countries? Can these employees—as well as the company—benefit from the cultivation of a global mindset? Our unambiguous answer is yes.

Consider, for example, the job of paint shop supervisors in a global car company such as Ford or DaimlerChrysler. The company is likely to have dozens of such individuals, and it is very unlikely that any of them will ever be sent on an expatriate assignment or engage in cross-border negotiations. Nonetheless, the company can build a global learning community of its own paint shop supervisors. They might, for instance, all receive and contribute to a global paint shop newsletter and might have easy connectivity to each other through electronic mail. Their children might enjoy being pen-pals. The net result would almost certainly be that, in a company with these types of practices, the need for a hierarchical push to create a learning organization deep within its operations would be dramatically reduced. In today's technology-networked environment, nothing—other than the lack of a global mindset—prevents even assembly line workers from developing their own global learning communities. In the absence of a global mindset, creating a global learning organization will almost certainly be a much tougher challenge.

This discussion is not meant to imply that the global mindset imperative is equally strong across the entire spectrum of employees. Although we contend that the returns to investment in cultivating a global mindset would always be positive, we do not expect them to be uniform. The value added by a global mindset, and the value subtracted by its absence, is likely to be strongest in the case of those individuals who are directly responsible for managing cross-border activities (for example, the president of GE Lighting), followed by those who must interact frequently with colleagues from other countries (for example, members of a cross-border research team at Rhone-Poulenc). Thus, if a company is in the early stages of becoming systematic about cultivating global mindsets, the highest returns would come from focusing on these more senior levels. Nonetheless, if the company's goal is to capture and sustain global market leadership in its industry, it absolutely has to regard the development of a global mindset as a goal that encompasses each and every unit and each and every employee.

CULTIVATING A GLOBAL MINDSET

In thinking about how to cultivate a global mindset, it is critical to remember that the key word is *cultivation,* and that the quest for a global mindset is a ceaseless journey. Living as we do in a complex and dynamic world, there is no upper limit to the extent to which one could continue to explore the world's diversity as well as the linkages across this diversity. No matter how developed the global mindset of a Nokia, a Toyota, or a Cisco Systems may appear to be today, surely 20 years from now, these companies' current mindset would appear, in relative terms, quite naive.

Remember too, as we described earlier, that mindsets represent knowledge structures (that is, cognitive templates). As a result, the development of mindsets follows the same generic path as the development of all types of knowledge: a child learning to walk, a team of scientists pushing the limits of microprocessor technology, or an organization like eBay learning about the world's cultures and markets. As we know from research in a variety of areas such as evolution of species, human development, cognitive psychology, and even technological innovation, all development occurs through a sequence of evolutions and revolutions. In other words, the ongoing cultivation of a global mindset, whether at the individual or the organizational level, must be seen as taking place through a series of S-curves (see Figure 5.3).

As a vivid illustration on a personal level, consider the experience of Jenny Stephens, a 35-year-old American executive working for the French subsidiary of an American multinational in Paris, whom we interviewed in 1997. She had moved to Paris seven years earlier, having met and married a Frenchman in New York. She spoke fluent French, interacted with French relatives, friends, and colleagues on an ongoing basis, and was by most standards very well informed about France. Yet when we asked her if she felt she now understood France and the French culture, she replied, "I have been here for seven years. In an almost predictable manner, I have found that whenever I begin to get a sense that now I really

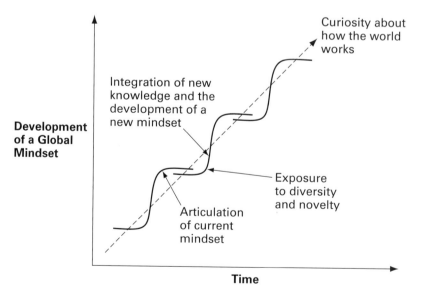

FIGURE 5.3 Development of a Global Mindset

do understand the French, something strange will happen that will throw me off completely. As I would reflect on the event and talk it over with my husband and friends, I would begin to develop a more complex view of the French. Then, things would seem to go fine for several months until the whole process would repeat itself in some other area."

As Jenny Stephens's experience points out, at any one time, we have a frame of reference, and we think we know how the world works. From time to time, however, something novel happens, an element of perplexity is introduced, and we are forced to go back to the drawing board. After some struggle, we emerge with a new frame of reference and begin to relearn and assimilate data within this new framework until the next discrepancy or challenge forces us to start the process all over again.

If we accept that the development of mindsets must take place through a series of S-curves, the interesting question then becomes: What can managers and companies do to accelerate the process of moving from one S-curve to another? Building on our own research as well as research in cognitive psychology and the development of knowledge, we would contend that the speed with which any individual or organization can cultivate its global mindset is driven by four factors:

- Curiosity about the world and a commitment to becoming smarter about how the world works
- An explicit and self-conscious articulation of current mindset
- Exposure to diversity and novelty
- A disciplined attempt to develop an integrated perspective that weaves together diverse strands of knowledge about cultures and markets

Cultivating Curiosity About the World

Curiosity and openness about how the world works reflects an attitude, an element of the individual's personality makeup. Like other elements of personality, it is shaped heavily by early childhood experiences and becomes more resistant to change as the individual gets older. Thus, although a company does have some maneuvering room in further cultivating curiosity among its existing employees, its greatest degree of freedom lies at the point of selection and in managing the company's demographic makeup.

In situations where a company has the luxury of hiring a younger workforce (for example, Nokia, where the average age across the entire company is around 30), it may be able to develop an inherent corporate advantage in the degree to which its employees will strive to develop a global mindset. In any case, every company has a good deal of discretion in including curiosity about diverse cultures and markets among the selection criteria at the point of hiring and again at the point of promotion. These considerations appeared to lie behind Daimler-Chrysler's appointment of Andreas Renschler as the head of executive management development in 1999, a role that gave him broad power to help shape the careers of the top two or three thousand managers in the merged corporation.

Renschler came to this job not with a background in human resource management but with a track record of having successfully managed the launch of Daimler-Benz's M-class sports utility vehicle out of a newly built U.S.–based car plant in Alabama, a challenge that required effectively melding a team of managers from diverse national and corporate backgrounds. According to Renschler, in his new role, he was looking for "people who are willing to change."[27]

Promotion decisions to senior executive levels that place high value on global experience and global mindsets, as illustrated by the example of Coca-Cola's CEO Douglas M. Daft (discussed in Chapter 1), also have a corollary effect in terms of sending strong signals regarding the increasing criticality of openness to and curiosity about diverse cultures and markets.

Articulating the Current Mindset

Mindsets evolve through a process of interaction between a person and the environment. Our current mindsets shape our interpretations of the world around us; in turn, these interpretations affect whether or not our mindsets change or remain unaltered. Unless this iterative process allows for new learning, it is easy to get trapped in one's own mental web. One powerful mechanism to reduce the likelihood of falling into this trap is to cultivate self-consciousness about one's mindset. This self-conscious articulation requires accepting the possibility that our view of the world is just one of many alternative interpretations of the reality. The thought process behind this articulation significantly enhances the likelihood of new learning.[28]

How might an individual manager or team of managers cultivate self-consciousness regarding their current mindsets? In our experience, two approaches work best: *direct mapping* and *indirect comparative mapping*. Direct mapping requires managers or teams to articulate their beliefs about the subject domain (for example, as Hewlett-Packard, what are our beliefs regarding the structure of the personal computer market in Europe?). In contrast, indirect comparative mapping works through an examination of how different people or companies appear to interpret the same reality (for example, as Hewlett-Packard, how does our view of the European personal computer industry compare with that of Compaq, IBM, Intel, and Microsoft?). Since indirect comparative mapping rests on the premise that any particular mindset is just one of several possibilities, we would argue that it is the more effective of the two approaches for helping a manager, a team, or a company to uncover its often deeply buried cognitive maps.

As an example of how the indirect comparative mapping approach works, consider the experience of one company where we succeeded in persuading the CEO that, at least once every quarter, the agenda for the board meeting must include a strategic review of why a different competitor behaves the way it does. After a year of this relatively simple exercise, the quality of discussions in the board meetings had changed dramatically. It became clear that the company's own perspective on the market potential of different countries and on whether or not joint ventures were a sensible entry mode in this particular industry were not necessarily shared by some of the key players. As a byproduct, board deliberations on action issues facing the company became more comprehensive and even led to the abandonment of what the CEO had earlier believed to be some of the seemingly "obvious" rules of this industry; in fact, this comparative mapping approach resulted in the CEO's becoming a proponent rather than an opponent of strategic alliances in this industry.

Cultivating Knowledge Regarding Diverse Cultures and Markets

Companies have recourse to two approaches for cultivating exposure to and increasing knowledge of diverse cultures and markets: They can facilitate such knowledge building at the level of individuals, and they can build diversity in the composition of the groups making up the company. These approaches complement each other: The former focuses on building cognitive diversity inside individuals' own mindsets, the latter focuses on assembling a diverse knowledge base within the organizational collectivity. Both approaches are essential for every company. Cultivating a global mindset at the level of individuals is a slow process that can take years of learning through experience in multiple cultures; thus relying exclusively on the globalization of individual mindsets would be woefully inadequate vis-à-vis industry and competitive imperatives.

The following are some of the most effective mechanisms available to help companies cultivate literacy of and enthusiasm for diverse cultures and markets.

Formal education: Formal education (language skills and knowledge building regarding diverse cultures and markets) can take place in the form of self-study courses, university-based education, or in-company seminars and management development programs. For example, at its Global Management Development Institute, South Korea's Samsung Group routinely offers substantive courses in international business management as well as in country histories, cultures, and economies, and in foreign languages. In-company programs have the added advantage that the learning occurs at multiple levels—not only in the classroom but through interactions with colleagues from other locations around the world, as well.

Participation in cross-border business teams and projects: Consider, for example, a leading U.S. bank creating a "Euro" team to coordinate the company's response to introduction of the new European currency. Should such a team be composed only of selected managers from the company's European units, or should the team also include a very small number of Americans from the company's U.S. operations? The latter approach, in our view, can be extremely effective in building in-depth knowledge regarding diverse cultures and markets—in addition to the obvious benefits of byproducts such as development of interpersonal ties.

Utilization of diverse locations for team and project meetings: This approach has been used successfully by VeriFone, a global market leader in the automation and delivery of secure payment and payment-related transactions. As one of several mechanisms adopted to keep becoming more attuned to the global environment, the company's top management team had instituted a policy of meeting for five days every six weeks at a different location around the globe (see Box 5.4 for a summary of the various mechanisms employed by VeriFone to cultivate a global mindset among its people and within the company as a whole). This generic approach can be implemented easily at any relevant level of the corporate hierarchy, from the board of directors to a multinational R&D team within one of the business units.

BOX 5-4

CULTIVATING A GLOBAL MINDSET: THE VERIFONE APPROACH—CIRCA 1997

VeriFone was a market leader in the automation and delivery of secure payment and payment-related transactions. Officially headquartered in Redwood City, California, the company was founded in 1981 and was acquired by Hewlett-Packard in June 1997 for $1.29 billion. VeriFone's stated mission was "To create and lead the transaction automation industry worldwide." In 1997, the company had 3,000 employees based at more than 30 facilities in North America, South America, Asia and Australia, Europe, and Africa. Here are some highlights of how VeriFone cultivated a global mindset among its people and more broadly at the level of the entire company:

- Hatim Tyabji, VeriFone's CEO, disdained the idea of an all-powerful corporate headquarters and preferred to view the company as a network of locations. He likened the company to a blueberry pancake where all berries were created equal and all had the same size. Many corporate functions (for example, human resource management and management information systems) were managed in a decentralized fashion out of multiple global locations such as Dallas (Texas), Bangalore (India), Taipei (Taiwan), and Honolulu (Hawaii).

- Virtually all employees of the company were provided with laptops and were connected to each other electronically. Every company facility was also equipped with videoconferencing facilities. Upon signing on to their e-mail systems, employees automatically saw a list of holidays and local times at various VeriFone locations.

- The top management team, consisting of the CEO and his 10 direct reports, met for five days every six weeks at a different location around the globe.

- The leadership was dedicated to instilling the company's core values (commitment to excellence, dedication to customer needs, promotion of teamwork, recognition of the individual, a global mindset, and ethical conduct) among all employees. The CEO wrote the corporate philosophy manual himself. This manual was then issued in a number of languages including English, Chinese, French, German, Japanese, Portuguese, and Spanish. When rolling out corporate programs, senior managers traveled personally to various locations to get local input and to provide guidelines regarding how the program could be tailored to the local context.

- Prior to its acquisition by Hewlett-Packard, VeriFone published the CEO's Letter to Shareholders (in its Annual Report) in multiple languages.

BOX *5-4*

(CONTINUED)

- The company conducted recruitment on a global basis and instituted a uniform performance assessment system and incentive structure around the globe.
- One of the company's recognized core competencies was its ability to leverage know-how from various locations in order to serve customers or pursue new opportunities. As an example, one of the company's sales reps in Greece learned from a large customer that a competitor had raised concerns about VeriFone's expertise in debit cards. The sales rep sent out an e-mail request to colleagues within the company for information and references on debit installations. Within 24 hours, he had 16 responses and 10 references, including the names and phone numbers of established customers with debit card installations. The next day, armed with this information and able to say that VeriFone had 400,000 installations worldwide, the rep closed a major deal with this customer. Stories such as these not only provide a concrete illustration of VeriFone's already well-developed global mindset, they also serve to reinforce the notion of what constitutes desirable attitudes and behaviors within the company—thereby leading to a further deepening of the global mindset.

Abstracted from D. B. Stoppard, A. Donnellon, & R. I. Nolan, "VeriFone," Harvard Business School Case #9-398-030.

Immersion experiences in foreign cultures: Immersion experiences can range from two- to three-month training assignments to more extensive cultural learning programs. Standard Chartered, a London-based global bank, has used the former approach, sending trainees recruited in London to Singapore and those recruited in Singapore to London. The Overseas Area Specialist Course, initiated by Korea's Samsung Group in 1991, is an example of an extensive program. Every year, each of more than 200 carefully screened trainees selected one country of interest, underwent three months of language and cross-cultural training, and then spent a one-year period devoted solely to understanding the chosen country. There was no specific job assignment and trainees were forbidden to make contact with the local Samsung office. While abroad, they were even encouraged to use modes of travel other than airlines, as these generally resulted in a deeper immersion in the local culture. At the end of the immersion period, trainees returned to headquarters in Seoul and reported on their experiences during a two-month debriefing period.[29]

Expatriate assignments: Multiyear expatriate assignments are by far the most intensive mechanism through which an individual can learn about another culture and market. However, this is also probably the most expensive mechanism for cultivating a global mindset—for the company and, given the increasing preponderance of dual-career marriages, often for the individual as well. Accordingly, companies need to pay greater attention to targeting expatriate assignments toward high-potential managers (as distinct from the common practice of selecting people that you don't want to see too much of) but also to ensuring that their stay abroad fosters cultural learning rather than cultural isolation. As Gurcharan Das, former head of Procter & Gamble India, has observed astutely:

> *There are powerful . . . rewards for an international manager on transfer overseas who chooses to get involved in the local community. When such people approach the new country with an open mind, learn the local language, and make friends with colleagues and neighbors, they gain access to a wealth of a new culture. . . . Unfortunately, my experience in Mexico indicates that many expatriate managers live in "golden ghettos" of ease with little genuine contact with locals other than servants. . . . The lesson for global companies is to give each international manager a local "mentor" who will open doors to the community. Ultimately, however, it is the responsibility of individual managers to open their minds, plunge into their local communities, and try to make them their own.*[30]

Cultivating geographic and cultural diversity among the senior management ranks: Notwithstanding the value of the various mechanisms discussed thus far, there do exist limits to the speed with which a company can cultivate a global mindset among its employees, the number of employees that it can efficiently target for this objective, and the rate of success in cultivating global mindsets. Accordingly, virtually all companies also face the imperative of expanding the cognitive map of the organization by cultivating geographic and cultural diversity more directly among the senior management ranks. Such efforts can be targeted at many levels of the organization, from the composition of the board of directors and the office of the CEO to the composition of business unit management teams. For example, in the late 1990s, IBM elected Minoru Makihara, the president of Mitsubishi, to its board, and General Motors elected Sweden's Percy Barnevik, the founding architect of ABB, to its board. Similarly, in the early 1990s, of the 22 people on Dow Chemical's senior-most management committee, 10 were born outside the U.S. and 17 had had significant international experience. At the level of individual lines of business, Hoechst, the German pharmaceutical company, serves as a good example. In the late 1990s, Hoechst's pharmaceutical business was led by an American CEO, a French CFO, and a Canadian COO.

Location of business unit headquarters: By dispersing business unit headquarters to carefully selected locations around the world, companies can also further their cognitive diversity (that is, their knowledge about diverse cultures and markets). Among major corporations, ABB was perhaps the pioneer in dispersing the locations of business area headquarters away from the corporate center. Other more recent examples would include Eaton Corporation, which has shifted the worldwide headquarters of its light and medium truck transmission business to Amsterdam, The Netherlands, and moved the world headquarters of its automotive controls business to Strasbourg, France.

Cultivating Ability to Integrate Diverse Knowledge Bases

Notwithstanding the fact that cognitive diversity is critical for navigating in today's complex and dynamic environment, it can also be paralyzing. A management team composed of seven people representing four nationalities adds value only when the diverse perspectives can be melded into a coherent vision and a coherent set of decisions and actions. Otherwise, what you get is conflict, frustration, delay, and at best either a forced or a compromise decision. To emerge as a winner in the global battle in its market—the overriding goal of every company—gaining knowledge must be accompanied by developing the ability to make and implement smart decisions faster than competitors. This, in turn, requires that the company be able to integrate the diverse knowledge bases so they become a usable resource.

Fortunately, many effective mechanisms are available to aid companies in developing an ability to integrate knowledge about diverse cultures and markets.

Defining and cultivating a set of core values throughout the corporation: By definition, core values are those values that cut across subsidiaries no matter where located. A set of deeply ingrained and widely shared core values (as in the case of companies such as Marriott, GE, Unilever, and Honda) can serve as an intellectual as well as social integrating mechanism. Intellectually, belief in core values implicitly requires people to make sense of their local observations from the perspective of the company's global agenda. And on a social level, shared values give people with diverse cultural backgrounds and diverse knowledge bases a common platform on which to base a constructive rather than unproductive, conflict-ridden dialog.

Widespread distribution of ownership rights on a global basis: Ownership rights in the global parent provide a powerful mechanism to ensure that every employee, regardless of location or nationality, would be inclined to look at local opportunities, local challenges, and local resources from a global perspective. Companies such as Eli Lilly (which issues stock options to every employee worldwide through the company's GlobalShares program[31]) significantly increase the likelihood that every employee becomes more cosmopolitan, more global in outlook.

Cultivation of an internal labor market driven by pure meritocracy: Companies such as McKinsey and Ford, which are committed to using merit rather than nationality as the prime driver of career mobility right up to the CEO level, create an environment in which all managers see themselves as global resources. Such an environment goes a long way toward removing impediments to viewing local knowledge as idiosyncratic and of only local value.

Job rotation across geographic regions, business divisions, and functions: Job rotations across countries have long served as an effective mechanism to promote openness to and knowledge about diverse cultures and markets. If well planned, they also help cultivate an ability to integrate across this diversity. Consider the approach adopted by Nokia. Jorma Ollila, Nokia's CEO, systematically and periodically switches the jobs of his key managers right up to very senior levels. In 1998, Sari Baldauf, formerly the head of Nokia's Asia-Pacific operations, was appointed to lead corporate R&D. Similarly, Olli-Pekka Kallasvuo, the former head of Nokia's U.S. operations, became the new corporate chief financial officer.[32] From a management development perspective, one major outcome of these shuffles is to cultivate a thorough understanding of diversity (through regional responsibilities for Asia or North America) as well as an ability to integrate across this diversity (through global responsibilities for R&D or finance).

Cultivation of interpersonal and social ties among people based in different locations: Typically, the frequency and openness of interaction between two people is a function of the strength of the interpersonal and social ties between them. Accordingly, the more successful a company is at cultivating interpersonal and social ties among people based in different subsidiaries, the more effective it should be at integrating their diverse perspectives and knowledge bases. For instance, in France's Rhone-Poulenc Group, the top 50 managers from across the world meet three to four times every year to socialize as well as to discuss business issues. In addition, people from various subsidiaries meet with each other through their involvement in cross-border business teams. As Peter Neff, the then-president and CEO of Rhone-Polenc Inc. said: "I sit on the boards of three worldwide business groups, and the leaders of these groups sit on the advisory board for the American company. These councils bring different perspectives to major decisions, considering such questions as whether a particular strategy is viable, the nature of product and business portfolios, and the potential for competitive leadership. They also decide on major capital expenditures. And, finally, they are a tool to facilitate socialization and alignment within the leadership structure."[33]

SUMMARY

The economic landscape of the world is changing rapidly and becoming increasingly global. For virtually every medium-sized to large company in developed as well as developing economies, market opportunities, critical resources, cutting-edge ideas, and competitors lurk not just around the corner in the home market but increasingly in distant and often little-understood regions of the world as well. How successful a company is at exploiting emerging opportunities and tackling accompanying challenges depends crucially on how intelligent it is at observing and interpreting the dynamic world in which it operates. Creating a global mindset is one of the central ingredients required for building such intelligence.

A global mindset is one that combines an openness to and awareness of diversity across cultures and markets with a propensity and ability to synthesize across this diversity. Some of the key steps in fostering the development of a global mindset are:

- Cultivating curiosity about the world
- Articulating the current mindset
- Cultivating knowledge regarding diverse cultures and markets
- Cultivating the ability to integrate across diverse knowledge bases

CHAPTER 6

LEVERAGING KNOWLEDGE ACROSS THE GLOBAL NETWORK

Market success is only part of globalization. We must globalize every activity in the company. We've made some progress in sourcing products and components so critical to survive and win in a price-competitive deflationary world, but our challenge is to go beyond that—*to capitalize on the vast intellectual capital available around the globe.*

—*John F. Welch Jr., CEO, General Electric Company, 1999*[1]

WHENEVER A company extends its presence across borders, it is confronted with diversity. Diversity, however, represents not just a challenge with which the firm must cope but also a critical resource that the firm can use to create value for customers as well as shareholders. The process of adapting products and processes to the vagaries of each location forces each subsidiary to engage in at least some local innovation. Every such local innovation represents the creation of new knowledge. Although some of the new knowledge may be too idiosyncratic to have much value outside the local environment, a good chunk of what starts out as locally created knowledge often has global relevance and value. For instance:

- Unilever has long fostered a culture of entrepreneurship among its subsidiaries. As one example, Hindustan Lever, the subsidiary in India, took the initiative to develop "Wheel"—a new laundry detergent targeted at the bottom tier of the economic pyramid. To create, market, and distribute a product that would be effective yet within the price reach of targeted customers, Hindustan Lever created a separate business unit and charged it with inventing a new business system. Wheel delivers significantly lower margins than other detergents on a per-unit basis; yet, given its very much higher asset turnover and a large market size, it has been an economic success. Unilever has since replicated this concept and business idea in other markets, most notably in the case of "Ala," a similar detergent brand in Brazil.[2]

- China is rapidly becoming one of the fastest-growing markets for Microsoft. However, given the vast linguistic differences between English and Chinese, both written and spoken, Microsoft's success in China depends very heavily on its effectiveness in customizing the user interface of its products, something more easily said than done. Not surprisingly, Microsoft has decided to locate one of its biggest research programs in language recognition and speech input in China. The technological knowledge emerging from these China-based activities should be of critical value to Microsoft's operations not only in China but in all corners of the world.[3]

Building on the premise that there exists a wide gap between the rhetoric and the reality of knowledge management, this chapter proposes that building an appropriate social ecology is a crucial requirement for effective knowledge management. We explicitly uncover the pathologies and pitfalls that prevent companies from realizing the full potential of knowledge management, and present a detailed analysis of how one company—Nucor Corporation, the world's most innovative and fastest-growing steel company over three decades—has created an exemplary social ecology for accumulating and mobilizing knowledge. We use these insights to present a general framework for converting any company into an effective knowledge machine.[4]

THE GAP BETWEEN RHETORIC AND REALITY

Despite widespread awareness of the economic value that can be unleashed by creating and mobilizing intellectual capital, for most companies, reality remains well below potential. As the CEO of a commercial services company lamented in an interview: "We provide pretty much the same services in every location. But my regional managers would rather die than learn from each other." Our research suggests that this anecdote is hardly an isolated case. As our survey research indicates (see Figure 6.1), not only is actual knowledge sharing well below corporate expectations, it also is notably below corporate executives' perceptions of today's reality.

UNPACKING THE KNOWLEDGE MANAGEMENT AGENDA

Since all knowledge starts as information, many companies tend to regard knowledge management as synonymous with information management. Carried to an extreme, such a perspective can result in a profoundly mistaken belief that the installation of a sophisticated information technology infrastructure is the be-all and end-all of knowledge management. Departing from such thinking, our central thesis is that effective knowledge management depends not merely on information technology platforms but more broadly on the social ecology of the organization.

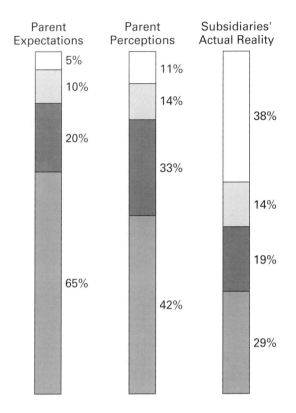

Parent Expectations / Parent Perceptions / Subsidiaries' Actual Reality

Parent Expectations: 5%, 10%, 20%, 65%

Parent Perceptions: 11%, 14%, 33%, 42%

Subsidiaries' Actual Reality: 38%, 14%, 19%, 29%

☐ Subsidiary is neither a provider nor a receiver of knowledge and skills

☐ Subsidiary is primarily a provider of knowledge and skills

■ Subsidiary is primarily a receiver of knowledge and skills

▨ Subsidiary is both a provider and a receiver of knowledge and skills

FIGURE 6.1   Potential Versus Reality of Knowledge Sharing: Survey Results from Three Large Global Corporations (Total number of subsidiaries = 79)

The Centrality of Social Ecology

We define *social ecology* as referring to the social system in which people are embedded. Social ecology drives the organization's formal and informal expectations from individuals; witness, for example, the impact of stock options on the motivation of people at Microsoft. Social ecology shapes the degree of freedom individuals have to pursue actions without seeking prior approval; witness, for example, the "15% Rule" that allows scientists to allocate part of their own time at 3M. It signals to the individual the desired norms of behavior; witness, for example, the power of "the credo" at Johnson & Johnson. It sends signals about which dimensions of performance are more or less highly valued by the organization;

witness, for example, the impact of Harold Geneen's financial controls on the behavior of people during his tenure at ITT. It defines the types of people who will be welcomed by the organization and those who will be rejected; witness, for example, the salience that Nordstrom attaches to hiring and retaining only those people who truly enjoy serving customers. It defines for people the meaning of important concepts such as quality; witness, for example, the implications of Jack Welch's passion for "Six Sigma" on the behavior of people at GE. It affects the way people interact with each other both inside and outside the organization; witness, for instance, the impact of Sears's Total Performance Indicators (TPI) approach on its employees' interactions with customers. In short, the social ecology of an organization is critical because it affects people's motivations and abilities and thereby shapes their behavior.

As illustrated in Figure 6.2, the determinants of social ecology are culture, structure, information systems, reward systems, processes, people, and leadership. The term *ecology* suggests that the social system should be viewed not as a random collection of disparate elements but as a package where the various elements interact with each other.

Information technology (IT) certainly plays a central role in knowledge management in any organization. Yet, in our view, information technology is only one part of the total picture and far from a panacea for the challenge of knowledge management. IT is perhaps the only viable mechanism to connect large numbers of people based far apart and located in different time zones. Yet, like any powerful tool, IT can be used effectively, misused in wasteful ways, and even abused. It also is important to note that we live in an era of open systems and the interest of technology providers lies in making the technology available to as wide a cus-

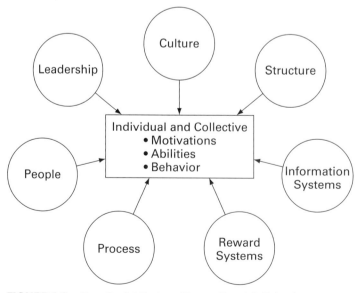

FIGURE 6.2   How Social Ecology Shapes People's Behavior

tomer base as possible rather than to only a select few. Thus, for most companies, IT platforms provide at best a temporary advantage. Sustainable advantage depends on how smart the company is in using the technology. That depends fundamentally on the social ecology of the organization. As the survey data in Figure 6.3 indicate, senior executives appear to echo our perspective.

Knowledge Accumulation and Knowledge Mobilization

The intellectual capital of any enterprise is a function of two primary factors: the stock of knowledge created or acquired by individual persons and units in the enterprise, and the extent to which such knowledge is shared and mobilized across the enterprise. A direct parallel exists between the concept of a company's intellectual capital and the concept of an economy's money supply. Economists measure money supply in the form of a multiplicative product of two factors: the stock of notes in circulation multiplied by the velocity of circulation. Similarly, we need to view an enterprise's intellectual capital as the product of individual- and unit-level stock of knowledge multiplied by the velocity at which such knowledge is shared and mobilized throughout the enterprise. This notion of a multiplicative relationship is rooted in the premise that an increase in either the stock of individual and unit knowledge or in the sharing of knowledge has an amplified impact on the magnitude of collective knowledge. Thus the knowledge management agenda of any firm must include boosting both the stock of knowledge among individuals and units and the sharing of knowledge across individuals and units.

As depicted in Figure 6.4, the knowledge accumulation task can be further disaggregated into three subtasks: *knowledge creation,* whereby individuals and

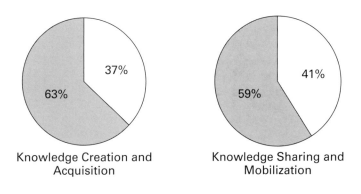

Knowledge Creation and Acquisition

Knowledge Sharing and Mobilization

☐ Relative importance of information technology

▨ Relative importance of leadership, organization, and culture

FIGURE 6.3 Drivers of Knowledge Management: Survey Results from Senior Executives Within Global Fortune 500 Companies (Data from one senior executive in each of 43 companies)

units learn from their own internal experiments and experience; *knowledge acquisition,* whereby individuals and units acquire and internalize knowledge developed by entities outside the company such as technology suppliers, competitors, and so forth; and *knowledge retention,* that is, minimizing the loss or leakage of internally created or externally acquired knowledge.

Also depicted in Figure 6.4 is the disaggregation of the knowledge mobilization task into a set of subtasks: *knowledge identification* (systematic uncovering of opportunities for knowledge sharing within the enterprise), *knowledge outflow* (creating willingness on the part of potential senders to share their knowledge), *knowledge transmission* (building effective and efficient channels for the actual transfer of knowledge), and *knowledge inflow* (creating willingness and ability on the part of potential receivers to accept and use knowledge from other units within the enterprise).

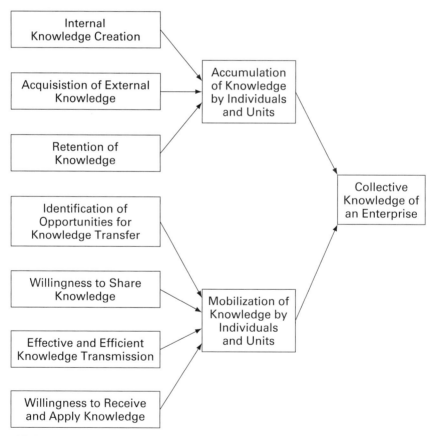

FIGURE 6.4 Unpacking the Knowledge Management Agenda

PATHOLOGIES AND PITFALLS IN KNOWLEDGE MANAGEMENT

Box 6.1 summarizes the myriad pathologies and pitfalls that can (and often do) bedevil every element of the knowledge management process in many organizations.[5]

BOX 6-1

COMMON PATHOLOGIES AND CHALLENGES IN KNOWL-EDGE ACCUMULATION AND KNOWLEDGE MOBILIZATION

Element of the Knowledge Management Process	*Common Pathologies and Challenges*
Knowledge Creation	• Complacence • Low decision-making discretion • Absence of an internal market for ideas (in most companies, lack of support from just one person, the immediate superior, kills the initiative)
Knowledge Acquisition	• Failure to be an early mover in knowledge acquisition • Inability to integrate and apply external knowledge
Knowledge Retention	• Employee turnover • Bleed-through of proprietary knowledge to competitors
Knowledge Identification (identification of knowledge-sharing opportunities)	• The "halo" effect (high performers have nothing to learn and low performers have no good ideas of value to other units) • "Garbage in, garbage out" syndrome (a common result of asking all units to upload their "best" practices into shared databases)
Knowledge Outflow (willingness to share knowledge)	• "How does it help me?" syndrome • "Knowledge is power" syndrome • Incentives tied to internal relative performance
Knowledge Transmission (effective and efficient transmission channels)	• Mismatch between structure of knowledge and structure of transmission channels • Use of multiple links in the transmission chain
Knowledge Inflow (willingness to receive knowledge)	• "Not invented here" syndrome • Reluctance to acknowledge the superiority of peers

Barriers to Knowledge Creation

The creation of new knowledge is always a nonroutine activity, involving some risk and requiring some resources. When a company finds that it is falling behind in discovering new ideas, it is almost always because of one or more of three pathologies: lack of motivation to experiment (complacence), lack of freedom to experiment (low decision-making discretion), and premature killing of new ideas (absence of a market for new ideas).

Complacence. By definition, complacence implies a lack of dissatisfaction with the status quo and thus an absence of felt need to experiment with new ways of doing things. It is no wonder that many companies commit some of their biggest blunders during periods when their financial performance is exceptionally strong; some notable examples would be IBM and Digital Equipment in the early 1980s.

Low decision-making discretion. Another pathology that impedes knowledge creation is not giving people the discretion and slack resources needed to explore new pathways. Without discretion, there can be no experimentation. Consider, for instance, companies such as Ikea or Marriott. The need for consistency demands that the basic format and standard operating procedures be replicated in every location. Yet, if carried too far, such an approach would put the burden of innovation solely on corporate headquarters and rob the company of the creative potential of its global network.

Absence of a market for ideas. Typically, in any firm, requests for approval of and financial support for new initiatives must go through the normal hierarchical channels. The net result is that a denial by just one person, the immediate boss, almost always results in the demise of the new initiative. Contrast this scenario with that of the independent entrepreneur who can shop any idea to multiple venture capitalists. Not surprisingly, most radical innovations occur not within but outside established corporations.

Pitfalls in Knowledge Acquisition

Failures at successfully internalizing externally available knowledge result from one or both of two types of pitfalls: weaknesses in accessing external knowledge, and weaknesses in integrating and applying such knowledge once it has been accessed.

Failure to be an early mover in knowledge acquisition. Externally created knowledge is almost always available to multiple acquirers. That being the case, creating competitive advantage requires that the company be an early mover in identifying and acquiring the relevant knowledge. This is precisely the challenge faced by companies such as Kodak, Fuji, Canon, and Sony, among others, as the photography industry makes the transition to digital imaging. The relevant question for Kodak is not whether the company can acquire (or create) digital imaging technologies, but rather, whether Kodak can do so faster and better than its competitors.

Inability to integrate and apply external knowledge. By definition, all external knowledge is created in a different organizational setting and culture. Even if they are aware of and able to access the external knowledge, companies will not profit from it unless they are able to integrate and use such knowledge within their own organizational setting and culture. We observed this relatively common pitfall in a large pharmaceutical company that acquired a biotechnology firm. Unfortunately, the acquiring company lacked the organizational capability to successfully integrate the knowledge base from the biotech side with its own pharmaceuticals know-how. After many years of losses, the acquired biotechnology firm had to be divested.

Pifalls in Knowledge Retention

Companies face two types of challenges in dealing with the retention of knowledge created internally or acquired from external sources.

Employee turnover. Useful and proprietary knowledge can be lost through the departure of people who possess such knowledge either voluntarily (due to dissatisfaction) or involuntarily (due to downsizing or layoffs during recession periods). Any company whose employee turnover is higher than the average for its industry runs the risk of significantly depleting the return on its investment in knowledge creation.

Bleed-through of proprietary knowledge. Another risk is the conversion of proprietary knowledge into a commodity, which can result from the leakage of such knowledge to competitors or alliance partners who could become future competitors. Otis Elevator rues to this day its post-WWII joint venture with Toshiba, now a major global competitor in the elevator industry. Toshiba got its start in the elevator industry by drawing heavily on staff and technology from the Otis joint venture.[6]

Pitfalls in Identifying Opportunities for Knowledge Sharing

As noted earlier, knowledge cannot be shared between or among units unless the source and target units or an intermediary recognize both the existence of leading-edge knowledge in the source unit and its potential value for the target unit. Two common pathologies prevent companies from uncovering a large proportion of knowledge-sharing opportunities.

The "halo" effect. This effect manifests itself in the form of a generalized belief that a unit with good financial performance has little to learn and a lot to teach, whereas a unit with poor financial performance has little to teach and a lot to learn. We have observed this syndrome most often in subsidiaries that have strong financial performance in major markets such as the United States, Japan, or Germany. The halo effect, when coupled with arrogance and complacence, can make the situation for these subsidiaries rather perilous.

"Garbage in, garbage out" syndrome. In studying a major service sector company, we discovered that this company had established a Lotus Notes-based system for knowledge sharing, and units were encouraged to enter information

about what they regarded as their own best practices into this internally public database. As it turned out, this database became less a forum to share knowledge and more a forum to engage in one-upmanship; no unit wanted to appear as if it had nothing to offer. The result, in the words of a senior manager, was that the database became flooded with "a lot of garbage" rather than becoming a catalog of validated and truly best practices.

Pathologies That Block Knowledge Outflow

There are at least three pathologies that can seriously inhibit a source unit's willingness to share valuable know-how and information with peer units: the "how does it help me?" syndrome, the "knowledge is power" syndrome, and incentive systems that reward relative performance.

"How does it help me?" syndrome. This syndrome manifests itself when units view sharing knowledge with other units as a diversion of scarce time, energy, and resources away from managing their own business. For instance, in our study, a marketing subsidiary in a multinational company was clearly more successful at generating new orders than most other peer units within the company. Any efforts by managers within this leading-edge unit to share their best practices with peer units would certainly have benefited those other units, but, within the unit itself, such efforts were perceived as an incurred cost without any compensating benefits. What managers in this unit really wanted to do was to remain focused on increasing their own competence base and not get "distracted" by the abstract notion of helping peer units catch up.

"Knowledge is power" syndrome. Managers and units within every company operate in a state of both cooperation and competition vis-à-vis each other. This natural tension has several sources. First, corporate resources are always finite, and units must compete with each other to get their share. Second, given the fact of pyramidal structures, managers are well aware that they compete with their colleagues for promotion to higher-level positions. Finally, at least some senior managers have a high need for power and value greater relative power for its own sake. The ubiquity of these phenomena implies that preserving an asymmetric distribution of power in one's own favor is often viewed as advantageous by those managers who are able to do so.

This pathology is illustrated well by the case of Alpha, a Europe-headquartered global engineering company. At the time of our interviews, the company had three business areas (BAs). Each BA president had complete responsibility for his business globally—except North America. In North America, all operations reported to the president of Market Area (MA)-North America who reported directly to the CEO. The three BA presidents disagreed with this arrangement, advocating that the MA-North America position be abolished and they be given direct control over activities in this region. The net result was an extremely limited transfer of technological know-how from Europe to North America. As one BA president explained: "People know that it is the BAs who create the technology and control it. They also realize that, in the middle of the technology pipeline between BA headquarters and MA-North America, there exists a control valve. The hands on that control valve belong to us. We can open that valve or we can keep it shut. Sooner or later, people are going to realize where the power in this company lies. Of course, we want to share our know-how with North America, but we will really do so only after we have obtained complete control over them."

Incentives tied to relative performance. In our research, we came across one company in the retail industry that relied heavily on the relative performance of different locations vis-à-vis each other in determining the incentive bonus for unit general managers. Coincidentally, within this company, the heads of two neighboring areas were married to each other. Interviews revealed that these two general managers had chosen not to share some of their best ideas even with each other. If incentives tied to relative performance can have this level of inhibiting impact on knowledge sharing between two managers who are married to each other, imagine the barriers they can create in the sharing of knowledge between managers who are simply colleagues.

Barriers to Effective and Efficient Knowledge Transmission

Assuming that valuable knowledge exists within a unit and that managers in this unit are motivated to share this knowledge with peer units, the next hurdle in the knowledge sharing process is to ensure that effective and efficient transmission channels exist. At least two pathologies can lead companies to create or rely on transmission channels that are highly inadequate for the task at hand: a mismatch between the structure of transmission channels and the structure of the knowledge to be transferred, and the use of multiple links in the transmission chain.

Mismatch between structure of knowledge and structure of transmission channels. As discussed earlier, knowledge exists in several forms: information, codified know-how, and tacit know-how. Instead of tailoring the channel to the type of knowledge being transmitted, many companies select the transmission channels on an ad hoc and almost random basis. In these cases, much knowledge transmission tends to be either highly inefficient or highly ineffective.

As an example, consider the case of a global product manager at one of the companies in our study. This company sells a relatively small number (less than 2,000 annually) of very expensive machines, often as part of large greenfield projects. Thus, in any particular geographic market, for any particular type of machine, the number of units sold can vary significantly from one year to the next. This product manager wanted to collect market knowledge to develop production plans for the next year. Falling into the trap of relying on the most efficient (but not necessarily effective) communication mechanism, he sent a fax to all sales subsidiaries asking for their forecasts for next year's sales. The response was deadly. Even after two reminders, less than 20 percent of sales subsidiaries had faxed back any response. When we interviewed the presidents of the sales subsidiaries, they indicated that it was not possible to develop accurate forecasts a year in advance, so that sending back single point forecasts would be misleading. They could, of course, have developed a probability distribution of likely sales next year, but, as this would require communicating complex judgment-level knowledge, the sales unit presidents felt that the product manager should have arranged a face-to-face meeting (or, at least, a lengthy telephone discussion) rather than merely sending out a fax. As one of the sales unit heads who did send back a fax reply indicated to us: "I hope that he (the product manager) does not actually believe in the forecast figures that I have sent to him. It's nothing but garbage. I sent it in because he was pestering me to respond to his fax."

Use of multiple links in the transmission chain. Between any source unit and any target unit that have useful knowledge to share, the number of intermediary links can vary enormously. As an example of how companies often create superfluous (and thereby counterproductive) links in the knowledge chain, consider the case of another company in our study. The norm in this company was that the sales units own the customers within their territories and that nobody else from the company was permitted to contact the customers directly. One of the unfortunate results of this norm was that global product managers learned about customers' evolving needs through the eyes and ears of the sales units rather than directly from the customers. In other companies, we observed the practice of attempting transfer of best practices from one unit to another solely through a dialog among the unit general managers rather than through direct interaction between the operating personnel in the source unit (the knowledge holders) and their counterparts (the knowledge users) in the target units.

Pathologies That Block Knowledge Inflow

Other common pathologies diminish managers' willingness to seek and welcome incoming knowledge from other parts of the organization.

The "not invented here" (NIH) syndrome. The roots of the NIH syndrome, a chronic malady in many organizations, lie in ego-defense mechanisms that cause some managers, particularly those with successful track records, to erect a mental barrier to any novel idea coming from a source outside their own unit. In our research, we encountered this syndrome in one of the world's leading consumer products companies. At the time of our interviews, the very successful Japanese subsidiary of this company had gained a reputation for being totally closed to any idea originating elsewhere in Asia.

Reluctance to acknowledge the superiority of peers. Even in situations where managers may privately concede the superiority of a practice originating elsewhere in the organization, ubiquitous power struggles lead some managers to deny that the know-how of peer units is unique or valuable. Such power struggles often get magnified in companies where the CEO believes strongly in a high level of autonomy for and competition among Strategic Business Units (SBUs). Over-reliance on the SBU concept may be good for building knowledge islands, but it does little to build bridges across these islands.

THE SOCIAL ECOLOGY OF A KNOWLEDGE MACHINE: THE CASE OF NUCOR

As of 1999, Nucor Corporation had been the most innovative and fastest-growing steel company of the past three decades. As an example of how a knowledge machine works, we see Nucor as a far more interesting company than, say, Accenture (formerly Andersen Consulting) or McKinsey, because unlike professional service firms whose only output is knowledge, Nucor's end product is steel, a tangible and nondifferentiable commodity. Yet for much of the three decades from 1970 onward, Nucor was a knowledge machine par excellence.

Since the late 1960s, the U.S. steel industry has faced numerous problems, such as substitution from other materials, foreign competition, slowing of demand, and strained labor relations, and has reported one of the poorest profitability and growth records in the American economy. Yet, despite operating in a fundamentally troubled industry, during this time period Nucor enjoyed an annual compounded sales growth rate of 17 percent, all generated organically. Furthermore, the company's profit margins were consistently well above industry medians, and average annual return to shareholders exceeded 20 percent. (See Box 6.2 for a business profile of Nucor Corporation.) Nucor achieved this phenomenal and sustained success by excelling at a single task: creating and mobilizing knowledge in order to become and remain the most efficient steel producer in the world. It did so by developing and constantly upgrading three competencies that were both strategic and proprietary: plant construction and start-up know-how, manufacturing process know-how, and the ability to adopt breakthrough technologies earlier and more effectively than competitors.[7]

Knowledge Accumulation at Nucor

Knowledge creation. Nucor's success at knowledge creation derived from three elements of its social ecology: superior human capital, extremely high-powered incentives, and a very high degree of empowerment, coupled with a high tolerance for failure as well as high accountability.

At Nucor, accessing superior human capital began with the company's policy of locating plants in rural areas, which tended to have an abundance of hardworking and mechanically inclined people. Nucor was a leading employer in these locations and offered a top-of-the-line compensation package, enabling it to attract an unusually large pool of applicants for every job opening (for example, 1,200 applicants for eight job openings at the plant in Darlington, South Carolina). As a consequence, the company was able to use stringent selection criteria to hire conscientious, dedicated, goal-oriented, self-reliant people. Furthermore, Nucor built on this foundation of superior human capital by investing in continuous on-the-job multifunction training.

Superior human capital ensures that people have the intrinsic ability to excel at tasks assigned to them. By itself, however, it does not ensure that people will be

BOX *6-2*

NUCOR CORPORATION: A BUSINESS PROFILE

Products: Steel and Steel-Related Products

Summary Financial Statistics

Year	Sales ($ millions)	Earnings/ Share ($)*	Year-End Stock Price ($)*
1970	51	0.02	0.27
1975	121	0.10	0.41
1980	482	0.55	5.82
1985	758	0.68	8.98
1990	1,482	0.88	15.50
1995	3,462	3.14	57.13
1999**	4,009	2.80	54.81

*Adjusted for stock splits

**During 1997–1999, along with other U.S.–based steel companies, Nucor was affected severely by fallout from currency devaluations in many emerging economies (Russia, Asia, and Latin America).

Source: Company documents

Nucor's Performance Cannot Be Explained by External Factors

External Factors	Comments
Industry structure	The median profitability and growth rate of the steel industry was among the lowest of all sectors in the U.S. economy.
Access to minimill technology	Entry barriers into the minimill segment were significantly lower than into the integrated steel mill segment. Further, the standard practice of minimill technology suppliers was to offer their technology on a nonexclusive basis to all customers including technology first movers such as Nucor.
Access to raw materials	Nucor purchased scrap steel through third-party agents at market prices.
Access to locations	Nucor located its plants in farm areas. Such locations were anything but scarce.
Access to distribution channels	Nucor used nonexclusive third-party steel service centers (50 percent of sales) as well as direct selling (50 percent of sales) to powerful Original Equipment Manufacturers (OEMs) who faced almost no switching costs.
Brand name and market power	Steel was a commodity product where Nucor's market share was less than 10 percent, giving it almost no market power to charge premium prices.

inclined to keep pushing the boundaries of knowledge rather than merely executing their current routines, albeit flawlessly. Nucor cultivated hunger for new knowledge through its extremely high-powered incentive system for every employee, from the production worker to the corporate CEO. (See Box 6.3 for a synopsis of Nucor's incentive systems.) As summarized in Box 6.3, there was no upper cap on the incentive payouts. In the 1990s, payouts for production employees averaged 80–150 percent of base wage, making Nucor's production employees the best-paid workers in the steel industry.

BOX *6-3*

NUCOR'S INCENTIVE SYSTEM

Nucor provided employees with a performance-related compensation system. All employees were covered under one of four basic compensation plans, each featuring incentives related to meeting specific goals and targets.

1. *Production Incentive Plan.* Employees involved directly in manufacturing were paid weekly bonuses on the basis of the production of their workgroups, which ranged from 25 to 40 workers each. Every workgroup included not only the production workers but also maintenance personnel and the production supervisor, all of whom received the same percentage of base wage as the bonus. In other words, the bonus was given not on the basis of an individual's output but on the basis of the group's output. Even if only one worker's tardiness or attendance problem caused the group to miss its weekly output target, every member of the group was denied the bonus for that week. No bonus was paid if the equipment was not operating. Further, the bonus was paid only for output that met quality standards and was based on a comparison between actual and "standard" output. For each workgroup, once the standard output was determined, the standard was not revised unless a significant change in the production process resulted from a source other than the workers in the bonus group. While there were no upper caps, in general, the production incentive bonus had averaged 80–150 percent of the base wage. Further, each production group's weekly output and the bonus received were visibly displayed at the front entrance to the factory.

   The incentive plan was designed to induce highly disciplined behavior from every member of the workgroup. A group member who was late by five minutes or longer lost the bonus for the day. One who was late by 30 minutes or absent for any reason, including sickness (with the exception of four forgiveness days per year) lost the bonus for the entire week.

2. *Department Manager Incentive Plan:* Department managers were the immediate superiors of the production supervisors and, in turn, reported directly to the general manager of their plant. Nucor department managers earned an annual incentive bonus based not on the performance of their own departments but on that of the entire plant to which they belonged. The targeted performance criterion here was return on assets. Every plant operated as a stand-alone business unit and was expected to realize a 25 percent or better

BOX 6-3

(CONTINUED)

return on the assets (ROA) employed within that plant. In recent years, these bonuses had averaged 82 percent of base salary.

3. *Non-Production and Non-Department Manager Incentive Plan:* This bonus was paid to all plant-level employees other than the general manager who were not on one of the first two plans. Its participants included accountants, engineers, secretaries, clerks, receptionists, or any of a broad number of employee classifications. The bonus was based primarily upon each plant's return on assets and was paid out on a monthly basis. The ROA data as well as the bonus payout figures were posted visibly in the employee cafeteria. In recent years, this bonus had averaged around 25 percent of base salary.

4. *Senior Officers' Incentive Plan:* The designation "senior officer" included all corporate executives as well as plant general managers. Their base salaries were set at less than what executives received in comparable companies. A significant part of each senior officer's compensation was based on Nucor's return on stockholders' equity above a certain minimum level. On the upside, officers' total compensation could be several times base salary. On the downside, their compensation could be only base salary and therefore significantly below the average pay for this type of responsibility.

These incentives motivated Nucor's employees to push the boundaries of manufacturing process know-how in several ways. First, because incentives were a function of production output, employees could earn higher bonuses only by discovering or inventing new ways to boost productivity. Second, because the incentive payouts depended only on output that met quality standards, employees were motivated to develop process innovations that would help them "do things right the first time." Finally, because the magnitude of the bonus payouts was not limited and employees' discovery of new process innovations had no adverse impact on resetting the standards, people were stretched to keep pushing the frontiers of manufacturing process know-how.

Attracting and recruiting superior human capital and offering them high-powered incentives helps ensure that people are able and eager to innovate. However, creating an effectively functioning social ecology for knowledge creation also requires that they have the necessary freedom to experiment—and even fail—with new ideas. Nucor created such freedom by regularly pushing the limits to which its organizational structure could be made and kept flat. Its organization consisted of only four management layers, which, for a company with $4.1 billion in sales and 6,800 employees, was radically flat. In addition, Nucor had only 22 people, including executives as well as clerical and other staff, located at the corporate head office. All other employees worked for and were responsible to one of the company's 25 business units. The flatness of Nucor's structure implied that the

25 business unit general managers reported directly to corporate headquarters without any intervening layer such as group vice presidents. Similarly, the typical production supervisor was responsible for a production team of 25 to 40 people.

Whenever employees are encouraged to experiment, there is always the possibility of failure. A company that does not tolerate failure will severely inhibit experimentation. On the other hand, a company that has only failures will not survive. Thus, a knowledge creation ecology requires high tolerance for failure within a context of very high accountability. The following observation by Ken Iverson, Nucor's architect and its chairman until 2000, illustrates how Nucor cultivated a culture of experimentation within a context of accountability:

> We try to impress upon our employees that we are not King Solomon. We use an expression that I really like, and that is—good managers make bad decisions. We believe that if you take an average person and put him in a management position, he'll make 50% good decisions and 50% bad decisions. A good manager makes 60% good decisions. That means 40% of those decisions could have been better. We continually tell our employees that it is their responsibility to the company to let the managers know when they make those 40% decisions that could have been better.... The only other point I'd like to make about decision making is, don't keep making the same bad decisions.... Every Nucor plant has its little storehouse of equipment that was bought, tried, and discarded. The knowledge we gather from our so-called "failures" may lead us to spectacular success.[8]

Knowledge acquisition. Nucor was consistently the first mover in the steel industry in acquiring and adopting breakthrough technologies. Not only was it the first American company to adopt the minimill technology, it was also the first company in the world to make flat rolled steel in a minimill and to commercialize thin-slab casting.

Being a first mover in adopting breakthrough process technologies is always risky, and particularly so in an extremely capital-intensive industry such as steel. Despite these risks, Nucor not only pioneered technology adoption within its industry but also succeeded in commercializing these technologies earlier and faster than competitors. The company's extraordinary success in technology acquisition over three decades can be traced back to various aspects of its abilities, mindset, and behavior. Specifically, Nucor had its operating personnel deeply involved in the assessment of emerging technology options, and had a unique and proprietary ability to remove the bugs in absorbing, implementing, and commercializing the acquired technologies.

As described earlier, Nucor's social ecology drove every employee to search for better and more efficient ways to make steel and steel-related products, so that, relative to other steel companies, Nucor's operating personnel had a deeper mastery of this industry's manufacturing processes. Nucor built on this foundation by employing a unique approach to technology adoption decisions. Whereas other steel companies sent senior executives and staff engineers to analyze emerging technologies being developed by equipment suppliers, Nucor's technology adoption decisions were made by teams composed not only of managers and engineers but also of operators. As a result, Nucor's technology assessment teams came to the equipment suppliers with a significantly deeper knowledge of technology as well as operational issues. Further, given an effectively functioning social ecology for knowledge creation, they also had greater confidence in the company's ability to resolve unknown bugs that would inevitably appear during the process of implementing and commercializing the new technology. In short, when assessing new technology options, Nucor not only understood the associated risks and returns more clearly than other companies, it also had justifiably greater confidence in its ability to reduce the risks and increase the returns during the process of technology absorption.

Nucor's ability to excel at knowledge acquisition is illustrated well by the company's lead in the adoption of thin-slab casting technology. Until the mid-1980s, minimills could not produce high-end flat steel products serving the needs of automotive and appliance customers; the flat steel market was the monopoly of integrated steel producers. Nucor made history in 1987 by building the first minimill (in Crawfordsville, Indiana) that could make flat steel, an innovation that moved the company into the premium segment of the steel industry. In the Crawfordsville plant, Nucor gambled on the thin-slab casting technology developed by SMS Schloemann-Siemag, a German company that had demonstrated this technology in a small pilot plant but had not yet proved it commercially. According to our interviews with an SMS executive, technical staff from more than 100 steel companies had visited SMS to explore the technology. Yet, in a seemingly bet-the-company move, it was Nucor that first adopted the thin-slab casting technology. Nucor's investment in the Crawfordsville plant almost equaled stockholders' equity for that year and represented approximately five times the company's net earnings. Despite some initial hiccups, Nucor succeeded and, by 1997, had built two more minimills that use the thin-slab casting process. Despite the fact that Nucor obtained this technology from SMS by signing a nonexclusive contract with an additional technology flow-back clause, the first plant built by a competitor using this technology appeared in 1995, fully eight years after Nucor's pioneering effort.

Knowledge retention.   Companies often lose sizable chunks of the knowledge they have created or acquired through the voluntary or involuntary departure of people possessing such knowledge. Nucor orchestrated an ecology to protect itself against such loss of knowledge by successfully implementing a policy of no layoffs during recessions and by cultivating very high loyalty and commitment among its personnel, thereby reducing voluntary turnover.

Nucor maintained a policy of not laying off or furloughing people during business downturns. Unlike other companies, when recession hit, Nucor reduced the workweek rather than the workforce. Given the company's rural locations and its role as the leading employer in these locations, employees regarded a reduced workweek and the correspondingly lower wages as a relatively attractive option.

Notwithstanding the no-layoffs policy, reductions in workweek did cause a reduction in wages and could potentially have weakened the fabric of loyalty and commitment between the employees and the company. To counter this threat, Nucor's workweek reductions were always accompanied by a "Share the Pain" program. Under this program, any reduction in workers' compensation due to workweek reduction was accompanied by a disproportionately greater reduction in managers' compensation and an even greater cut in the CEO's pay (by as much as 70 percent). In this way, Nucor's response to recessions ended up strengthening the mutual sense of trust and respect within the company. It further cemented this loyalty and commitment through policies such as college scholarships for employees' children, a profit-sharing plan, and a stock purchase plan. The net result of the high loyalty was that Nucor enjoyed the lowest turnover rate of any company in its industry. Moreover, Nucor's very low personnel turnover provided additional benefits in its efforts toward knowledge accumulation. First, the no-layoffs policy motivated employees to pursue process improvements vigorously without the fear of eliminating jobs—either their own or their colleagues'. Second, the prospect of a long-term relationship between the employee and the company strengthened mutual incentives to invest in the building of human and organizational capital.

Knowledge Mobilization at Nucor

Knowledge identification. As described earlier, in every company, different units typically have different levels and areas of competence. Given this disparity across units, a company's success in creating value through knowledge sharing depends first on its ability to identify best practices. Nucor was fervently systematic in measuring the performance of every work group, every department, and every plant, and in making these performance data visible inside the company. With this routinized measurement and distribution of performance data, the units themselves, as well as corporate headquarters, could uncover myriad opportunities to share best practices.

Creating willingness to share knowledge. Nucor's social ecology was fashioned to encourage eagerness on the part of every work unit to proactively share best practices with all the others. The genesis of this ecology lay in Nucor's reliance on group-based incentives at every level in the organization from shop-floor workers to plant general managers. More concretely, the bonus of shop-floor workers depended not on their own performance but on the performance of their entire 25- to 40-person workgroup, which was responsible for a particular stage of production. Similarly, within every plant, department managers earned an annual incentive bonus on the basis of the performance of the entire plant, rather than just their own department. For plant general managers as well, incentive bonuses depended on the performance of the whole company rather than on their individual plants. These group-based incentives, in the context of their large magnitude, implied that any individual's (or unit's) superior competence would have a minimal impact on the bonus amount if the performance of other individuals (or units) in the bonus group remained subpar. This provided a strong motivation to share one's own best practices with peer units in order to boost the performance of the entire bonus group.

Constructing effective and efficient transmission channels.

A company's knowledge base encompasses a wide spectrum of different types of knowledge, from highly structured, codified, and thus mobile forms of knowledge (such as monthly financial data) at one end to highly unstructured, tacit, and embedded forms of knowledge (such as plant start-up know-how) at the other. Generally, information technology is a highly effective and efficient mechanism for the transfer of codified knowledge, and Nucor, like many organizations, exploited the power of information technology. Unlike many organizations, however, Nucor also excelled at the sharing of nonroutine and unstructured forms of knowledge—a key driver for building and leveraging core competencies. The ability to transfer these forms of knowledge requires much richer transmission channels (such as face-to-face communication and transfer of people). Later we describe in some detail Nucor's approach to constructing these knowledge transmission channels within each plant as well as across plants.

Nucor's goal within each plant was to build a social community that promoted mutual trust and open communication, where each person knew everyone else personally and they all had ample opportunity to interact with one another. Achieving this goal began with the company's policy of keeping the number of employees in each plant between 250 and 300. This small number, coupled with employees' long tenure, fostered the development of very high interpersonal familiarity. In addition, each plant general manager routinely held annual dinner meetings for groups of 25 to a 100 at a time so that every employee could be invited. Like traditional New England town meetings, the format was free and open, but there were ground rules. All comments were to remain business-related and not be aimed at specific individuals. Management guaranteed that it would carefully consider and respond to every criticism and suggestion.

In the arena of interplant knowledge transfers too, Nucor made use of multiple transmission channels. First, detailed performance data on each mill were regularly distributed to all plant managers. Second, all plant general managers met as a group with headquarters management three times a year (in February, May, and November) to review each facility's performance and to develop formal plans for the transfer of best practices. Third, not only plant general managers but supervisors and machine operators as well periodically visited each other's mills. These visits enabled operations personnel who were the true holders of process knowledge to go beyond performance data and to understand firsthand the factors that make particular practices superior or inferior. Fourth, recognizing the special difficulties inherent in the transfer of complex know-how, Nucor engaged in the selective assignment of people from one plant to another, "detailing" them on the basis of their expertise.

In addition to sharing best practices across existing plants, Nucor strove to be systematic in recycling its process innovations from existing plants to new plant start-ups. The company's philosophy was to build or rebuild one or more mills a year. Rather than rely on outside contractors to build mills, Nucor put together a small group of engineers from its existing mills. This internal group was responsible for designing and managing the construction of new building or rebuilding projects. To top this off, the actual construction on these projects was done by workers hired from the local area, who were informed that they were likely to be recruited to subsequently operate the mills.

Nucor's unique approach to building or rebuilding mills yielded a handful of benefits. First, the existing process knowledge was recycled into new plant design and construction. Second, the construction workers knew that they were building the plant for themselves and had a natural incentive to build it well. Third, knowledge of the underlying process technology embedded in the plant design was carried over in the workers' minds from the construction phase to the operations phase. Fourth, the company was able to accumulate an additional core competence in plant start-up know-how.

Creating willingness to receive knowledge. Earlier, we discussed how the "not invented here" syndrome and the reluctance to acknowledge the superiority of others often inhibit units from seeking or welcoming knowledge from peer units. Nucor's social ecology countered such tendencies in two ways. One, both the magnitude and the steepness of the incentives signaled strongly to people that relying solely on one's own efforts at knowledge creation (and, thus, slower competence development) was likely be very costly in terms of forgone compensation. Two, by making every unit's performance highly visible to others in the company, Nucor made the workplace somewhat of a fishbowl. Strong performers were showcased while weak performers were exposed and were likely to feel the intense heat of peer pressure.

Figure 6.5 depicts how Nucor's social ecology is the foundation of its position as the leading knowledge machine within the steel industry.

GUIDELINES FOR BUILDING AN EFFECTIVE KNOWLEDGE MACHINE

In a world in which the half-life of new knowledge is becoming ever shorter, an effective knowledge machine must excel at two central tasks: creating and acquiring new knowledge, and sharing and mobilizing this knowledge throughout the global network. Unless new knowledge can be continuously generated, the enterprise will soon find itself playing tomorrow's game with yesterday's tools. And unless knowledge is pumped efficiently throughout the network, the enterprise will not only pay the price of reinventing the same wheel many times over, it will also risk becoming prey to competitors who are able to replicate and roll out the innovator's ideas more rapidly.

Building on our discussion of the pathologies that bedevil many companies and our in-depth analysis of Nucor Corporation, we would advance the following

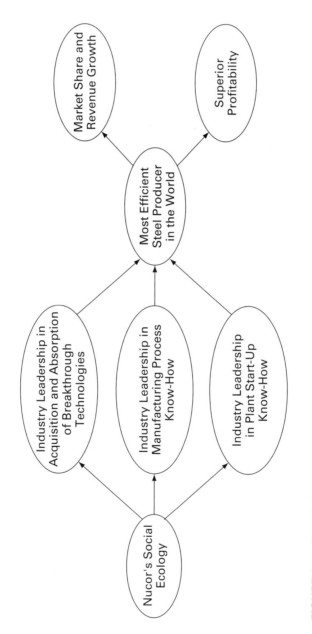

FIGURE 6.5 Nucor's Knowledge Machine

guidelines that companies can use to move toward becoming a more effective and efficient knowledge machine.

Maximizing Knowledge Accumulation

Stretch goals. The easier the target, the less the need for new approaches. Hence, the starting point for developing a culture of knowledge creation is to set targets that cannot be achieved without some innovation. As Jack Welch, the legendary former CEO of General Electric, has observed, "If you *do* know how to get there—it's not a stretch target.... The CEO of Yokogawa, our Japanese partner in the Medical Systems business, calls this concept 'bullet-train thinking,' i.e., if you want a ten-miles-per-hour increase in train speed, you tinker with horsepower— but if you want to *double* its speed, you have to break out of both conventional thinking *and* conventional performance expectations."[9]

Provide high-powered incentives. By definition, stretch goals increase a person's level of risk in performing a task. Unless the potential reward matches the higher level of risk, it would be irrational for smart people to stay with the company. Stretch goals without high-powered incentives are likely to end up as lofty exhortations lacking the real power to stir people to seek new approaches.

Cultivate empowerment and slack. Stretch goals and high-powered incentives stimulate a demand for new ideas. In contrast, empowerment and slack are supply-side tools that play a critical role in increasing the creative capacity of subunits. The "15% Rule" at 3M Corporation is a good example of how empowerment and slack foster innovation. Under this rule, scientists at 3M are allowed, indeed expected, to use 15 percent of their working time on projects of their own choosing and for which they do not need prior approval from superiors.

Equip every unit with a well-defined sandbox for play. By definition, creating a culture that values experimentation means encouraging a willingness to undertake risks. Although senior executives, in concert with the board of directors, must from time to time undertake bet-the-company types of moves, it would be suicidal to have a culture in which the power to make such moves is widely distributed in the firm. One mechanism that permits companies to sidestep this dilemma is to give people or units well-defined *sandboxes*—discretionary areas—for experimentation and play. If an experiment proves to be a fiasco, the risks are likely to be acceptable. Again, 3M's 15% Rule is one example of a well-defined sandbox. Here are some other potentially useful, although hypothetical, examples of a sandbox approach: a hospitality chain could specify that every hotel general manager has the freedom to experiment with 10 percent of the rooms on the property, or a specialty retailer could specify that every store manager has the freedom to design and create one new merchandise department. Within the limitations of the sandbox, employees can experiment with their own new, even radical, ideas.

Cultivate a market for ideas within the company. As the abundance of new product failures bears witness, not all new ideas that at first appear promising will prove to be promising in hindsight. Every company must have a screening mechanism to determine which of the many ideas emerging from the various subunits deserve further support and which should be abandoned. When we read or hear about senior managers stifling good ideas emerging from the subunits, the problem usually is not that the company has screening mechanisms, but that the screening mechanisms are dumb rather than intelligent. Companies must accept the fact that no single individual, howsoever smart, has a monopoly on wisdom. Accordingly, they should create a culture whereby an idea that is rejected by the would-be innovator's immediate superior can still be shopped around to other potential sources of support within the company, without creating a perception of insubordination.

Maximizing Knowledge Mobilization

Ban knowledge hoarding and turn knowledge givers into heroes. Cultural norms that treat knowledge hoarding as a violation of the company's core values and treat knowledge givers as heroes are the best foundation for building an ecology that maximizes knowledge sharing. Every company must decide, implicitly or explicitly, which resources are to be treated as if they were corporate resources ("loaned, licensed, or leased" to the business units) and which resources are to be treated as if they were owned by the business units. Consider, for example, brand names such as Nokia, Honda, or IBM. In each of these companies, business units use the corporate brand name as a critical resource. It is clear, however, that the brand name does not belong to any single business unit or subsidiary; in fact, through their actions, subsidiaries are expected to strengthen the value of the brand. To maximize knowledge sharing, companies must view knowledge similarly, that is, they must treat knowledge as a corporate resource that cannot be hoarded by any particular subsidiary or business unit. GE, Procter & Gamble, and the consulting firm McKinsey & Company are examples of companies with such policies.

Rely on group-based incentives. Group-based incentives, especially if they are high-powered, reinforce knowledge-sharing as a cultural norm. In companies such as Nucor, incentives take the form of cash compensation. In other companies, such as Microsoft, they take the form of sizable stock options. The power of group-based incentives stems from the fact that they direct attention to maximizing the performance of the whole system rather than just an individual unit. Of course, a potential disadvantage of group-based incentives is that they can lead to free-rider problems. However, this side effect can be minimized by ensuring that incentives are large enough to be meaningful, making individual behavior visible within the group, and giving the group power to expel the chronic underperformer.

Invest in codification of tacit knowledge.   By definition, codified knowledge is much more mobile than tacit knowledge. A company's investment in codifying tacit knowledge can have very high payoffs. Consider the case of Marriott International. In 1998, the company increased the total number of its hotels worldwide from about 1,500 to about 1,700. Given an average of more than 300 rooms per hotel and about 1.3 employees per room, this growth meant the addition of some 80,000 new employees in that year alone. With this level of growth, Marriott has been compelled to convert virtually everything it knows about the operation of a hotel into codified SOPs (standard operating procedures). Without codification, the outcome would be either highly inconsistent service or a much slower growth rate. Companies, of course, must recognize that there is a limit to how much knowledge can be codified. Even in a company such as Marriott, many critical types of knowledge (for example, how to integrate acquisitions) must remain at least partly tacit. Notwithstanding these limits, the returns from investments in codification can be very high in terms of both a wider sharing of knowledge within the enterprise and of spurring the development of new knowledge. Often, an explicit mapping of what we know today is the basis for discovering what we do not know.

Match transmission mechanisms to type of knowledge.   The transfer of all knowledge occurs through one or more of the following transmission mechanisms: exchange of documents, conversations and coaching, and transfer of people and teams who carry the knowledge in their heads. To be both effective and efficient, transmission mechanisms must be tailored to the type of knowledge being transferred. By *effectiveness* of transmission channels, we refer to the extent to which the receiver receives what the sender has sent. And by *efficiency* of transmission channels, we refer to the cost and speed of the transmission channels. Document exchange (paper-based or electronic) is a highly effective and efficient mechanism for sharing codified knowledge. For transmitting tacit knowledge, however, this mechanism is often highly ineffective. Conversations and people transfer, on the other hand, are relatively inefficient mechanisms for knowledge sharing, yet for the transfer of tacit knowledge, they may be the only effective mechanisms. Efficiency without effectiveness, as we know well, is useless.

SUMMARY

As any company begins to operate in multiple countries, it must deal with the challenge of diverse cultures and markets. Diversity, however, should be viewed not just as a challenge but also as a critical source of knowledge and innovation. Notwithstanding the potential benefits from global learning, for most companies, the gap between the rhetoric and reality of global knowledge management remains quite large. Our detailed analysis of knowledge management at Nucor Corporation illustrates how companies can overcome the numerous pathologies that can hamper their efforts to accumulate new knowledge and to mobilize such knowledge across individuals and units.

For managers, the key point to remember is that effective accumulation and mobilization of knowledge depends not just on sophisticated information technology platforms but also on an internally coherent and supportive social ecology. The key elements of social ecology are culture, structure, information systems, reward systems, processes, people, and leadership. As implied by the term *ecology,* the social system is not a random collection of these elements but is a system where all of these elements interact with each other. Nucor Corporation is one excellent example of how a social ecology can be created that drives an organization to excel at knowledge accumulation and mobilization.

CHAPTER 7

CREATING AND MANAGING GLOBAL BUSINESS TEAMS

We are all angels with only one wing. We can only fly while embracing each other.

—*Luciano De Crescenzo*[1]

GLOBAL BUSINESS teams (GBTs) typically consist of executives from multiple subsidiaries and their task is to coordinate certain activities across borders within the global firm. GBTs are becoming increasingly important in the ongoing management of global networks. Nonetheless, most GBTs do not achieve their intended objectives. The unique challenges that derail the effective functioning of GBTs are: building trust among team members and overcoming communication barriers. In this chapter, we present a framework for designing high-performing GBTs. This framework revolves around appropriate choices in team charter, team composition, and team process.

GLOBAL BUSINESS TEAMS

In 1999, Ford acquired the car division of Volvo for $6 billion and immediately gained a larger market share, more production facilities, more product development centers, more distribution outlets; in short, a significantly larger scale of operations. As we've noted earlier, however, this kind of enlarged global presence does not automatically become global competitive advantage. A firm must be able to convert "scale" into "economies of global scale." Notwithstanding the preservation of various distinct brands (Volvo, Jaguar, Lincoln, and so on), creating strategic advantage out of the acquisition would require a rationalization of product development, manufacturing, and some aspects of marketing and distribution.[2] Global teams consisting of members from different subsidiaries in Ford and Volvo had to undertake several essential tasks: identify, understand, and evaluate the key assets, capabilities, and resources of both companies; identify potential areas for sharing resources across the two companies (such as engineering

129

facilities and production capacity); identify areas where the two companies' core competencies could be combined and leveraged to create new business opportunities (such as safer and more environment-friendly car designs); and prepare a plan to build world-class competencies in locations where activities would be concentrated, along with a plan to ensure the smooth coordination of activities located in different geographical locations.

For Groupe Schneider, a French multinational enterprise that specializes in electrical distribution, industrial control, and automation, managing global customer accounts (such as major automobile companies, petrochemical firms, and large pharmaceuticals) is a key challenge. When, for instance, Schneider automates a production line or installs a control and monitoring system for General Motors in China, Schneider's performance and service is expected to be just as efficient and effective in Beijing as in Detroit. Consistency across countries must be cultivated in every step of the value chain—project engineering, delivery, operator training, equipment maintenance, and after-sales service. Schneider has created global customer account management teams—cross-border, cross-functional teams—to provide a coordinated and consistent response to global customers such as General Motors, Renault, Volkswagen, Merck, and Glaxo-Wellcome. Management issues paralleling Groupe Schneider's dominate virtually all business-to-business marketing contexts (for example, IBM, Cisco Systems, McKinsey & Co., and even Procter & Gamble in its dealings with global retailers such as Wal-Mart).

ABB's competitive advantage is derived, in part, from its ability to transfer knowledge across countries. To quote Sune Karlsson, business area manager for ABB's Power Transformers unit in the early 1990s: "Our most important strength is that we have 25 factories around the world, each with its own president, design manager, marketing manager, and production manager. These people are working on the same problems and opportunities day after day, year after year, and learning a tremendous amount. We want to create a process of continuous expertise transfer. If we can do that, it is a source of advantage none of our rivals can match."[3] ABB created dozens of cross-border teams to facilitate knowledge transfer within and across its many lines of business.

In each of the cases described so far—Ford's attempt to integrate Volvo, Schneider's management of global customer accounts, and ABB's efforts to maximize knowledge transfer across countries—the underlying organizational thread is the global business team concept.

Multinational enterprises typically use one of three formal organizational structures: a global area structure, a global product structure, or a global matrix structure. We will not analyze the pros and cons of these structural alternatives here—formal organization is a topic that already has received considerable attention.[4] In addition, formal organization is merely the starting point in addressing the challenge of building and managing the global network. One could even argue that the formal organization is not the most critical variable. Companies often focus on issues of organizational structure not because they are the most critical but because they are the easiest to tackle. Changing the organizational structure—the boxes and arrows—is much easier than changing people's motivation, behavior, and mindset. However, it is the informal organization that makes the formal structure work. Having the right organizational structure but inappropriate informal processes and behavior is much more problematic than having an inappropriate organizational structure but the right informal processes and behavior.

No matter whether the formal organization is based on an area, a product, or a matrix structure, every company operating across borders requires a multidimensional perspective. Less formal and more flexible processes are needed to make the global network function effectively and efficiently. The concept of the GBT is one of the most important of these process mechanisms. *By a GBT, we refer to a cross-border team of individuals of different nationalities, working in different cultures, possibly in different businesses and across different functions, who come together to coordinate some aspect of the multinational operations on a global basis.* These teams go by a variety of names: global management committees, world business boards, global product councils, global launch teams, global quality task forces, global supply chain teams, global purchasing forums, and global strategy teams, among others.

It is virtually impossible for any global enterprise to leverage its global presence (exploit economies of global scale and scope, maximize knowledge transfer, and so forth) without understanding and mastering the effective management of GBTs. Yet, in our survey of 70 GBTs, only 18 percent of the teams considered their performance "highly successful" and the remaining 82 percent fell short of intended outcomes. In fact, fully one-third of the teams in our sample rated their performance as largely unsuccessful.[5] In this chapter, we focus on the dynamics of creating and managing high-performing GBTs by addressing two issues: why GBTs often fail, and what steps can be taken to make GBTs more effective and efficient.[6]

WHY GBTs FAIL

Some of the same problems that plague domestic teams also plague global teams: misalignment in the goals of individual team members, missing elements in the bundle of knowledge and skills necessary for the team to accomplish its task, and lack of clarity regarding team objectives. (Box 7.1 presents details regarding these three problems.) However, given geographical-distance, differences in languages, and cultural diversity, GBTs face some unique problems. These unique problems relate to the difficulty of cultivating trust among team members and of overcoming communication barriers.

Inability to Cultivate Trust Among Team Members

By definition, trust implies "the willingness of a party to be vulnerable to the actions of another party based on the expectation that the other party will perform a particular action important to the trustor, irrespective of the ability to monitor or control that other party."[7] Trust is critical to the success of GBTs in that it

BOX 7-1

GENERIC CHALLENGES FACED BY ANY BUSINESS TEAM

Business teams—whether domestic or global—often fail to accomplish their expected objectives because of misalignment in the goals of individual team members, lack of needed knowledge and skills, or lack of clarity regarding team objectives. Here is a quick review of these problems, which—although not unique to global teams—may well rise up to plague them, and may complicate efforts to deal with the problems discussed at greater length in the body of the chapter.

Misalignment in the goals of individual team members. The goals of individual members can often be at cross-purposes. This was the case when, following a cross-border acquisition in 1998, a U.S.–based industrial products firm set up a team consisting of plant managers from different countries belonging to both companies in an effort to consolidate the number of manufacturing facilities. Despite the clarity of its charter, the team had a great deal of trouble in rationalizing the plants on a global basis because individual plant managers were intent on protecting their territory and operations rather than working for the larger good. Because the team lacked a leader with clout to steer the team toward tough, unpalatable decisions, the misalignment of goals derailed the team.

As this example highlights, members often join teams with incompatible goals. An unresolved conflict between members' personal goals and corporate goals is almost always a sure path to failure.

Team lacks the needed bundle of knowledge and skills. Business problems generally assigned to a team are multifaceted and complex in nature. To successfully tackle such problems, every team must include among its members the requisite bundle of differentiated knowledge and skills. This fact is often overlooked.

For instance, take the case of Epsilon and Alpha (one European and the other American), two companies of equal size in a certain segment of the process machinery industry. Around 1990, these two companies merged with the goal of becoming a globally dominant player. As one of the major post-merger tasks, the new company created a cross-border product development team charged with designing a common product line. The outcome was dismal failure. Not only did the team take twice as long as expected to accomplish its task, the basic platform for the new product was overengineered and too costly to manufacture. A post-audit revealed that the team had had no representation from any marketing subsidiary from any country. Rather, the team had gotten wrapped up in pursuing technological sophistication for its own sake and in accommodating the historical proclivities of the technology experts on the different sides of the Atlantic.

Lack of clarity regarding team objectives. This problem manifests when team objectives are defined too vaguely. For example, a major European multinational firm in the luxury goods sector formed a cross-border, cross-business team and defined the team's charter as "Make the principal customer more productive." The team struggled to understand the meaning of this mission and gave up on the project after two frustrating meetings.

If the team charter is unclear or incorrectly specified, team members can get caught in a web of fruitless and directionless debates since almost any plan of action or point of view can be rationalized or justified within a vague charter. And without

BOX *7-1*

(CONTINUED)

a framework for conflict resolution, team members also have difficulty resolving substantive disagreements. In such a context, team deliberations can easily degenerate into endless debates with no resolution.

Even when the charter is reasonably clear, teams can fail if the broad charter is not translated into specific, measurable goals. In the absence of specific performance targets, teams struggle to define intermediate work plans and often flounder or lose momentum. In addition, they lose the opportunity to celebrate small victories along the way, which are critical in building confidence, momentum, and social cohesion among team members.

encourages cooperation and minimizes unproductive conflict.[8] Owing to differences in national backgrounds, subsidiary affiliations, and functional orientations, each member of a GBT brings a unique cognitive lens to the group. If harnessed effectively, cognitive diversity can yield significant synergies, developing a collective wisdom that is superior to that of any single individual. However, without cohesiveness and a sense of trust, team members may shy away from revealing their true beliefs or, if they do share their viewpoints, they may not be heard. In one way or another, the absence of mutual trust is likely to turn a team's cognitive diversity into a liability rather than an asset.

If we look at the drivers of trust, it becomes obvious why GBTs tend to be particularly prone to start their work with problems of low trust among their members. Among the myriad factors that determine the level of trust among people, some of the most important are individual characteristics, quality of communication, and the broader institutional context. More specifically, research has discovered that, on average, people tend to trust each other more when they are more similar to each other, have more frequent communication with each other, and operate in a mutually embraced institutional and cultural context that imposes tough sanctions for behaving in an untrustworthy manner.[9] For obvious reasons, GBTs by their very nature suffer from severe limitations along all three dimensions. Not surprisingly, in our experience, when GBTs fail, it is usually the case that team process was not managed with an eye toward cultivating trust.

Communication Barriers

One of the more obvious barriers to the effective functioning of GBTs arises from differences in geography, language, and culture.

Physical distance. With members living in different countries, separated by time zones and physical distance, and with often-conflicting schedules, arranging team meetings generally poses logistical challenges. Undoubtedly, technology (e-mail, teleconferencing, and videoconferencing) can enable team members to work together despite geographical distances. However, technology is a complement to and not a substitute for team meetings. Face-to-face meetings foster familiarity and build trust among team members, something that is not easily established through virtual meetings. Without the benefit of seeing body language and directly experiencing others' reactions, the emotional dimension—critical to team success—gets unduly downplayed. Moreover, certain types of team deliberations simply require face-to-face meetings. Brainstorming, for instance, requires unstructured, free-form interaction over an extended period of time, something not readily achieved in the context of a virtual meeting.

Language. Inability to understand what the other person is saying is always a barrier to communication, and is much more likely to occur in cross-cultural settings. One extreme would be a team where every member speaks a different language and has very poor facility in a common language such as English. Such a team would undoubtedly require interpreters, who, regardless of their skills, are unlikely to capture the full richness of body language and other forms of nonverbal communication.

Even in the case of global teams where people speak the same language, differences in semantics, accent, tone, pitch, and dialect across different countries can become impediments. For example, whereas "table a motion" means to postpone discussion in the United States, in the United Kingdom it means to discuss the issue right away. If language barriers are not adequately dealt with, the likelihood of creating an atmosphere conducive to open and candid sharing of different viewpoints and perspectives is greatly diminished, as is the team's ability to achieve creative solutions.

Culture. The diversity of cultures frequently represented in GBTs means that their members are likely to bring different values, norms, assumptions, and patterns of behavior to the group. Consider, for example, cultural differences along the spectrum from "individualistic" to "collectivistic" norms for decision making.[10] The need for consensus deemed critical in collectivistic cultures is a relatively low priority in individualistic cultures. Take the case of a GBT in which some of the members come from highly individualistic cultures (such as the United States and Britain) and others from highly collectivistic cultures (such as Japan and Venezuela). Unless the differences in assumptions and beliefs inherent in such cultural diversity are explicitly dealt with during team process, the cohesiveness of the members is likely to suffer—which, in turn, will impede the group's effectiveness.

The results of our survey of 58 senior executives from five U.S. and four European multinational enterprises (see Table 7.1) confirm the importance of the global team challenges identified here. It should be emphasized that the unique problems of global teams—difficulty in establishing trust and communication barriers—tend to exacerbate the generic problems found in all teams that were outlined in the preceding box.

TABLE 7.1   The Challenge of Managing Global Business Teams (*n* = 58)

Importance of the task in determining the effectiveness of GBTs (on a 1–7 scale where 1 = "not at all important" and 7 = "very important")	Task Element	Ease or difficulty in accomplishing the task (on a 1–7 scale where 1 = "very easy" and 7 = "very difficult")
6.52	Cultivating trust among team members	6.06
6.35	Overcoming communication barriers	5.56
6.04	Aligning the goals of individual team members	5.44
5.62	Ensuring that the team possesses the needed bundle of knowledge and skills	4.66
6.05	Obtaining clarity regarding the team objectives	4.61

The performance of any team is a function of correct choices and decisions in three areas: team charter, team composition, and team process. Needless to say, the same three elements must be managed for a GBT, with a view to overcoming the unique challenges facing such teams. As Figure 7.1 indicates, a clear charter without an appropriate mix of team members would lead to failure. Similarly, when team composition is sound but team process is not, team effectiveness will suffer.

DEFINING TEAM CHARTER

As we have discussed in the preceding section, given diversity and distance, GBTs are prone to communication problems and trust issues. Hence, structuring and obtaining clarity regarding the team charter is particularly critical to the success of GBTs. In this context, three questions need to be addressed: Is the charter defined correctly? Is the charter framed correctly? And, is the charter clearly understood?

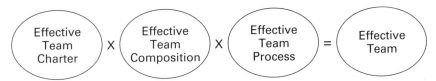

FIGURE 7.1   A Framework for Designing and Managing High-Performing GBTs

Is the Charter Defined Correctly?

The substantive validity of any GBT's charter depends, of course, on the specific situation. One of the first agenda items for any GBT (or, if the team is yet to be formed, for those championing it) must be to explicitly discuss and ensure that the team agenda is defined clearly and correctly. Many GBTs are doomed from the start because this step is skipped or the issues are not resolved. Likewise, GBTs that succeed tend to be the ones where this step is given proper weight.

Consider the case of a European company that manufactures industrial components. In 1995, this company set up a global customer account team to coordinate its marketing, sales, and service offerings to one of its largest customers. In setting up this team, the company was actually being proactive. Since this particular customer engaged in decentralized and uncoordinated sourcing, there was no immediate or obvious external pressure to establish a global account team.

At its first meeting, the team identified three possible alternative objectives: to encourage and help the customer move toward coordinated global sourcing at a faster pace, to offer the customer global volume discounts and thus lower prices, and to offer a more attractive bundle of products and services based on a better, more comprehensive understanding of the customer's global needs than the customer's individual buying locations might have. After considerable discussion, the team decided against the first two alternatives and embraced the third. The logic behind this choice was as follows. They decided that the first alternative was imprudent because, other things being the same, a coordinated supplier is better off dealing with an uncoordinated rather than a coordinated customer. However, were the customer to move toward coordinated global sourcing in the future, this team, having the advantage of its internal coordination, would be able to read the signals and quickly offer an appropriate response. The second alternative was rejected because the company's prices were already competitive, and the company's long-term strategy was to win on the basis of superior products and services rather than lower prices. The third alternative was seen as the most appropriate because it accomplished several key corporate objectives simultaneously: It eliminated internal price competition across plants, thus boosting gross margins; it made the company's product and service offerings to the customer more comprehensive; and it dramatically enhanced the company's ability to respond appropriately to any moves that the customer might make toward coordinated global sourcing.

Is the Charter Framed Correctly?

Ensuring that the charter is framed correctly is a more subtle challenge. By *framing*, we mean the way an idea is expressed or a problem is formulated. Decision issues can usually be framed in multiple ways. In turn, different frames for the same problem can result in different outcomes.[11]

As the following example illustrates, it is generally best to frame the GBT's charter in terms of the company's position vis-à-vis the external marketplace (the external capital market, the external product market, and so forth), rather than giving it an internal focus—so as not to exacerbate any preexisting internal conflicts.

In the mid-1990s, senior executives of a consumer products company assembled a global manufacturing team with the objective of rationalizing the company's production network. Given this objective, there were at least two alternative ways of framing this team's charter. Consider the following approach: "The team's charter is to cut costs by reducing the number of factories in our worldwide network from fifteen to nine and downsizing the workforce." Compare it to the following approach: "We want to be the clear industry leader in terms of creating customer and shareholder value. This goal requires that we be world-class in manufacturing—better than our best-in-class competitor in terms of cost, quality, and service. Given these targets, the team's charter is to propose the optimal network of factories for our business."

We contend that framing the charter using the second approach would yield more benefits than the first. An external and somewhat broader focus tends to encourage benchmarking and fosters greater creativity. Furthermore, in this case, it would provide a more compelling rationale for making the tough decisions inherent in any manufacturing rationalization and consequent workforce reduction.

Is the Charter Clearly Understood?

When teams have frequent face-to-face meetings, it is possible to iron out ambiguities in the team charter. If the team members meet less often, it becomes critical that the team charter be made clear so as to facilitate effective delegation of task execution. Because of physical distances, global teams tend to meet face-to-face very infrequently indeed. Given the resulting communication problems, it is imperative that the team members clearly understand the specifics of the charter—in particular, the scope of the project, the expected deliverables, and the time line.

The team must be sure about the raison d'être for the project. It must be clear from the start as to which topics are included within the charter, and which topics the team should *not* be working on. Furthermore, the expected output of the team must be fully understood as well. Is the team expected only to make recommendations on the best course of action? In such a case, what would be the process of hand-off to the implementation phase? Or is the team expected not only to make recommendations but also to implement the decisions? And, in terms of the time line, the team must know if it is intended to be an ongoing, permanent team. Such teams might be needed where the project scope extends to the implementation of decisions. Or is it a one-shot project team? Such teams might be appropriate when the project involves only recommendations, in which case the team must be clear about when it is expected to complete its assignment.

The successful experience of an industrial products firm illustrates this point. This company formed a team to examine the organizational design of its global businesses. Several meetings were arranged between the sponsor and the team members to ensure that the team charter was clearly understood. The project scope was defined to include the following:

- Analysis of the current organizational design across the company's five growth platform businesses. Part of the diagnostic phase was to focus on the question of whether a single organizational design made sense across the five businesses.

- External benchmarking of world-class global organizations and latest research on the best approaches to organizational design.

- Development of the business case and recommendations for an organizational design that would optimize global growth potential across the five businesses. Recommendations were to include approaches to capture potential synergies across the businesses in areas such as research and development, information technology, human resources, and supply chain.

The project was also intended to be a personal learning experience, designed to make the team members experts on the topic of organizational design and to expose them to the many facets of globalization within the company's businesses. Furthermore, the team members were explicitly told *not* to work on nongrowth business units or subsidiaries, or to reformulate the global strategies of the five businesses.

Finally, two deliverables were expected from the project team: a set of recommendations on the optimal worldwide organizational design for the five major growth platform businesses, and a presentation of the team's key findings, including a process or a methodology for tackling potential global organization issues.

The specificity of the objectives, project scope, and deliverables, along with the time spent at the start of the project getting the team members to internalize and accept the charter, helped them to stay on course and make progress.

CONFIGURING THE GLOBAL BUSINESS TEAM

Differences among team members along with factors such as age, education, organizational tenure, and personality imply that every team, global or nonglobal, has some degree of diversity within its composition. Global business teams, however, are characterized by particularly high levels of diversity for at least three reasons. First, they are composed of members from diverse cultural and national backgrounds. Second, team members generally represent different subsidiaries whose agendas may not be entirely congruent. In fact, given the ever-present possibility of consolidation or rationalization, peer subsidiaries often coexist in a state of both collaboration and competition. Third, because team members often represent different functional units (marketing and manufacturing, for example), their worldviews and priorities may well be quite different.

Is the inevitably high level of diversity within a typical GBT a necessary evil that must be curbed or a source of strength that must be cultivated? We believe that the answer to this question depends very much on which dimension of diversity we focus on: "cognitive diversity" or "behavioral diversity."[12]

Ensuring Requisite Cognitive Diversity

We use the term *cognitive diversity* to refer to diversity in the substantive content of how the various team members perceive the challenges and opportunities, the options to be evaluated, and the optimal course of action. Cognitive diversity can originate from a variety of underlying factors such as differences in nationality, subsidiary history and charter, and functional background. Differences in nationality can account for substantive differences on issues such as whether the Indian economy is ready for hypermarkets, whether the free Internet service model pioneered in the United Kingdom can be sustained, and so forth. Differences in subsidiary histories and charters can account for substantive differences on issues such as whether Singapore, Hong Kong, or Tokyo should serve as the optimal location for the company's Asia region headquarters, whether it matters that Norway is not yet a member of the European Union, and so forth. Similarly, differences in functional background can account for substantive differences on issues such as the relative importance of market-pull versus technology-push considerations in the company's new product development efforts.

Since no single team member can ever have a monopoly on wisdom, cognitive diversity is almost always a source of strength. Divergent perspectives foster creativity and a more comprehensive search for and assessment of options. There is, of course, an obvious requirement. The team must be able to integrate the diverse perspectives and actually come to an integrative resolution. Otherwise, the GBT's outcome may well be little more than intellectual development of the team members. However, in that case, because there have been no decisions and no action, the business itself has not benefited from the GBT's collective wisdom.

The case of TRW-UK illustrates well how a company can benefit from assembling team members with the required base of knowledge and skills. TRW is a global supplier of automobile components to Nissan. In 1993, Nissan expressed dissatisfaction with the performance of TRW-UK, specifying both the high defect rate and the high cost structure of the steering assemblies supplied by TRW-UK. An examination of TRW-UK's internal operations indicated that these deficiencies resulted from communication and execution problems across engineering, product design, and process design. In response, TRW created the Nissan Global Team to address the specific problems in TRW-UK. This team was composed of six members: a top-flight engineer and a salesperson with customer support responsibilities from each of three regions—the United States, Japan, and the United Kingdom. This team "represented TRW's best capabilities in lean principles as they applied to product and process engineering and design, manufacturing, shop floor issues, and customer service,"[13] and was highly successful. Within three years, the U.K. plant had become one of TRW's most efficient and highest-quality operations. As a further testimony to the success of its efforts, the Nissan Global Team was reassigned to work on enhancing business opportunities with customers other than Nissan.

Minimizing the Negative Effects of Behavioral Diversity

We use the term *behavioral diversity* to refer to diversity in language as well as culture-driven norms of behavior—body language, the importance of "face," norms regarding punctuality, norms regarding team representation, and so forth. Behavioral diversity causes differences in how people communicate what they believe in rather than in the content of the beliefs themselves. Consider, for example, a cross-border business team in a Franco-American company such as Vivendi or Accor. The typical norm in most American teams is that the most senior member will present the team's perspective. In contrast, in most French teams, the typical norm is exactly the opposite—it is often the most junior member who presents the team's perspective. Thus, unless the members of the Franco-American team are sensitized to these differences, misunderstandings can easily emerge, blocking and distorting current and future communication.

We believe that behavioral diversity is best regarded as a necessary evil—something that you cannot avoid per se but whose effects you must attempt to minimize or even eliminate through language training and cultural sensitization. There is no merit whatsoever in accepting or sustaining communication barriers that do nothing other than foster misunderstanding.

Creating a GBT often poses a dilemma. On many occasions, in order to secure needed substantive knowledge and skills, a GBT may need to include one or more individuals whose behavioral skills and attitudes fall short of the ideal. In this case, the team composition generally should be driven by substantive considerations; process mechanisms should then be designed to deal with the consequent challenge of team integration. This issue is discussed later in this chapter.

The Question of Team Size

What is the optimal size of a team? As a guideline, we would argue that the ideal size of a GBT is one that can ensure the required knowledge and skill base with the smallest number of people.

There is an inherent dilemma in deciding on the optimal team size. On one hand, the need to represent every required knowledge and skill would call for a very large team. On the other hand, the need to work smoothly and develop mutual trust would call for a small one—very large teams can be cumbersome and dysfunctional. It is not only difficult to foster broad participation and bring out diverse viewpoints in a very large group, it is also hard to unify the group in determining a meaningful course of action.[14] An effective solution to this dilemma is to establish a core team and supplement it as needed with other individuals, thereby creating an extended team. Membership in the core team would be limited to a relatively manageable number, say, up to about 10 members. Then, if the core team requires input from other individuals, they could be brought into the team on an ad hoc basis. In this way, the extended team could include all relevant knowledge-holders and stakeholders, both within and outside the organization. For example, many global customer account teams include even the corporate CEO on an ad hoc basis. This becomes necessary if, for instance, the team needs to renew its contract with the customer and it is deemed important for the company's CEO to meet with the CEO of the customer organization.

If, for some reason, the core team itself must be very large, then it is best to break it into subteams, each assigned to tackle specific aspects of the overall team objectives. This is the approach adopted by companies such as Microsoft when creating teams for major product development projects. Given the need to integrate multiple technologies and market requirements, having a large team is often unavoidable. However, the large team is then disaggregated into a number of subteams, each of which focuses on a specific product feature, component, or market adaptation.

Selection of Team Leadership

Structuring the leadership of a GBT involves decisions on three roles: team leader, external coach, and sponsor.

Choice of an effective team leader.

Despite increasing emphasis on self-management by teams, in the case of cross-border teams, self-management is often problematic. The organizational, linguistic, cultural, and physical distances that separate members of a typical GBT can create severe communication barriers, impede the development of trust, and contribute to the misalignment of team members' goals. These are just some of the reasons the role of the team leader in a GBT can be pivotal.

An effective GBT leader is likely to have a big stake in the outcome of the project. Other important qualities of an effective GBT leader would be credibility as a result of proven track record, conflict resolution and integration skills, and expertise in process management including diagnosis, situation assessment, option generation, and option evaluation.

Need for an external coach.

By external coach, we refer to someone who serves as an ad hoc member of the team and who is a process rather than content expert. The more complex and challenging the process to be managed, the greater the need for and value added by an external coach. It is precisely these considerations that led GE Capital to recognize the value of using an "integration manager" to help ensure rapid and effective post-merger integration. By design, this integration manager is someone other than the business leader and comes from outside the particular business.

Figure 7.2 provides a framework that depicts the conditions under which a GBT is likely to find using an external coach beneficial. The need for such a coach is likely to be particularly high when the process management task is complex and the team leader's own process management skills are inadequate. This framework would have been useful in the case of a global financial services firm that set up a cross-border task force to rationalize the number of its offices spread across three continents. The appointed leader, a team member with a major stake in the project's outcome, turned out to be rigid, inflexible, and overbearing to the point that alternative views and ideas were stifled. The team was able to make progress only when an external coach was brought in.

Role of the GBT sponsor. The sponsor of a GBT is typically a senior executive who has a credible interest, even passion, for the success of the team. A sponsor who performs this role well can indirectly encourage open and candid conversations among team members drawn from different countries and cultures. Among the responsibilities of the sponsor are to clarify and interpret the charter; clarify performance expectations and deliverables; provide ongoing guidelines, input, and support; facilitate access to needed resources; manage political road-blocks on behalf of the team; be an intellectual sounding board on content; review team progress; and hold the team accountable.

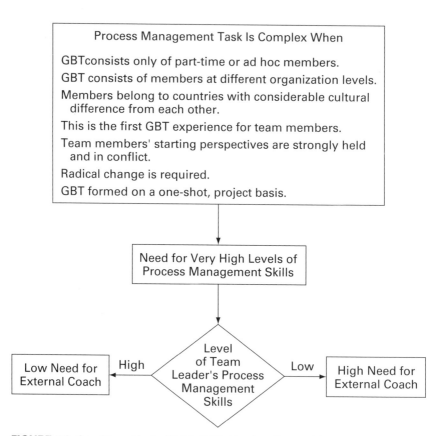

FIGURE 7.2 Conditions Under Which GBTs Need an External Coach

MANAGING TEAM PROCESS

Team charter, team composition, and team process work as a system to determine team effectiveness. Having a clearly and correctly defined charter and an optimally constituted team is merely the foundation. Without skillful management of the team process, even a well-constructed team is more than likely to fail in accomplishing its objectives.

In the case of a global business team, the primary goals of an effective team process would be to facilitate open and rich communication among the team members and to cultivate a culture of trust among them. Accomplishing these goals is essential in order to exploit the full potential of the diverse knowledge and skill base represented in the team, to integrate these diverse perspectives into creative, meaningful, and implementable solutions, and to further develop team members' knowledge, skills, and mindsets so that their participation in the GBT enriches them intellectually.

The following sections discuss the primary process levers that can be used to overcome communication barriers and to cultivate a culture of trust.

Overcoming Communication Barriers

We have argued earlier that global teams are particularly prone to communication barriers. Several process mechanisms can be used to overcome communication issues.

Language and cross-cultural training. To overcome barriers to communication created by the obvious linguistic and cultural distances separating members of the typical GBT, companies need to invest in language and cross-cultural training. Investments in language training reduce the need for third-party mediators such as translators and thus foster more direct, more spontaneous, and freer communication. The ABB Group provides a good example of how even halfway progress on linguistic skills can go far toward reducing communication barriers. Goran Lindahl, ABB's former CEO, was explicit in referring to his company's official language as "poor English" to drive home the point that no one should be embarrassed to express an idea simply because his or her English is not perfect.

Investments in cross-cultural skills also help GBT members in several ways. A better understanding of team members' disparate cultures can be expected to improve the richness of communication: People would pick up the signals in each others' verbal and nonverbal communications more comprehensively and more accurately. Also, investment in cross-cultural skills can be expected to improve team members' ability to understand and respect diversity and turn it into competitive advantage.

Agreement on norms of behavior. Establishing ground rules that reflect the desired norms of behavior can serve as a powerful self-policing mechanism to overcome communication barriers, enrich the content of team discussions, and keep the team operating as an integrated network.

A global customer account management team created by a European industrial packaging company illustrates how explicit agreement on certain ground rules can facilitate a team's smooth functioning. This team established two ground rules: Whenever a member of the account team had any meeting with the customer, that member would send a briefing to every other member of the team, and the customer's primary contact would be with one or more of the members of the global account team—no other employee of the firm was authorized to discuss or decide policy and strategy issues with the customer. These ground rules proved beneficial especially in circumstances when the customer tested the relationship. Occasionally, the customer would contact employees other than those on the account team, but the employees would always refer them to someone on the team. In cases where the global customer would contact different members on the account team about issues such as prices and delivery times, the ground rules ensured that the customer always got the same answer from each member.

Bias for data-driven discussions.   In the absence of facts, people tend to resort to opinions. As everyone knows, discussions based solely or largely on opinions can easily degenerate into personal attacks. On the other hand, if the opinions are accompanied by factual data, conflicting ideas can be evaluated more objectively and are less likely to be viewed as personal attacks. Fact-based discussions encourage team members to be more forthcoming in sharing their viewpoints even if their views may be at odds with the prevailing wisdom.[15]

A global consumer products firm formed a cross-border team to recommend ways to improve the profitability of one of its global businesses. The team, with the help of a consulting firm, assembled a detailed fact base including the fundamental shifts in the industry, competitors' moves, and the company's current positioning. The concrete factual data helped elevate the team's level of discourse. Instead of denying the problem, shifting the blame to uncontrollable external factors, or focusing on individual personalities, the team was able to brainstorm and come to terms with the critical vulnerabilities in the company's competitive positioning. A clear agreement emerged that these vulnerabilities required immediate, decisive, and visible action.

Developing multiple alternatives to enrich the debate.
Explicitly surfacing multiple alternatives is often very useful in ensuring the expression of diverse views within a GBT. The "dialectical inquiry" and "devil's advocate" approaches are two of the well-recognized formal mechanisms aimed at uncovering multiple alternatives.[16] In a dialectical inquiry, for every potential solution, the team is instructed to develop a full-fledged counterapproach based on different assumptions; then a debate ensues on the merits of the plan and the counterplan. In the devil's advocate approach, the team is told to critique a potential solution (but not necessarily to develop a full-blown counterapproach). Both

approaches can benefit the process as well as the outcome of team discussions by adding a sense of creativity while giving members license to express different views.[17]

The industrial products firm team described earlier (under the section "Is the Charter Clearly Understood") used the approach of explicitly seeking multiple alternatives to draw out the intellectual diversity represented within the team. Their mission was to make recommendations on the optimal worldwide organization for the five major global businesses. For each global business, the team collectively generated three distinct organizational forms and assigned subsets of the team to develop the best set of arguments for each form. The team's final recommendations reflected the comprehensive discussions that followed each subteam's presentation of its approach to solving the problem.

Rotating the location for meetings. Rotating the geographic location of team meetings to different parts of the world is yet another mechanism to enrich the cognitive base of the team and also legitimize the expression of divergent viewpoints. In Chapter 5, we discussed the case of VeriFone, a market leader in the automation and delivery of secure payment and payment-related transactions. VeriFone uses this approach to keep the top management team well informed about the global environment. The team, consisting of the CEO and his direct reports, meets for five days every six weeks at different locations around the globe.[18]

Cultivating a Culture of Trust

As discussed earlier, global business teams are also particularly prone to perennially low levels of trust. Firms can engage in several process mechanisms to cultivate trust among team members.

Face-to-face meetings. It is critical that the first few meetings of a GBT occur face-to-face. Other things being equal, the more deeply the members of any GBT know and understand each other, the greater the likelihood that they will trust one another. It is well known that different modes of communication differ in terms of the richness (or bandwidth, to use the current popular term) of communication that they permit. Face-to-face interaction enables the richest form of communication and can help develop a solid social foundation and mutual trust that can be subsequently leveraged through distance technologies.

In our interviews, the CEO of a global consumer products company underscored the importance of early face-to-face meetings in cultivating trust: "There is an enormous premium on good, clean non-bureaucratic communication and that depends enormously on a high level of trust. That's why at the start of the team process, you have to be together personally. You can't start them with memos or telephone calls or things like that. You've got to get the group together to know each other and get a level of comfort and trust with one another. After that you can resort to the phone calls and videoconferences."

Rotation and diffusion of team leadership.

Rotating team leadership across the various decisions that a GBT may have to make is beneficial but it is even more important to diffuse team leadership for different GBTs across different countries. By rotating and diffusing team leadership across countries, managers in several subsidiaries learn to appreciate the need for cross-border coordination. Moreover, diffusion of team leadership creates mutual interdependencies across countries because typically a country manager will lead one GBT while acting as a contributing member in another. Mutual dependence does not eliminate all conflicts, but it certainly minimizes politicking and harmful conflicts, since managers are forced to iron out and resolve conflicts en route to achieving their objectives and outcomes.

To quote John Pepper, chairman of the board of Procter & Gamble: "We felt that if each subsidiary manager also led a team, they would come to understand the value and challenge of working on a regional basis. We set up a brand team on Lenor, another on Pampers, another on Pantene, and so on. We assigned different country managers to lead these. Really wanting to get everybody into the fire so to speak in experiencing it. What made the teams work was the mutual interdependency that grew."[19]

Linking rewards to team performance.

Consider two scenarios. In the first scenario, the subsidiary manager's incentive bonus is based solely on country-level performance, even though part of the manager's time is devoted to being a member of a GBT. In the second scenario, this manager's bonus is partly linked also to the attainment of the expected outcomes of the GBT.

In the second scenario, as compared to the first, the subsidiary manager's motivation to resolve conflicts and reach an effective solution would be higher since his or her incentive bonus depends on team outcomes as well. Thus in the second scenario there will be less incentive for team members to behave in a distrusting manner since such behavior would work against self-interest in terms of rewards. These considerations lie behind Procter & Gamble's policy to give explicit weight to both country and team performance in computing annual incentive payments to its country managers.[20]

Investments in building social capital.

At any given time, a global firm typically has many GBTs working on different cross-border coordination issues. It therefore makes abundant sense for the firm to undertake corporate-wide initiatives to create interpersonal familiarity and trust among key managers of different subsidiaries. Such corporate-wide initiatives could take many forms: bringing managers from different subsidiaries together in executive development programs, horizontal rotation of managers across locations, and building language skills among these managers so that these "get to know each other" encounters have high value.

Unilever, the Dutch-British multinational, has used several mechanisms to build social capital among its employees.[21] In each country, the company uses sophisticated recruitment techniques to attract the best and brightest local nationals to come and work for its subsidiaries in that country. Unilever couples this foundation of local recruitment with a strategic expatriate program. This involves rotating high-potential executives across countries, across different tasks in a given function (such as advertising, selling, and brand management within the marketing function), and across different businesses (such as exposure to diverse businesses such as ice cream, tea, and detergents). These job rotations help build strong social networks. To quote Flores Maljers, the former cochairman and CEO of Unilever: "Exposure to another environment not only gives them [that is, expats] more know-how but also improves their 'know-who.' In addition, cross-postings between companies are very important for establishing unity, a common sense of purpose, and an understanding of different national cultures and attitudes."[22]

Unilever started its management development center, Four Acres, in the mid-1950s. Every year about 400 executives from all over the world are selected and sent by the headquarters to Four Acres for learning and development. Each executive program typically consists of about 30 participants drawn from different subsidiaries and countries. One of the objectives of these courses is to help participants get reacquainted with old friends and make new friends.

Through careful attention to global human resource management—selection, training, and development of global managers—Unilever has attempted to build social capital. Such human resource initiatives build strong personal networks that can facilitate the smooth functioning of multiple GBTs.

Our framework for designing high-performing GBTs is summarized in Figure 7.3.

SUMMARY

GBTs have become a ubiquitous phenomenon among global firms. Yet making such teams achieve their intended outcomes is far from easy. The unique factors that cause GBTs to fail are communication barriers and difficulties in cultivating trust among team members. Correct choices in team charter, team composition, and team process can increase a GBT's likelihood of achieving its objectives.

When the GBT is composed of members with unique and distinct knowledge and skill bases drawn from different subsidiaries in different countries, the potential for cognitive diversity is high. Since no individual has a monopoly on wisdom, such intellectual diversity constitutes a source of strength. However, intellectual diversity within a GBT almost always brings with it some degree of interpersonal incompatibility and communication barriers due to cultural and linguistic differences. Recognizing and anticipating these pitfalls, a company should put process mechanisms in place to enable the team to reconcile diverse perspectives and arrive at better, more novel solutions by integrating the best of individual members' ideas and contributions.

	Low Integration	High Integration
High Cognitive Diversity	Fragmented team, unable to converge on a decision	Effective global business team
Low Cognitive Diversity	A team that cannot add value	High-speed decision-making but also high risk of poor-quality decisions

Configuring the GBT

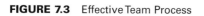

Low Integration   **High Integration**

Management of Team Process

FIGURE 7.3   Effective Team Process

CHAPTER 8

TRANSFORMING THE GLOBAL GAME

The rise of a globally connected world offers a truly rare opportunity: The chance to start something totally new. This is what we believe at IBM. And it is the core idea we are taking to customers (and pursuing ourselves): how to seize this unique moment and rethink what you do, reconceive what you offer and, along the way, reinvent who you are.

—Louis V. Gerstner Jr., Chairman and CEO, IBM, 2000[1]

PRIOR TO 1995, most books were purchased in bookstores or from printed catalogs. Further, book retailing was almost totally a country-centric, multilocal industry. In July 1995, Amazon.com began offering books for sale on its Web site. By mid-2000, more than 20 million customers worldwide were buying books, CDs, and other goods worth $2.5 billion annually from Amazon.com via the Internet. Relative to conventional retailers, the virtual store format of Amazon.com provided several advantages: better convenience (24-hour, 7-day-a-week shopping), global reach, a wider and deeper product mix (Amazon.com offered 4.7 million titles versus 200,000 titles in the biggest bricks-and-mortar retail outlet), better price (as a result of lower investments in inventory and fixed assets), and better customer service (as a result of personalized recommendations based on purchase patterns of customers). By December 2000, a mere five years after it started, and despite the massive stock market correction during the preceding nine months, Amazon.com's market capitalization was $8.8 billion—more than three times as much as the combined market value of the two largest established booksellers, Barnes & Noble and Borders.[2]

As the Amazon.com example demonstrates, competitive advantage is not just a function of how well a company plays by the existing rules of the game but, more important, it depends upon the firm's ability to radically change the rules themselves. This is as true of a newcomer such as Amazon.com as it is of an established player such as Ford in the automotive business or General Electric in the aircraft engine business.

There are three ways a corporation can change the rules of the game: redesign the value chain, reinvent the concept of customer value, and redefine the customer base. In this chapter, we present a framework to systematically attack in these three arenas.

A FRAMEWORK FOR CHANGING THE RULES OF THE GLOBAL GAME

Transforming the game, no doubt, is fundamentally a creative undertaking; it cannot result from a purely deliberate and purposeful process. Neither is industry transformation solely a function of luck, accident, or opportunism. In fact, an explicit and systematic framework is needed to guide the creative process of changing the rules of the global game. This chapter illustrates the framework through detailed examples.[3]

Why Cultivate a Bias for Changing the Rules?

There are several reasons why every company must cultivate a bias for changing the rules by which it plays the game within its industry.

Major discontinuities in the external environment. The external environment of the firm is constantly changing—sometimes incrementally and at other times in a quantum and discontinuous fashion. Changes in the external environment almost always require the business to invent at least some new rules of the game. For example, from the perspective of a financial services firm such as Merrill Lynch, the aging of the population represents an incremental change whereas the emergence of Internet trading represents a radical change.

Proactive reshaping of the industry structure. Changes in the external environment do not always originate from external forces. Firms large and small can often reshape the external environment. For example, in late 1999 Sun Microsystems announced that it would offer application software such as word-processing programs over the Internet. Unlike the historical approach to application software, these programs need not be purchased for installation on the personal computer (PC); instead, they could be rented from Web servers on an as-needed basis. Sun's move was aimed squarely at undercutting the power of the Windows operating system, the core product of Microsoft, a much larger competitor. Despite its market dominance, Microsoft was forced to follow suit and to announce that it too would embrace the renting of application programs over Web servers.

Need to break out of the competitive pack. In the absence of collusion, it is a given that competitors inevitably will find themselves pursuing conflicting goals. For example, in the PC industry, at least three of the major players

(Compaq, Dell, and Hewlett-Packard) had at various times declared their intention to be the market share leader in the industry. In a situation such as this, continuing to play by the old rules leaves the firm highly vulnerable to preemption by more innovative competitors.

Three Arenas for Attack

A business model (see Figure 8.1) results from answering three questions:

- Who are my target customers?
- What value do I want to deliver to these customers?
- How will I create that customer value?

The answers to these three questions operate as a *system* (that is to say, the individual answers must be self-reinforcing and internally consistent). As an example, take the case of Procter & Gamble's Ivory soap. The target customer segment for this product is consumer households. This segment values hygiene. P&G has assembled a value chain (R&D, sourcing, manufacturing, marketing, distribution, and so forth) that can deliver a low-cost, basic soap that is gentle to the skin and has the necessary cleaning ability.

To recap, a business model is the result of internally consistent choices in three areas: customer definition, identification of customer value, and design of the value creation process. It therefore follows that the rules of the game can be changed in three arenas, as shown in Figure 8.2. It should be emphasized that when a firm changes the rules of the game, the new rules have to be winning rules looked at from the customers' point of view. The three arenas for changing the rules of the game are

- Dramatic redesign of the end-to-end value chain architecture—that is, how do we dramatically improve the efficiency of the end-to-end value chain?
- Dramatic reinvention of the concept of customer value—that is, how do we dramatically change the value customers receive?
- Dramatic redefinition of the customer base—that is, how do we dramatically expand the size of the market?

These three arenas are highly interconnected. Changes in any *one* arena will almost always have implications for the other two arenas as well. Dramatic redesign of the value chain could fundamentally change the concept of customer value. Similarly, dramatic redefinition of the customer base would require a

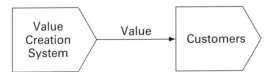

FIGURE 8.1 Elements of a Business Model: An Overview

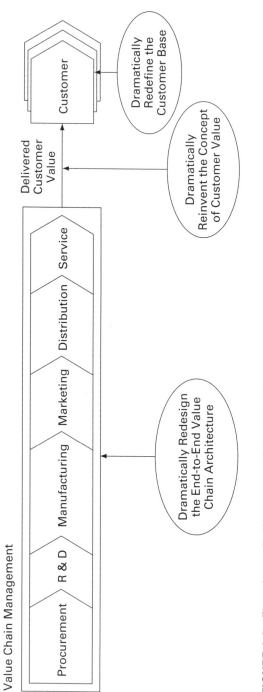

FIGURE 8.2 Three Arenas for Changing the Rules of the Game

radically different value creation system. *When one internally consistent business model is converted into another internally consistent business model, the rules of the game are changed.*

REDESIGNING THE END-TO-END VALUE CHAIN ARCHITECTURE

Value chain refers to the linked set of value-creating activities all the way from basic raw material sources for component suppliers through to the ultimate end-use product delivered into the final consumers' hands.[4] The first arena for changing the rules of the game is to radically redesign the end-to-end value chain architecture. A superior architecture is one that, viewed from the customers' point of view, has either dramatically lowered costs or dramatically increased value, or both. Examples of companies that have designed far superior value chain architectures include

- Nucor, the world's most efficient steel manufacturer
- Ikea, the world's largest furniture retailer
- Wal-Mart, the world's largest general retailer
- Amazon.com, the world's largest virtual bookstore
- Dell, the world's largest direct sales computer company

In the rest of this section, we discuss in detail how Dell Computer radically redesigned the end-to-end value chain architecture in the global personal computer industry.[5]

Dell Computer—Background

As of 2000, Dell Computer Corporation was the world's largest direct-selling computer company, with 36,500 employees in more than 30 countries and customers in more than 170 countries. Headquartered near Austin in Round Rock, Texas, the company was founded in 1984 when Michael Dell pioneered the process of selling custom-built computers directly to customers. Within a short life of 16 years, Dell had become the number-one retailer of personal computers, outselling IBM, Hewlett-Packard, and Compaq.[6] Businesses of all sizes, government agencies, educational institutions, and individual customers ordered Dell's desktop and notebook computers, workstations, and network servers by phone or via the Internet. In 1996, Dell embraced the Web. By late 1999, more than 40 percent of the company's sales emanated from this channel.[7] On the Internet, customers were in control. They could use the Web any time of the day or night at their own convenience to configure, price, and order computer systems; they could get current order status and delivery information and access technical reference materials on hardware and software. Dell computer systems were assembled one at a time, as ordered, at factories in Austin, Texas; Limerick, Ireland; and Penang, Malaysia. Dell outsourced delivery to other firms with far superior core competencies in logistics, to ensure that custom orders were delivered within a few days.[8] Dell provided an extensive range of value-added services, including system installation and management, after-sales service, and technology-transition planning and execution. Its own on-site systems engineers and consultants and employees of strategic service partners gave Dell an army of more than 10,000 service providers around the world.

Comparative financial data on Dell, IBM, Hewlett-Packard, and Compaq are given in Table 8.1. Dell outpaced its competitors in both growth and profitability. Dell's market capitalization was about $700 million at the June 1988 initial public offering. By December 2000, it had grown to nearly $50 billion, an increase of more than 70 times over a 12-year period—a gain dramatically above that of Standard & Poor's 500. At age 35, Michael Dell was the richest man in the world under 40. Dell had created enormous value for customers and shareholders by adopting a radically different value chain architecture in the PC industry.

TABLE 8.1   Comparative Financial Data on Selected Companies in the Global Computer Systems Industry ($ billions)

	Five-Year Average: 1994–1998			
	Dell	**IBM**	**Compaq**	**Hewlett-Packard**
Five-year return on capital (percentage)	52	14	24	19
Five-year sales growth (percentage)	43	5	41	19
Five-year net income growth (percentage)	86	27	49	21

	1998 Data			
	Dell	**IBM**	**Compaq**	**Hewlett-Packard**
Sales ($B)	12.3	81.7	31.2	47.0
As percentage of sales:				
Cost of goods sold	78	63	75	68
Gross margin	22	37	25	32
Selling and administration	9.7	20	16	17
Research and development	1.3	6	4.5	7
Operating income	11	11	loss	8
Net income	8	8	loss	6
Inventory turnover	53 times	16 times	20 times	8 times
Return on equity (percentage)	77	32	deficit	18

Source: Based on company annual reports and *Forbes,* 11 January 1999, p. 150.

The Traditional Value Chain in the PC Industry

The traditional value chain in the personal computer industry can be characterized as "build-to-stock" (Figure 8.3A). PC manufacturers designed and built their products with preconfigured options based on market forecasts. Products were first stored in company warehouses and later dispatched to resellers, retailers, and other intermediaries who typically added a 20–30 percent markup before selling to their customers. PC manufacturers controlled the upstream part of the value chain, giving the downstream part to middlemen. Retailers justified their margins by providing several benefits to customers: easily accessed locations, selection across multiple brands, opportunity to see and test products before purchasing, and knowledgeable salespeople who could educate customers regarding their choices.

Two trends in the early 1980s allowed Michael Dell to radically reengineer the PC industry value chain. First, corporate customers were becoming increasingly sophisticated and therefore did not require intense personal selling by salespeople. By the late 1980s even individuals—especially those buying their second or third PC—had become savvy and experienced technology users. Second, the different components of a PC—monitor, keyboard, memory, disk drive, software, and so on—became standard modules permitting mass customization in the system configuration of PCs.

A. Traditional Value Chain: The Indirect Model

Personal Computer Manufacturers

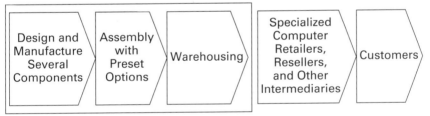

B. Dell Computer's Redesigned Value Chain: The Direct Model

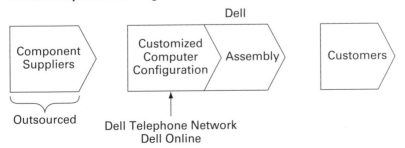

FIGURE 8.3 Redesigning the End-to-End Value Chain Architecture in the Global Personal Computer Industry: From Build-to-Stock to Build-to-Order

How Dell Computer Redesigned the Value Chain

Dell Computer's direct model is shown in Figure 8.3B. Dell dramatically changed the value chain architecture by departing from the industry's historical rules on several fronts. Specifically, the company outsourced all components but performed assembly. It eliminated retailers and shipped directly from its factories to end customers, and took customized orders for hardware and software over the phone or via the Internet. In addition, Dell designed an integrated supply chain linking its suppliers very closely to its assembly factories and the order-intake system. As recounted by Michael Dell: "We tell our suppliers exactly what our daily production requirements are. So it's not 'Well, every two weeks deliver 5000 to this warehouse, and we'll put them on the shelf, and then we'll take them off the shelf.' It's 'Tomorrow morning, we need 8,562, and deliver them to door number seven by 7 A.M.'"[9] Three major benefits ensued from Dell's new value chain architecture: technology advantage, cost advantage, and customer knowledge advantage.

Technology advantage.   Dell custom-built its machines *after* receiving an order, instead of making machines for inventory in anticipation of orders. Thus, Dell had dramatically low levels of components as well as finished goods inventory (on average, 7 to 11 days for Dell versus 70 to 100 days combined for other PC manufacturers and their resellers). Low inventory translated into a huge technology advantage.

Microprocessor and other component technologies kept advancing at a relentless pace. Since Dell essentially had no finished goods inventory in the pipeline, it enjoyed a first-mover advantage in bringing leading-edge component technology to the marketplace. Dell's PC components were 60 to 80 days newer than those in IBM or Compaq PCs. Thus Dell was able to introduce new products faster than its competitors.

Cost advantage.   Dell derived cost advantage in three areas: component purchase costs, inventory and working capital costs, and selling and administrative costs.

Cost of computer components kept declining. Because Dell purchased components on a just-in-time basis, it enjoyed a nearly 6 percent lower cost of components relative to its competitors.[10]

Radical reductions in inventory gave Dell other cost advantages as well. Dell saved on the interest cost of financing the inventory and warehousing costs to store the inventory. Because of its direct channel with customers, Dell eliminated the need to mark down inventory not sold by retailers. Thus Dell minimized the cost of product obsolescence. Dell's direct dealings with individual customers ensured immediate payment via credit card. That meant that in general, accounts receivable investment was lower as well, and bad-debt risks were insignificant. Furthermore, Dell enjoyed normal credit terms from its component suppliers. As a consequence, Dell operated with negative working capital. In 1998, Dell had 36 days in accounts receivable, 7 days in inventory, but 51 days in accounts payable—for a negative 18 days of sales in working capital!

Eliminating the retailer and establishing direct interface with the customer via phone and the Internet significantly lowered Dell's selling and administrative costs. Dell eliminated the typical markup of middlemen. In the traditional indirect model, PC manufacturers maintained a sales force, as did the middlemen. In the direct model, only Dell had a sales force. Thus, sales force costs tended to be lower for Dell. The company also avoided the cost of physical space at the distributors' showrooms. Finally, the Internet helped to reduce sales costs even further. A business that uses telephone operators to interface with customers must pay for telephone personnel salaries, toll-free calls, and the bricks and mortar for the telephone service center. Communication with customers via the Internet reduced many of these costs.

Customer knowledge advantage.

Traditional PC producers dealt with middlemen, not with the end customer. Dell's direct dealings with each individual customer gave the company several advantages. First, direct contact with customers helped Dell gain a superior understanding of specific customer needs. Each of its several market segments—multinational corporations, medium-sized businesses, small companies, individuals, federal government, state and local governments, and educational institutions—had unique computing needs and different buying processes. Global service capabilities were critical for multinational corporations, for example, while medium-sized businesses placed a high value on presale, product repair, and help-desk support. By organizing its marketing and sales functions around distinct customer groups, Dell was able to address varying customer needs with greater precision and speed.

Second, proprietary information about customers' buying patterns gave Dell superior ability to forecast demand, which in turn helped it maintain minimum inventory without suffering the problem of stock-outs. As Michael Dell observed, "This closeness [to end use customers] gives us access to information that's absolutely critical to our strategy. It helps us forecast what they're going to need and when. If you look at the complexity and the diversity of our product line, there's no way we could [maintain very low inventory] unless we had credible information about what the customer is actually buying. If you don't have the tight linkage [with end customers] then trying to manage to 11 days of inventory would be insane."[11]

Finally, based on customers' past purchasing patterns, Dell forged lifelong customer relationships. For instance, Dell understood better than its competitors which customers would benefit most when newer versions of hardware and software were available and therefore was able to proactively market new products to the right customer segments. By owning the relationship with customers, Dell not only avoided getting filtered information from third-party retailers but also insulated itself from poor service and lack of product knowledge on the part of retailers.

Dell's Virtuous Cycle

In sum, Dell achieved leadership by radically redesigning the industry value chain (Figure 8.3B) and created a *virtuous cycle*—the opposite of the vicious cycle that plagues so many businesses—by rewriting the rules of the PC industry (Figure 8.4). Dell custom configured PCs through direct dealings with end customers. Customer intimacy gave Dell superior ability to forecast market demand. This allowed Dell to pursue just-in-time manufacturing with very low levels of finished goods and components inventory, with little risk of stock-outs. Radical reductions in inventory not only lowered costs but also enabled Dell to be first to market with the latest products. The net result was that Dell had the dominant share of the PC market. This in turn led to more customer contacts, thereby restarting the cycle.

Dell's value chain architecture also enabled the company to globalize faster and more profitably than its competitors for two reasons. First, Dell's direct model yielded the same benefits in non–U.S. markets as it did in the U.S. market. Thus Dell's direct model was superior to its competitors' indirect model in non–U.S. markets as well. Second, because of its direct channel, Dell—in contrast to IBM and Compaq—did not require access to local distribution channels, so it faced lower entry barriers into non–U.S. markets. Thus Dell was able to globalize its business model faster than its competitors. For instance, although

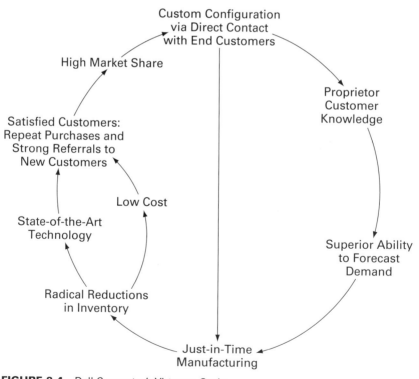

FIGURE 8.4   Dell Computer's Virtuous Cycle

many multinationals found it difficult to make money in China, Dell had achieved profitability within a year of its August 1998 entry into that market.[12]

IBM, Compaq, and Hewlett-Packard might have found it difficult to imitate and neutralize Dell's direct model for fear of alienating their dealers. The bulk of the sales for these corporations came through third-party dealers. If they set up direct channels, their distributors would be upset since direct channels took market share away from retailers and resellers. Therefore, companies using the indirect model could not run the risk of angering their critical constituency. To quote Michael Dell, "Our competitors are prisoners of their history. They're stuck with their dealers."[13]

Key Ideas Regarding Value Chain Redesign

As the analysis of Dell Computer illustrates, three principles should guide the redesign of the end-to-end value chain architecture. First, creating a new value chain involves redesigning its two central attributes: the set of activities that will constitute the new value chain, and the interfaces across the activities. In eliminating the middleman role altogether, Dell redesigned the set of activities comprising the value chain. However, the company did not stop there. It built deep relationships at both ends—with suppliers as well as customers. This attempt at virtual integration without vertical integration represents a redesign of the interface across activities on Dell's part.

Second, the new value chain must create dramatic gains in one or more of three areas: cost structure, asset investment, and speed of responsiveness to external changes. Relative to traditional competitors, Dell's direct model had the following unique combination of features: significantly lower costs, negative working capital investment, custom-built machines, first-mover advantage in offering leading-edge component technologies, high quality and reliability, an efficient and convenient purchasing process, speed of delivery, and excellent after-sales service.

Third, the new value chain must enhance the scalability of the company's business model to ensure rapid growth in market share, high-velocity globalization, and scope expansion into other related products and services. On the upstream side, Dell had relied totally on third-party component suppliers; on the downstream side, it had completely eliminated reliance on local distribution channels; and the Internet-based Dell Online channel had allowed Dell to sell a large variety of PC-related peripheral products such as printers, cameras, and so forth. As a result, Dell's business model had perhaps been the most rapidly scalable within the PC industry.

REINVENTING THE CONCEPT OF CUSTOMER VALUE

The typical approach firms can take to dramatically reinvent the concept of customer value is to shift from selling discrete products to supplying total systems and solutions. Consider several examples:

From selling hardware and software	To	Supplying total business solutions
From country-by-country advertising campaigns	To	Coordinated global advertising campaigns
From selling insurance, banking, mortgages, mutual funds, and the like as discrete products	To	Providing financial security and freedom through an integrated system of products and services
From selling automotive paint	To	Providing a complete paint shop
From selling packaging materials	To	Supplying total packaging systems

In the next section, we analyze how Tetra Pak changed the rules of the game in the global liquid packaging industry by reinventing the concept of customer value.

Tetra Pak—Background

Tetra Pak, a Swedish multinational, is dedicated to the development, manufacture, and sale of systems for the processing, packaging, and distribution of liquid food products.[14] Tetra Pak is the only company of its kind capable of supplying customers with comprehensive systems that integrate processing lines with packaging and distribution systems.

Tetra Pak was a division of Tetra Laval and accounted for 70 percent of the sales of the Tetra Laval group. Two brothers, Hans and Gad Rausing, transformed Tetra Pak from a small Swedish milk carton firm into a global liquid-packaging powerhouse. The company was a niche player focused on only one product category: liquid packaging for food items. The firm did not make cartons for shampoos, detergents, or other nonfood items, or diversify outside the packaging sector. Tetra Pak's growth, therefore, necessarily had to come from global expansion in its product category. Although the privately owned company did not publish financial data, several indicators pointed to its phenomenal growth and financial success:

- Tetra Pak had minimum presence in the paper carton business 25 years ago, when other companies such as Enso (Finland) and International Paper (United States) dominated this segment. Yet by 1999, Tetra Pak produced packaging materials at 57 plants, sold 90 billion containers a year in more than 165 countries, and had captured a 40 percent share of the European liquid-packaging market.

- In 1991, Tetra Pak paid £1.4 billion in cash to acquire Alfa-Laval, a Swedish firm that produced and sold systems for separation, heat transfer, and fluid handling for the food industry.

- In 1993, the Rausing brothers, who lived in England, surpassed the queen as the richest individuals in the United Kingdom.

- In 1998, Gad Rausing paid $7 billion to acquire his brother's 50 percent share in the firm, placing the value of the firm at $14 billion.

Tetra Pak's success can be attributed to the way it changed the concept of customer value in the global liquid-packaging industry.

Traditional Value Chain

There were many options for packaging materials, including steel, aluminum, glass, plastic, paper, and fiber-foil (metal and paper composite). Typically, package manufacturers made the containers and then shipped them to processors of milk, juice, and other liquids. The processors filled the containers and transported them to supermarkets for sale to consumers.

Tetra-Pak's New Business Model

Whereas traditional players offered containers to customers, Tetra Pak changed the value proposition by offering customers total systems: filling equipment, packaging materials, and distribution equipment such as conveyors, tray packers, and film wrappers. Customer value was transformed from the traditional model, liquids poured into containers, to Tetra Pak's model, containers made at the point where beverages were ready to be packed.

The Tetra Pak system had two unique features. First, the company installed its filling equipment on the premises of beverage producers. Inside each machine was a continuous roll of paper with four layers of plastic coating and an additional layer of aluminum coating. When liquid was poured, the roll of paper curled into a tube, which was then heat sealed and cut into a carton. Thus there was essentially *zero* time lag between making and using the container. Second, air and light inside cartons tended to cause much faster decay in liquids. Tetra Pak employed a two-step process to ensure that cartons were airtight and lightproof.[15] The first step was perhaps more critical. The fact that cartons were formed *after* the liquid was poured enabled Tetra Pak to use a special vacuum-filling technology which kept air out of the liquids during the filling process. In the second step, once the package was sealed, plastic and aluminum coatings kept air out of the cartons and created a secure barrier against light. Thus, Tetra Pak cartons had an "aseptic" property. That is to say, they did not require refrigeration to preserve the shelf life of liquids. For instance, in an aseptic package, milk had a shelf life of six months and juices had a shelf life of twelve months.[16]

Tetra Pak's business model changed the concept of value at every stage of the traditional industry chain.

For container manufacturers. Tetra Pak completely eliminated this stage of the value chain, thereby yielding several benefits. There were obvious savings in factory space as well as labor and overhead costs involved in making the containers. Tetra Pak also saved the cost of "transporting air" from container manufacturers to beverage producers. Not only was transporting containers expensive, but containers such as glass bottles were breakable in transit. Finally,

Tetra Pak avoided handling costs at two points: loading the empty containers onto the truck at one end and unloading and storing containers by beverage processors at the other.

For beverage processors.   As noted earlier, Tetra Pak eliminated the cost of inbound handling of empty containers for beverage processors. Several additional benefits accrued at this stage of the chain. Perhaps the most important benefit of the Tetra Pak system was that cartons were made only when needed, thereby ensuring zero inventories of empty cartons in the pipeline. This saved financing costs and storage space. Also, beverages, once filled and sealed, did not require refrigerated trucks to send to supermarkets, even when they had to be transported on long hauls.

Glass bottles, plastic jugs, and gabled-top (that is, the traditional triangular fold closure) paper cartons could not be stacked neatly on each other. Thus transporting glass bottles, plastic jugs, and paper cartons involved several inefficiencies. First, they required crating. Second, in the case of glass bottles, partitions were needed between bottles to prevent breakage. Third, the narrow neck of glass bottles and plastic jugs and the triangular top of paper cartons wasted space. In contrast, the box-shaped Tetra Briks could be stacked easily. The rectangular and flat structure of Tetra Briks ensured efficient utilization of space.

Beverage producers enjoyed the benefit of one-stop shopping for complete systems from Tetra Pak, with matching equipment at every stage. This enabled customers to have a single point of accountability, ensuring uninterrupted production. Tetra Pak, in turn, assembled an experienced and technically well trained service force that assured customers fast, efficient repairs and equipment maintenance.

Its close relationships with beverage companies prompted Tetra Pak to dedicate more than 1,000 research and development engineers worldwide to focus on customer needs, develop new packaging designs, and continuously improve processing and distribution systems. As a result, Tetra Pak had up-to-date technology in its filling and sealing systems, which were rated the best in the industry.

Tetra Pak leased its filling machines. From the standpoint of customers, the leasing program had two attractive features: low capital outflow, and protection against technological obsolescence of the machines. Having locked up beverage companies on long-term machine leases, Tetra Pak entered into contracts with customers to supply them packaging materials at attractive margins. The packaging materials were custom designed for Tetra Pak machines, effectively giving the company a virtual monopoly on providing raw materials to the filling machines. Once familiar with Tetra Pak machines and invested in training employees to operate those machines, beverage companies had little incentive to switch to other suppliers.

For supermarkets.   A significant value added for supermarkets was the savings in handling—a major cost element. Because Tetra Briks could be stacked, the beverage producers usually loaded them onto trucks on a wheeled cart. At the supermarket, the driver of the truck wheeled the cart inside the store onto the display space. By contrast, other types of packages, such as glass bottles, plastic jugs, and paper cartons, could not be stacked—and therefore required unloading and handling by supermarket personnel. Further, unlike Tetra Pak cartons, other types of packages required refrigerated sections inside the supermarket to preserve the liquids—another major cost item.

For end-use customers.   A major value for end-use customers was the convenience of the Tetra Pak cartons. Glass bottles were heavy, bulky, and breakable. Plastic jugs and paper cartons required refrigeration and therefore were not as convenient in school lunches and on picnics. Tetra Pak cartons, on the other hand, were compact in size, convenient to use, appealing in appearance, and competitive in price.

To sum up, Tetra Pak's business model changed the value proposition for beverage producers, supermarkets, and end customers (Figure 8.5). In emerging countries such as India, China, and Brazil, sizable populations live in places with minimum or no refrigeration facilities. The Tetra Pak system was well suited for such huge and growing markets. Without Tetra Pak cartons, such markets would be largely underserved.

Key Ideas Regarding Reinventing Customer Value

When a firm redefines its value proposition from selling discrete products to selling an integrated system of products and services, as the Tetra Pak example illustrates, customers' dependence on the firm significantly increases. Customers typically do not like a single source since the sole-source provider has the ability to exploit the resulting bargaining power. As a result, from the customers' standpoint,

Customer Type	Tetra Pak's New Concept of Value
Beverage Processors	Bought total systems
	Zero inventory
	Convenience in handling
	Savings in transportation to supermarkets
	One-stop shopping
Supermarkets	Convenience in handling
	Savings in display
End customers	Compact size
	Convenience
	Handsome packaging
	Competitive pricing

FIGURE 8.5   How Tetra Pak Dramatically Reinvented the Concept of Customer Value

offering total solutions will be a winning value proposition *only* if the following three conditions hold:

- The firm is best-in-class in each of the products in the bundle. If the firm is not best-in-class in one product that is offered under the one-stop-shopping umbrella, by definition, customer value is reduced since customers could obtain that product from another, superior source.

- The integrated solution is genuinely superior to the alternative whereby the customer buys discrete products and services and bundles them together. Such superiority can result from one or more of several sources: superior systems design, superior system assembly, and superior customization to the user's needs.

- The firm offers the bundle at a lower cost than what it would cost customers to assemble the individual products from separate world-class providers. That is to say, the firm should not only demonstrate that the bundle is superior but should be willing to share the gains with customers.

As the Tetra Pak analysis illustrates, the company's success has been the result of paying careful attention to meeting all three of these conditions.

REDEFINING THE CUSTOMER BASE

By *redefining the customer base,* we mean the discovery of a hidden customer segment so large as to result in a dramatic enlargement of the industry's total customer base. Companies that have discovered and created whole new customer megasegments include

Apple: Personal computers for every man, woman, and child at a time when computers were used by corporations, scientific establishments, educational institutions, and governments.

Schwab: Financial products for do-it-yourself, knowledgeable individual investors with small trading volumes, at a time when such products were primarily sold to institutional investors and wealthy individuals.

Canon: Personal copiers for individuals and small businesses at a time when copiers were sold to large corporations.

In the rest of this section, we analyze how Canon changed the rules of the game in the global photocopier industry by redefining the target customer base.

Canon—Background

Canon was a latecomer to the copier business. The first mover was Haloid Corporation—renamed Xerox Corporation in 1961—which bought the patents for the electrostatic copier process from the inventor, Chester Carlson, in 1956.[17] The introduction of the 914 machine in 1959 signaled the emergence of the company as the dominant force in the copier industry. The name of the machine sprang from its ability to copy documents 9"x14" in size. The 914 machine was the first of its kind to make multiple copies and made the largest number of copies per minute, thereby opening up the "era of mass copying."[18] Xerox seized the initiative by assembling a business model targeted at large corporations that required high-volume copying.

The results were spectacular. By 1961, a mere two years after the introduction of the 914, Xerox became a Fortune 500 company. The cover of *BusinessWeek* displayed the 914 copier, and *Fortune* went a step further, declaring the 914 to be "the most successful product ever marketed in America."[19] The Smithsonian displays a 914 original. By 1970, Xerox had reached Fortune 60 status. Xerox crossed the $1 billion sales mark in 1968—the fastest company to reach that landmark at that time. The company wasted no time in pursuing global markets. It created a joint venture with the United Kingdom's Rank Organization to form Rank Xerox, which dominated the European market. In addition, Rank Xerox and Fuji Photo Films (Japan) created another joint venture, Fuji Xerox, which dominated the Asian market. By 1970, Xerox held a 95 percent market share in the global copier industry.

Canon, a Japanese multinational and an upstart in the copier industry in the mid-1970s, created entirely new market segments for copiers not served by Xerox in the United States—that is, small companies and individuals. In the late 1970s, Canon designed a value delivery system that offered a $1,000 personal copier that targeted these segments. For almost a decade, Xerox largely ignored the new market space created by Canon at the low end. In fact, in 1978, Fuji Xerox was willing to sell low-end copiers to Xerox to counterattack Canon in the United States. Xerox, however, refused Fuji Xerox's offer.[20] Canon's leadership in low-end copiers illustrates the power of changing the rules of the game by radically redefining the customer.

Xerox's Big Copier Business Model

Xerox's decision to serve large corporate customers allowed it to build a business model with huge barriers to entry. Xerox had more than 500 patents that protected its plain paper copying (PPC) technology. The alternate technology at that time was coated-paper copying (CPC). CPC technology was inferior to PPC for two reasons: The coated paper required by CPC machines was more expensive than the plain paper used by PPC machines, and CPC machines produced one copy at a time whereas PPC machines could provide high-volume, multiple copies. Corporate customers had massive duplicating needs and therefore preferred scale-efficient big machines. PPC patenting effectively ruled out new entrants.

The choice of corporate customers allowed Xerox to build a direct sales force since there was a limited number of customers to serve. By 1970, Xerox had created an enviable sales force capability: tremendous technical expertise, long-term customer relationships, and deep product knowledge. Any new entrant who wanted to imitate Xerox's business model would have to replicate such a sales network, a high-fixed-cost activity and thus a major entry barrier.

Xerox's customers—Fortune 500 companies—did not care as much about price as they did about the need for 100 percent uptime on their machines. Since central copy centers typically had one large machine, the entire copy center came to a standstill when that machine went down. Thus it was not enough for Xerox to offer excellent service; it had to guarantee outstanding service, 24 hours a day. As soon as a machine went down, Xerox sent service staff to fix it. By 1970, Xerox had built a world-class, around-the-clock servicing capability—another formidable entry barrier.

Instead of selling machines outright, Xerox leased them. Lease financing of a technologically complex product in a context of rapidly evolving technology is always a high-risk activity. Xerox understood and controlled the pace of technological evolution much better than any other photocopier company. Therefore, Xerox's level of risk in lease financing was much lower than for its competitors.

Through a decade of expenditures on marketing and advertising, Xerox established a powerful brand name in the industry. In fact, copying and "xeroxing" virtually became synonymous. Any new entrant had to contend with Xerox's strong brand image.

Xerox's combined entry barriers were simply overwhelming for a start-up firm. These entry barriers posed significant problems even for an established office equipment supplier like IBM. Certainly, IBM faced an insurmountable barrier in the form of technology patents over PPC. It is true that IBM sold mainframes to corporate customers through a sales force and serviced the computers through an extensive servicing network in the 1960s. Even so, IBM's sales and service staff at that time were not easily transferable to the copier market without significant additional investments in technology and product-specific training. It is not surprising, therefore, that Xerox enjoyed a virtual monopoly in the big copier industry.

Canon's Distributed Copier Business Model

By identifying new customer segments that were not using copiers at that time—small businesses and individuals—Canon not only opened up a new market space but in the process was able to get around Xerox's powerful entry barriers.

Canon dedicated research efforts during the 1960s to developing an alternative to Xerox's PPC technology. In 1968, Canon invented what it called "New Process" (NP) technology, which used plain paper to photocopy but did not violate Xerox's patents. Canon deployed two of its existing competency bases—microelectronics (from its calculator business) and optics and imaging (from its camera business)—in developing the NP technology. Further, Canon benefited from a ruling by the Federal Trade Commission in 1975 that forced Xerox to license freely its dry-toner PPC technology to competitors.[21]

In the late 1970s, Canon successfully designed personal copiers at a price point significantly below Xerox's big copiers to appeal to small businesses and individuals. At that time, Canon's personal copiers, which made 8–10 copies per minute, ranged in price from $700 to $1,200. In contrast, Xerox's high-speed machines, which made 90–120 copies per minute, had a price range of $80,000-$129,000.[22] Canon's effect on the copier industry was similar to its earlier effect on the camera industry when it introduced AE-1, the first mass-market 35 mm single-lens reflex camera with microprocessor control that could produce close to professional-quality photographs but sold for significantly less than Leica, the high-end German camera targeted at the professional market.[23]

Because Canon's target segments involved millions of customers, it could not use the direct sales force approach. Instead, the company chose to distribute its personal copiers through traditional third-party distributors: office products dealers, computer stores, and mass merchandisers such as Sears. This distribution approach not only eliminated Canon's need for huge cash outlay but allowed it rapid market entry.

Canon overcame Xerox's formidable advantage in 24-hour servicing capability through several means. First, Canon designed its machines for reliability; its copier had just eight units that could be assembled on an automated line by robots without any human help.[24] There is obviously an inverse relationship between product reliability and the need for service. Second, Canon made replacement parts modular so that end-use customers could replace them when they wore out. Copier drum, charging device, toner assembly, and cleaner were combined into a single disposable cartridge that the customer was expected to remove and replace with a new one after making 2,000 copies.[25] Third, Canon's design was so simple that traditional office products dealers could be trained to repair the machines. Finally, under distributed copying, people were willing to go to other departments to photocopy when their machines were down. Thus, unlike central copying, distributed copying did not require 24-hour servicing capability.

Finally, Canon's low-cost personal copiers were sold outright for cash, so leasing was not an issue. Also, Canon had built a strong brand name for high quality and low cost in the camera business. It successfully leveraged this brand name when it launched personal copiers. To summarize, Canon achieved leadership in low-end copiers by radically redefining the customer base (Figure 8.6).

There are several possible reasons why Xerox did not respond soon enough to Canon's attack with its own version of distributed copying. First, Xerox might not have perceived Canon as a serious threat since Canon did not initially go head-to-head against Xerox. Perhaps Xerox simply did not expect low-end copiers to become a huge market segment. In fact, during the 1970s, Xerox was most worried about IBM and Kodak, which entered the copier industry at the high end playing by Xerox's rules.[26] Second, big machines had a high profit margin per unit. Personal copiers, on the other hand, were low-margin products. Xerox might have feared cannibalizing its high-margin business for low-margin copiers. Third, Xerox had invested heavily in a sales force and servicing network. Its own sales force might not have welcomed use of third-party dealers to sell personal copiers, a competitive product to big copiers. Similarly, Xerox's service network, which operated as a profit center, had little incentive to support programs to

	Xerox	Canon
Target Customer Segments	Large corporations	Small offices Individuals
Concept of Customer Value	Centrally controlled photocopying	Individually controlled, decentralized photocopying
Value Chain Elements		
R&D	Focus on product Technology	Focus on product and process technology
Design	Complex Many parts Customized components Minimum acceptable quality*	Simple Fewer parts Standard components High reliability
Manufacture	Discrete High cost Acceptable quality*	Mass production Low cost High quality
Product Attributes	High price High speed	Low price Low speed
Marketing	Own sales force	Third-party dealers
Financing	Leasing	Outright sale
Servicing	Own service	Third-party dealers Self-service

*Backed up by excellent after-sales service

FIGURE 8.6   How Canon Radically Redefined the Customer Base

produce quantum improvements in product reliability. Fourth, under the leasing policy, Xerox had not fully recovered its investment on its installed base. Therefore, it might not have wanted to risk making its installed base obsolete prematurely by offering personal copiers. Finally, Xerox's customers—heads of copy centers in large corporations—were extremely critical to Xerox's success and therefore might have had an important influence in Xerox's internal decisions. Heads of copy centers would naturally resist introduction of distributed copying for fear of losing their power base.

Key Ideas Regarding Redefining the Customer Base

The Canon case represents an example of a company that discovered a hidden megasegment and built the necessary capabilities to serve it. Such an approach can change the rules of the global game in three ways:

- *The new segment changes the value potential of the industry.* Its discovery dramatically increases the size and growth rate of the overall marketspace. Further, the higher growth rate of the new segment begins to draw resources away from the established segment toward the new segment.

- *Solutions designed for the new segment begin to substitute for the historical solutions of the original segment.* As the distributed copying concept pioneered by Canon penetrated the large corporate market, personal copiers began to chip away at least partly at Xerox's sales of medium and high-end copiers. Such partial substitution can also be observed in many other industries such as PCs versus mainframes and the discount brokerage model of Charles Schwab versus the full-service model of Merrill Lynch.

- *Technological, financial, and organizational capabilities accumulated in the process of discovering and dominating the new segment can be leveraged to launch a direct attack on the incumbent players.* This turned out to be the case in the global photocopier industry. Canon used its stronghold in the low end of the copier industry to build technological capabilities, market understanding, and financial muscle. It then leveraged these strengths in the mid to late 1990s to move upscale and attack Xerox head-on in high-speed copiers.

SUMMARY

Our central premise in this chapter has been that every company should cultivate a bias for changing the rules of the game. The external environment is constantly changing along a host of dimensions such as technology (for example, the emergence of e-business), global landscape (for example, China's entry into the WTO), demography (for example, the aging of the population in the United States, Europe, and Japan), and so forth. In addition to exogenous changes, firms often also have the power to proactively reshape the boundaries, structure, and dynamics of their industry's environment. Being a first mover in responding to impending environmental change or being a pioneer in initiating change in one's industry environment can give the firm a major competitive advantage.

When exploring the opportunities for changing the rules of the game, we have identified three potential arenas for analysis and radical transformation: boundaries of the targeted customer base, conceptualization of the value to be delivered to customers, and design of the end-to-end value chain architecture.

In terms of redefining the customer base, we have proposed that the opportunity to change the rules of the game lies primarily in discovering and serving a previously hidden but potentially very large customer segment. As in the Canon case, such redefinition of the customer base can not only provide the innovator with a large, profitable, and undefended marketspace, it can also serve as the platform from which the newcomer can challenge the incumbent in its own historical arena.

In terms of reinventing the value proposition for the customers, we have proposed that the typical opportunity for changing the rules lies in turning from the selling of discrete products and services to a comprehensive customer solution whereby the customer is offered an integrated bundle of products and services to address a generic underlying need. Such a move would not only deepen the firm's relationships with its customers but is also likely to be seen by the customers as potentially increasing the supplier's market power. To guard against any negative responses by the customer, the firm must not only make sure that the comprehensive solutions approach is genuinely superior (in terms of effectiveness and efficiency) but also share the resulting benefits with its customers.

In terms of redesigning the end-to-end value chain architecture, we have proposed that the opportunities to change the rules lie in redesigning not only the set of activities comprising the value chain but also the interfaces across the activities. As the Dell Computer case illustrates, redesign of the value chain architecture should be governed by the following criteria: Will the new architecture allow us to market, sell, and provide the intended products and services to the target customers in a dramatically more effective and efficient manner? And will the new architecture allow us flexibility to scale up, expand the product and service bundle, and, if needed, switch to a superior value chain architecture in the future?

In conclusion, we believe that the quest for changing the rules of the game should be a never-ending process. As competitors wake up to the reality of your new and superior business model, every one of your innovations will eventually be imitated. However, before your current competitive advantages are neutralized, you must already have moved ahead—in exploiting new developments in your external environment or in proactively initiating a change in industry dynamics, or both. The relevant question for most firms is not *whether* the rules of the game will change; rather, it is *who* will take the initiative to do so—you, your competitors, or a new entrant.

CHAPTER 9

GLOBALIZATION IN THE DIGITAL AGE

Global yet decentralized, the Net is inherently transnational.
—*Esther Dyson, Release 2.0: A Design for Living in the Digital Age[1]*

THE EMERGENCE of the digital era has done more to bridge distance than perhaps any other development of the past few decades. How is digitization reshaping the economic landscape? How should newly formed information technology-driven firms, operating at the leading edge of the digital revolution, deal with the imperative to globalize? And how will the digital revolution transform the established global enterprise? These are some of the issues that we address in this chapter. Our analysis of the impact of digital technologies on the global enterprise also sheds light on the emerging shape of tomorrow's global corporation.

THE DIGITAL REVOLUTION

We use the term *digital revolution* to signify the emergence of a number of complementary technologies:

- Convergence of computers and communications and emergence of the Internet. The number of Internet users around the world is expected to grow from over 350 million in 2001 to more than one billion over the next five to ten years.
- Emergence of ubiquitous point-and-click interfaces that are based on open standards, are cheap to set up and run, and are global. Also, HTML, the language currently used to define Web pages, will be supplanted by XML, a more powerful one. XML, unlike its predecessor, attaches invisible metatags to objects on a Web page so that data elements are always tagged with relevant information about themselves. This means that in an online business-to-business (B2B) marketplace, the specifications, price, and availability of each product could be labeled with metatags enabling computers to make easier and faster price comparison across different vendors.[2]

- Roll-out of xDSL, cable modem, and other broadband communications technologies that enable always-on connection to the Internet at communication speeds of up to 40 times faster than the typical telephone modem. Broadband connections are expected to become a reality in more than 70 percent of households in developed countries over the next five to ten years.[3] In addition, at the level of the Internet backbone, the current first-generation Internet is expected to give way to a much faster second-generation Internet 2.

- Explosive growth in the use of mobile telecommunications globally not merely for voice telephony but, fueled by industry-wide agreements on standards such as third-generation cellular communications (3G), Wireless Application Protocol (WAP), or i-Mode (pioneered by Japan's NTT DoCoMo), increasingly also for Internet access. Nokia, the global leader in mobile phones, has projected that the number of mobile phone subscribers would exceed one billion well before the end of the current decade. The company has also projected that, within the next few years, the number of wireless devices with Internet access would exceed the number of wired ones.[4]

- Industry-wide backing of technologies such as Bluetooth (led by Ericsson, Nokia, Toshiba, Intel, and IBM and supported by more than 500 firms) that define how wireless devices should transmit data to each other. Industry analysts expect that within two years, more than 75 percent of mobile phones will carry the Bluetooth chip—enabling wireless connections with PCs, printers, or any other similarly equipped digital device located within about 30 feet (10 meters).[5]

- Rapid development and deployment of speech recognition and machine-based language translation technologies that might make it possible for people speaking or writing different languages to communicate with each other in real time. According to John Patrick, an IBM executive and a founding member of the World Wide Web Consortium, these technologies could turn the Internet into a "multilingual real-time intercom."[6]

It is clear from these trends that digital technologies are making the world highly interconnected. Instantaneous, or if desired asynchronous, multiway communication (voice, text, graphics, and video) with an unlimited number of people, and with complete disregard for geographic distance, is in some ways already a reality, and will become increasingly so over the coming five to ten years. In such an environment, whether you are a wine producer from France, a steel producer from Brazil, or a blue jeans producer from the United States, you have no choice but to become "netcentric,"[7] that is, to employ the full power of the Internet and other networking technologies to reinvent every aspect of your company's internal and external operations. Of course, some companies (such as Amazon.com, eBay, Yahoo!, FreeMarkets, and Sycamore Networks) were born netcentric. However, every existing enterprise (be it Ford, Toshiba, or ABB) must now transform itself and also become netcentric.

Let us now examine in greater detail two questions. What unique opportunities and challenges do newly formed netcentric firms such as Yahoo! face as they grapple with the global market-place? And how will the move to netcentricity transform established global enterprises, such as Ford or Procter & Gamble?

GLOBALIZATION IMPERATIVES FOR NEWLY FORMED NETCENTRIC FIRMS

In terms of explosive growth from the very start, newly created netcentric firms appear to have no precedent. eBay, the world's largest online auction house, was founded in 1996. By early 2002, it had more than 42 million registered users, enabled more than $30 million worth of transactions each day, and had a market value of over $15 billion. Yahoo!, the world's leading Internet portal in terms of traffic, advertising, and household and business user reach, was founded in 1994. By early 2002, it was serving more than 220 million users every month, had a lineup of thousands of advertisers along with a growing portfolio of merchants worldwide, and a market value of nearly $6 billion.

What are the opportunities and dilemmas that confront companies such as Amazon.com, eBay, Yahoo!, or Sycamore Networks as they look at the global landscape? Should they think of themselves as "born global" or should they chart a more methodical and step-by-step path toward building global presence?

Sitting on the Horns of a Dilemma

For newly formed netcentric companies, the pressures to globalize at Internet speed are indeed enormous. They come into being on the strength of new business models that either create an entirely new marketspace (for example, Yahoo! and eBay) or offer dramatically superior value relative to existing alternatives (for example, Amazon.com and Sycamore Networks). The basic concepts behind these new business models tend to be globally applicable, the underlying networking technology is in use globally, and the value proposition they offer is large enough to have relevance everywhere. In other words, once a netcentric start-up has created a new business model for one market, it has essentially created one for the entire world.

Cross-border transferability of the business model also implies that, if a significant portion of the fixed costs associated with creating and deploying the model could be spread over a global customer base, then there might accrue significant economies of scale. In addition, certain business models are subject to the network externalities effect (popularly known as Metcalfe's Law) whereby, as in the case of a social club, the value of the network rises exponentially with the number of people connected to it. This effect manifests very clearly in the case of ventures such as eBay, whose mission is to act as a market-making intermediary between fragmented sellers and buyers.

Finally, but no less critically, information transparency and the economic values inherent in these new business models create conditions such that, if the pioneer does not take preemptive action, it will get imitated rapidly. Look at Amazon.com as it entered the European market in 1998. In Britain, it faced the online operations of existing bookstores such as WH Smith, Waterstone's, and Blackwell. In Germany, it faced Booxtra (owned by the publishing house Axel Springer and Deutsche Telekom) and Libri (the online arm of a book retailer from Hamburg). In France, it faced FNAC (an established retailer that was now selling books online) and Alapage (a new start-up). In addition to these and other local competitors, Amazon also had to face BOL, the online book-retailing unit of Bertelsmann, in virtually every market.[8] In short, the opportunity cost of delayed globalization can potentially be high.

On the other side of the story, consider the overwhelming challenges faced by newly formed companies in the first few years of their lives. They must implement, continuously fine-tune, and, if needed, even dramatically change their business model as it moves from concept to reality. They must secure a stronghold in their home market, especially critical if the home market is the United States, the largest and leading-edge market for most Internet-based innovations. They must fend off technologically savvy, alert, well-informed, and well-financed domestic imitators. And they must learn how to manage explosive domestic growth while rapidly adding to their managerial, organizational, and financial capabilities. Thus, on the issue of rapid globalization, most newly formed netcentric firms find themselves sitting on the horns of the proverbial dilemma, "damned if you do and damned if you don't." Delayed globalization would imply high opportunity costs. On the other hand, early globalization might end up in a mess. No wonder that, in reflecting on the apparent sluggishness of many U.S.–based netcentric firms in entering European markets, an industry analyst observed: "I can't figure out what they are waiting for. Are they being really smart or really stupid?"[9] Despite the phenomenal success of Amazon in the U.S. market, even Jeff Bezos, the company's founder, has quipped, "What do they say about the British and Americans: 'A common people divided by a common language?' That's really true. It's a complex endeavor, setting up operations outside of your home country."[10]

Resolving the Dilemma

Unless the goal of the new start-up is to stay domestic and wait to get acquired, the key questions boil down to timing (how early in its life should the company start to go abroad) and speed (how rapid should be the pace of the venture's global expansion). Our research suggests that firms tend to pursue one of four archetypal strategies: born global, preemptive globalization, acquisitive globalization, and slow globalization. Figure 9.1 depicts a venture's global evolution under each of these four strategies.

A *born global* strategy implies living as a global enterprise literally from the very start. Some prototypical examples of born global companies would be Internet infrastructure firms such as Broadvision (the developer of software purchased by companies to enable one-to-one business commerce) and Selectica (the developer of software purchased by companies such as Cisco to enable self-configuration of

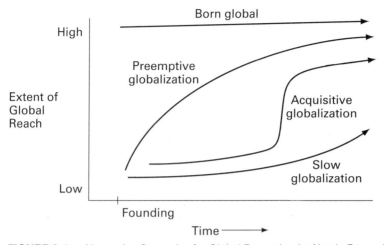

FIGURE 9.1   Alternative Strategies for Global Expansion by Newly Formed Netcentric Firms

complex systems by customers). Both companies started hunting for customers worldwide right from day one and received some of their earliest orders from outside the United States.

A *preemptive globalization* strategy also implies an early start. Unlike the born global case, however, this strategy rests on a sequential (yet high-velocity) approach to new market entry allowing the venture to learn from early moves and to accumulate resources and capabilities as it expands. A prototypical example would be Yahoo! This company was incorporated in 1995. By the end of 1996, Yahoo! was among the first companies, foreign or domestic, to set up local operations in Japan, Germany, the United Kingdom, and France, the four largest Internet markets outside the United States.

An *acquisitive globalization* strategy implies a relatively more delayed start. During the early years, this strategy allows the venture to focus solely on establishing a stronghold in the domestic market. When the venture does start to spread its wings abroad, it does so largely by acquiring similar start-ups and other imitators in foreign markets at a rapid pace. A prototypical example would be eBay, which has used a combination of new launches and acquisitions to enter foreign markets.

Finally, a *slow globalization* strategy implies a more measured and cautious pace of globalization. A prototypical example would be Amazon.com. While Amazon began selling and exporting books from its U.S.–based operations soon after its founding, over the six years from 1995 to 2000, its non–U.S. operations were limited to the United Kingdom, Germany, France, and Japan.

Our research also suggests that the choice among these strategies rests primarily on the *cross-border scalability* of the venture's business model. We use this concept to signify the extent of additional financial, infrastructural, managerial, and knowledge resources needed to enter a new market abroad. The lower the need for additional resources and local market knowledge, the more globally scalable the business model becomes. Figure 9.2 depicts the twin drivers of cross-border scalability—need for local infrastructure and need for local adaptation.

The stronger the imperative for setting up a local footprint while serving customers abroad and the larger the investment required for doing so, the less scalable the business model becomes in financial and organizational terms. Companies selling pure information goods—products or services that can be delivered online (such as eBay or Yahoo!)—generally have much less need for local infrastructure than have those selling physical goods (for example, Amazon) who must also establish a supply chain infrastructure that can reach customers in foreign markets. On the other hand, the greater the need for local adaptation of the company's products, services, and other elements of marketing mix, the less scalable the model becomes in terms of market knowledge and product or service design. Certain products or services require very little adaptation across borders. Others (such as Amazon's portfolio of books targeted to customers in a specific country) require considerable adaptation to the unique needs of the various markets.

Scalability matters because greater cross-border scalability increases the potential returns and reduces the potential risks associated with rapid global expansion. The lesser the need for investment in a local footprint, the greater the scale economies available from cross-border leveraging of the footprint established in the home country. And the lesser the need for local adaptation, the lower the need for new learning—and thus the lower the risk of failure.

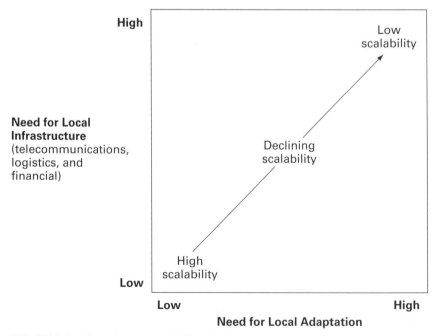

FIGURE 9.2 Cross-Border Scalability of a Business Model

Two important clarifications are in order. First, it should be noted that, depending on the specific nature of the business, the scalability of a business model across borders can be quite different from its scalability within currently served markets. Consider, for example, Amazon.com—whose business model rests on data mining, cross-selling, and building the company's own warehouses and order fulfillment system. Once customer data have been collected and warehouses built, these assets are highly scalable across a whole diversity of products—but within the current geographic markets. However, the cross-border scalability of these assets is severely limited. Second, the choice of an appropriate globalization strategy (in terms of the timing and speed of global expansion) does not guarantee that the strategy would indeed yield the expected results. Each strategy is associated with unique implementation challenges that must be met effectively to ensure that the venture will be successful. For example, take the case of an acquisitive globalizer such as eBay. For this strategy to succeed, the company must also possess highly developed competencies in such areas as timing, deal making (including not overpaying for acquisitions), and postmerger integration.

Notwithstanding the imperatives to globalize, if the business model is not easily scaleable, it can be disastrous to globalize too early and too rapidly. As a highly instructive example of a company that overlooked this important idea, look at the saga of Boo.com, a London-based company founded in 1998 by Swedish entrepreneurs. The founders were successful in raising more than $100 million from a group of high-profile investors including some of the world's best-known retailers and blue-chip investment banks. The founders envisioned Boo as a global retailer of fashionable sportswear. The company launched commercial operations in November 1999 simultaneously in 18 countries (the European Union, Switzerland, the United States, and Canada) encompassing multiple languages, multiple currencies, and local fulfillment infrastructures. Barely four months later, in March 2000, Boo announced plans to launch commercial operations in 13 additional countries spread across the world (Norway, Argentina, Australia, New Zealand, South Africa, Israel, Hong Kong, Singapore, Japan, Taiwan, Malaysia, Saudi Arabia, South Korea, and Thailand). Given such a strategy, it simply could not be very long before the scarcity of financial, organizational, and managerial resources collided with the massive complexity that high-velocity globalization was creating for the company. Just two months later, in May 2000, Boo was liquidated! It is true that Boo has not been the only start-up in the nascent online business-to-consumer market to have foundered. However, given systematic deficiencies in its approach to globalization, it was almost certainly one of the earliest, best-funded, best-connected, and highest-profile failures.

Like Boo, Amazon uses a business model that suffers from relatively low scalability. However, unlike Boo, Amazon has wisely chosen to pursue globalization at a radically slower pace. Of course, to the extent that a non–U.S. customer wanted to buy U.S.–targeted products and pay for shipping costs from the United States, Amazon was ready for global business from the very first day. However, that is not the same as having a strategy to become a dominant online retailer for customers on a global basis. Because of language and cultural differences, there is a huge difference in the portfolio of books, music, and videos that the majority of customers in different markets wish to buy. Also, given the fact that in the 1990s these were still physical products, Amazon needed to build a supply chain infrastructure in each market. Finally, credit card usage, ubiquitous in the United States, was much less widespread in many other countries, including some highly developed ones such as Germany. Reflecting the lower cross-border scalability of its business model, by 2002 (fully eight years after its founding), Amazon had entered only Germany (1998), the United Kingdom (1998), France (2000), and Japan (2000).

In contrast to Boo and Amazon, Sycamore Networks represents an example of extremely high global scalability. Sycamore was the brainchild of serial entrepreneurs Gururaj ("Desh") Deshpande and Daniel E. Smith, who had also cofounded Cascade Communications in 1991 and, in 1997, sold it to Ascend Communications for $3.7 billion. Thus, Deshpande and Smith were well-known and well-connected figures in the global network infrastructure industry. Sycamore designed and sold software-based intelligent optical networking products. Its target customers were network service providers who needed the ability to quickly and cost-effectively provide bandwidth and create new high-speed data services. Typically, these customers themselves were technologically sophisticated and shopped globally for best-of-breed solutions. The buying decisions were made by well-trained scientists and engineers who were fluent in English and tried to stay well informed about new technologies being developed by incumbent players such as Cisco and Nortel or new start-ups such as Sycamore. Further, while Sycamore's products might need some customization for a specific buyer, such customization depended largely on factors other than local language, culture, or other national characteristics. Also, in terms of the value chain, Sycamore had decided to outsource all manufacturing and distribution logistics and directed its own resources and energies toward technology development, product development, marketing, and customer service. Given these characteristics, Sycamore rightly concluded that early and rapid globalization was the only appropriate strategy for the company.

Yahoo!'s business model represents an intermediate level of global scalability—somewhere in between that of Amazon and Sycamore. As a portal providing free Internet navigation services to its users, Yahoo!'s product is pure information. Thus Yahoo! did not need any warehousing, logistics, or financial infrastructure in local markets. Nonetheless, as a consumer service provider, Yahoo! had to engage in significant localization. Before Yahoo!'s business model could be replicated in a new market, it required development of local content (search and classification of information about local Web sites), partnerships with local media, advertisers, and merchants, and localization of language. Reflecting the intermediate degree of its business model's scalability, Yahoo! has globalized at a rate that is much faster than Amazon's and yet much slower than Sycamore's. After its U.S. launch in 1994, the company set up local portals in other markets at the following rate: 1996 (Canada, Japan, the United Kingdom and Ireland, Germany, France), 1997 (Australia and New Zealand, South Korea, Denmark, Norway, Sweden), 1998 (Italy, Spain, Yahoo! Spanish for the global Spanish-speaking diaspora, and Yahoo!

Chinese for the global Chinese diaspora), 1999 (Singapore, Taiwan, Hong Kong, China, Mexico), and 2000 (Argentina and India).

To sum up, companies would be wise to keep the following guidelines in mind as they contemplate globalization at Internet speed:

- Adopt a global mindset and global product architecture from the very start. However, that does not imply that you must start to hunt for customers worldwide from the first day.

- Delay actual globalization of market presence until the market is close to ready in terms of the underlying infrastructure and purchasing power.

- Align the speed of global expansion to the cross-border scalability of your business model.

- Pace the speed of global expansion to the buildup of your organizational and managerial capabilities. Invest early and preemptively in organizational capability. At the same time, where necessary, reduce the demands on organizational capability by relying on partnerships and alliances.

- Think of extreme globalization not as extreme standardization of your products and services but as extreme mass customization. Modularization of product and service design is a well-established mechanism to deal with the need for dynamic variety created by a push toward mass customization.

We now shift gears and focus on how digital technologies are likely to transform the strategies of established global enterprises.

HOW NETCENTRICITY WILL TRANSFORM THE ESTABLISHED GLOBAL ENTERPRISE

There are many ways to look at any enterprise. Take Ford Motor Company. It produces and sells cars in most of the world's largest markets. It is also a professional home to many thousands of people. And it is a financial entity with billions of dollars worth of tangible and intangible assets. However, in terms of the impact of the digital revolution, what really matters is that Ford is a complex information processing organism embedded in an even bigger information ecosystem extending all the way from suppliers' suppliers to customers' customers and beyond. Every activity in this ecosystem—research and development, management of the production and logistics chain, finding customers, understanding their needs, marketing and selling to them, managing people, managing relationships with investors, and so forth—depends crucially on the speed, effectiveness, and efficiency of mechanisms to collect, store, share, process, and use information.

As we discussed earlier, with each passing day, digital technologies are increasing the richness of potential communication between multiple parties, instantaneously and directly without any need for mediation, with complete disregard for distance, without loss of content or memory, and at cost levels moving ever closer to zero. Thus it should be expected that these technologies will transform, on an ongoing basis, what any industry's ecosystem looks like and how it operates. The net result will be radically transformed business models for virtually every company in every industry. Figure 9.3 provides an overview of the various ways in which the digital revolution is likely to transform business models.

As already discussed at considerable length in the preceding section, every company will have significantly enhanced access to the worldwide base of potential customers. If the customer has access to the Internet, you will have the possibility to reach that customer—and vice versa. This is why Harrods, the London-based retailer, has launched an online shopping service;[11] why Christie's, the 234-year-old fine art auctioneer, has started to link all its sales to the Internet;[12] and why Canadian banks (such as Royal Bank of Canada, CIBC, and Toronto Dominion) are using the Web as a potentially much less expensive way than opening branches to build a U.S. customer base.[13] Also for these reasons, we would argue that, over time, the direct as well as indirect costs of anything less than global reach are likely to increase.

The next sections discuss in greater detail how the digital revolution is likely to transform the other two elements of any business model—delivered customer value, and design and management of the value chain.

Transformation of Delivered Customer Value

Development of new information-based products and services. Digital technologies enable companies to collect as well as provide far richer information to customers. Take a paper manufacturer selling its product to catalog printers. Using digital technologies, the paper supplier has much greater ability to engage in consultative rather than transactional selling. Internet connections can be used to educate the customer about the pros and cons of various types of papers and inks, help the customer in managing paper inventory, and even provide guidance with respect to finding new customers with printing needs.

The potential to develop new information-based products and services exists in virtually every industry. As Jacques Nasser, the former CEO of Ford Motor Company, observed, one could even view the car as an "Internet on wheels."[14] As another example, consider Gildemeister, a machine tool manufacturer based in Germany. Gildemeister has made it possible for customers located anywhere in the world to link each of their machines over the Internet to one of the company's three special service centers. This link allows Gildemeister service engineers to diagnose and fix problems faster and more accurately. The result is a win-win for both sides. Customers are able to reduce downtime on their production lines and Gildemeister is able to capture a bigger slice of the after-sales service business.[15]

More customized products and services. A richer database of information about customers' needs, perfect memory about the history of every customer's past purchases, a significantly improved ability to analyze these data, and more responsive value chains will make it increasingly possible for companies

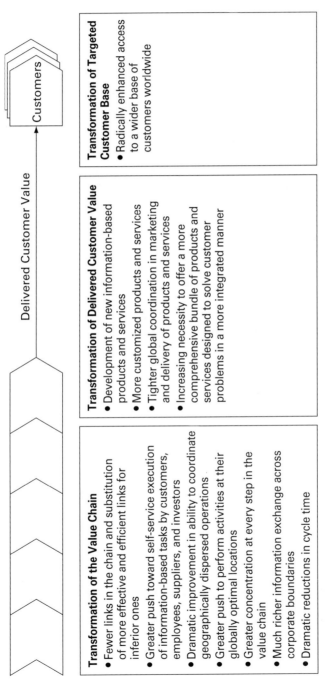

Transformation of the Value Chain

- Fewer links in the chain and substitution of more effective and efficient links for inferior ones
- Greater push toward self-service execution of information-based tasks by customers, employees, suppliers, and investors
- Dramatic improvement in ability to coordinate geographically dispersed operations
- Greater push to perform activities at their globally optimal locations
- Greater concentration at every step in the value chain
- Much richer information exchange across corporate boundaries
- Dramatic reductions in cycle time

Transformation of Delivered Customer Value

- Development of new information-based products and services
- More customized products and services
- Tighter global coordination in marketing and delivery of products and services
- Increasing necessity to offer a more comprehensive bundle of products and services designed to solve customer problems in a more integrated manner

Transformation of Targeted Customer Base

- Radically enhanced access to a wider base of customers worldwide

Delivered Customer Value

Customers

FIGURE 9.3 How Netcentricity Will Transform the Established Global Enterprise

181

to offer customized products and services. Such customization is already beginning to manifest itself in forms such as MyYahoo!, custom-fitted Levi's jeans, custom-configured PCs, and precisely tailored e-mail marketing by airlines. Over the coming years, mass customization is likely to become the norm in virtually every industry—be it cars, clothing, or entertainment.

Tighter global coordination in the marketing and delivery of products and services. For any global buyer, digital technologies increase the ease and reduce the costs of pursuing globally coordinated procurement. For the same reasons, they also make it easier and less costly to serve a global customer in a coordinated fashion. Thus, driven by both demand- and supply-side reasons, companies serving global customers will find that the need for tighter global coordination will increase steadily. Interestingly, however, this is likely to be true even for companies not serving global customers. The Internet will continue to increase individuals' and companies' ability to compare prices for similar goods not merely across domestic vendors but also across countries (as with the global reverse auctions for raw material and components facilitated by FreeMarkets). This development, coupled with ever more efficient and faster delivery systems, will imply that companies must develop increasingly more coordinated global marketing strategies; otherwise, they are likely to find their own subsidiaries competing with each other for the same customers.

An increasing necessity to offer a more comprehensive bundle of products and services to solve the customer's problem in a more integrated manner. Virtually every product or service is always part of a larger and more integrated bundle of complementary products and services. Companies selling PCs are likely to find that they must be ready to sell not just PCs but also complementary products and services such as printers, scanners, digital cameras, Internet access service, memory disks, and so forth. Similarly, companies selling airline tickets are likely to find that they must also be willing to sell hotel rooms, car rentals, and other related services. There are at least two reasons why we expect such a trend. First, companies will have a richer information base about customers and their needs, giving them a better understanding of customers' needs for a wide variety of complementary products. Second, offering a larger bundle of products and services increases the complexity of the coordination task facing the supplier; the greater power of digital technologies can be expected to reduce the difficulties and costs associated with such coordination dramatically.

Digital Transformation of the Value Chain

Fewer links in the chain and substitution of more effective and efficient links for inferior ones. Any value chain can be seen as a system comprising two interlinked subsystems: a physical supply chain and an information supply chain. Because of their obvious power to transmit even complex information over long distances without any loss of content, digital technologies will sharply reduce the number of links needed in any information pipe. This will apply to virtually all contexts—a CEO communicating with a shop-floor worker, a U.S. investor buying the shares of a South Korean company, or a customer in Boston buying a car from DaimlerChrysler. Clearly, some links will continue to be essential. Even here, the remaining links will increasingly be transformed from analog to digital.

Consider the case of Am-Teck, an electrical engineering company based in Lexington, Kentucky.

> *In the old world, field superintendents made lists of their needs by hand. They faxed them to an Am-Teck purchasing agent. He typed them up and faxed them to about 20 suppliers. The suppliers faxed back prices to the purchasing agent, who would then fax back to negotiate, select a supplier, create a purchase order, fax that out and let all the other bidders know they were losers. Enter PurchasePro.com, which does all this electronically, using a much larger, potentially unlimited list of suppliers, spreadsheets that analyze the bids and identify the best ones, and email to place orders. At Am-Teck, PurchasePro reduced the workload of procurement by 75 percent.[16]*

Virtually every supplier-customer interface, particularly in the business-to-business commerce context, will get streamlined and move over to the Net in order to become more direct, more efficient, and more agile. According to many projections, of the total business-to-business activity worldwide (about \$47 trillion as of 2000), approximately 65 percent (about \$30 trillion) will eventually be conducted online.[17] Markets will never really be frictionless, but it is inevitable that the extent of marketplace friction will decline dramatically.

Greater push toward self-service execution of information-based activities by customers, employees, suppliers, and investors.

Digital technologies are leading toward a generalization of the technology-enabled self-service concept pioneered by the banking industry in the form of the automated teller machine. As a customer of Dell Computer, you can now search for available options, self-configure the system that you want to buy, price it, pay for it, and track the shipment schedule on a totally self-service basis without the need for direct human assistance. If you are an employee of the company and want to check the company's policies on medical leave or find out about other jobs within the company, you can do that too via a Net-based self-service system. And if you are an investor looking for data on the company's performance and major events, you can download that information by going to the company's Web site. Because the self-service concept benefits all parties, it will spread. First, the needed information is accessible 24 hours a day, from anywhere in the world, on an instantaneous basis, at virtually no cost. Second, you get information directly from those who created it, thereby eliminating the possibility of information loss or distortion by intermediaries. Third, the whole process is far more efficient in terms of the underlying cost structure.

Dramatic improvement in ability to coordinate geographically dispersed operations. This will be increasingly true not just for large corporations with huge investments in information technology but also for small firms with relatively simple devices. Consider, for example, Lee Hung Fat Garment Factory Ltd., a Hong Kong–based clothing manufacturer. Lee Hung Fat has established some of its production facilities in mainland China and Bangladesh. A network of cameras on factory floors and in the offices at various locations, all connected through the Internet, allows the company's operations director to transmit scanned pictures of samples or even parts of samples to his customers abroad, to track the operations at each of his factories, and to hold video-conferences with his dispersed managers.[18]

Greater push to perform activities at their globally optimal locations. An important byproduct of dramatic improvement in ability to coordinate geographically dispersed operations will be that physical co-location of complementary activities will become less critical. As coordination across locations becomes better and cheaper, companies will face increasingly greater pressure to tap into the comparative advantage of different locations for every subactivity (whether internally performed or outsourced) in the value chain. For the same reasons, companies will also have much greater access to a wider base of resources and suppliers worldwide. In the industrial sector, this is one of the major value propositions behind the emergence of independent or industry-owned market-makers (such as FreeMarkets) whose added value lies in serving as a more comprehensive, more agile, and more efficient intermediary between suppliers and buyers located anywhere in the world than any of them can find locally. In short, the digital revolution should enable companies to lower their cost structures, to overcome the constraints imposed by scarcity of talent and other resources at current locations, provide 24-hour customer service from anywhere in the world, and to pursue round-the-clock R&D projects by setting up interdependent teams in different time zones.

Concentration and exercise of stronger customer power at every step, thereby intensifying the search for cost efficiencies on the part of every supplier. First, the establishment of procurement exchanges like the ones already discussed will enable buyers to harness and apply their global purchasing power more completely. Second, these procurement exchanges will also enable groups of firms, both within and across industries, to pool their purchasing power and exert even greater pressure on suppliers. Witness, for example, the creation of procurement exchanges set up by consortia of buyers such as Covisint in the auto sector, Worldwide Retail Exchange in the retail sector, and TradeRanger in the energy and petrochemicals sector. Third, Internet connections will allow buyers to more easily compare the offerings of different suppliers while also reducing the switching costs dramatically.

Much richer information exchange across corporate boundaries. Consider, for example, the case of Sumerset Houseboats, the world's oldest and largest houseboat manufacturer. Historically, the company updated its clients on the progress of their boats by phone and mail. Since customers wouldn't normally see the boat until it was finished, this considerably increased the risk of a mismatch between the final outcome and expectations. For the same reasons, it also was virtually impossible (or at least very costly) for customers to propose midcourse changes in boat design. With the company's adoption of the Internet, clients are now able to view boat concepts online, collaborate with Sumerset engineers during the design phase, and view the progress of their boats on an ongoing basis. The outcome has been a win-win for everybody: lower cost and greater satisfaction for customers, an expansion in Sumerset's global reach, and an increase in the company's sales of profitable accessories.[19]

Dramatic reductions in cycle time. Cycle time reductions are a corollary of many of the developments noted thus far: elimination of unnecessary links, substitution of more effective and efficient links for inferior ones, and richer and synchronous information exchange among all relevant parties. Take the case of National Semiconductor Corporation's (NSC) Southeast Asian operations in the early 1990s. Given the huge diversity in languages, cultures, rules, infrastructure, and transportation modes, NSC had a complex supply chain with a cycle time averaging 60 days—a major constraint in an industry with declining product life cycles. By outsourcing its logistics management and execution to Federal Express and relying on the latter's global information systems and well-established transportation network throughout Southeast Asia, NSC was able to reduce the cycle time to two days.[20]

To sum up, the cumulative effect of these developments will be that the ecosystem within which firms operate will become an Internet-driven ecosystem where Internet-connected suppliers will do business with Internet-connected customers, and virtually every aspect of the company's internal and external activities will be managed via or with the assistance of the Internet. Cisco Systems, the networking equipment and services company, is one of the leading examples of a global enterprise that is striving to become such an organization. Here is a profile highlighting Cisco's moves to run the entire company over the Web.

Running the Company on the Internet: The Case of Cisco Systems

In 2002, Cisco was clearly the worldwide market leader in providing hardware, software, and related services to enable networking for the Internet. Founded in 1984 by computer scientists from Stanford University, the company had grown into a global enterprise that employed over 36,000 people around the world. Even after the stock market collapse of the technology sector in late 2002, Cisco still had a market value of more than $76 billion. Of the company's FY 2002 revenue of $18.9 billion, approximately 41 percent came from outside the United States. Cisco was widely regarded by industry experts as a company at the cutting edge of running every aspect of its own business on the Web. In the more colorful words of a Silicon Valley observer we interviewed, Cisco believed in "eating its own dogfood."

Cisco had codified the algorithms that its technical salespeople employed to configure network systems for their corporate customers and put these on the Web for use by purchasing engineers. Network systems tended to be complex, were highly customized, and required careful configuration. By 2002, 80 percent of all Cisco orders were coming over the Web self-configured by the customer. As a media article, commenting on Cisco's exports to South America, observed: "Ninety-two percent of its orders from South America now arrive electronically, as faraway customers at screens type in specifications of the systems they want, working out details of configuration with special software. The orders are transmitted across the Internet, and the products are built to order, then loaded aboard jets and sent down south."[21] Customer self-configuration yielded two important benefits. First, there were large savings in selling expenses. Second, unlike the pre-Net days, when one-third of all incoming orders would be incorrect and had to be checked and respecified, nearly all Web-based orders came in correct from the very start.

Cisco outsourced much of its manufacturing. Using Web-based dynamic replenishment software that disaggregated the incoming orders, it automatically sent its suppliers information about what material and components they should ship to which assembly factories and when. The assembly factories also received relevant information about each order over the Internet and, as soon as the incoming material arrived, were ready to assemble, test, and ship the final system to the customer. Over half of Cisco's customer orders were being transmitted to and fulfilled by the company's subcontractors without a Cisco employee ever touching a piece of paper.[22]

Given the complexity of Cisco's products, customers needed a fairly heavy dose of after-sales technical support. Cisco had also put most of its technical support and troubleshooting know-how on the Web. By 2002, more than 80 percent of customers' technical support needs were being met online. The net result: During the preceding five years, Cisco's sales went up six times, yet the size of the technical support staff only doubled. Cisco also encouraged its customers to use the Internet to share their own experience with using Cisco equipment not just with the company but also with other customers, thereby creating "a self-inflating balloon of knowledge."[23]

Cisco also ran many aspects of its human resource management function over the Web. Job candidates were recruited and screened over the Web. Internal job postings were listed on the Web for employees to browse and, if desired, take action. Cisco had also launched a large-scale e-learning initiative that significantly changed the way it educated and trained its employees, channel partners, and customers. With this initiative, Cisco was aiming to shift its entire training structure to an e-learning model. In addition, employees could check corporate policies, look into the details of their benefits packages, buy or sell shares in the company—all on the Web. Even travel arrangements and expense submission procedures had been put entirely on the Web so that people could obtain reimbursement within two days.

Cisco regarded its own core competencies to be research and development and customer relationship management. Given the global spread of the company's own as well as its customers' operations, both of these activities were geographically dispersed. Here again, Cisco relied on the Internet to facilitate cross-border R&D collaboration as well as global customer account management.

Finally, Cisco managers believed that, by striving to put all aspects of the company's activities on the Web, they also had real-time access to operational and financial data. Cisco was aiming to become the first company in the world that could "virtually" close its books within one day of any day in any quarter. As Cisco CFO Larry Carter noted, "This is not just showing off. Knowing where you are all the time allows you to respond faster than your competitors. But it also means that the 600 people who used to spend ten days a quarter tracking transactions can now be more usefully employed on things such as mining data for business intelligence."[24] In overall terms, Carter estimated that, by running the company on the Web, Cisco was saving about $500 million per year (equal to one-sixth of its operating income of $3 billion). He added that, given the scarcity of technically trained manpower and the complexity of the company's operations during the 1990s, Cisco simply could not have grown at a nearly 50 percent annual rate without living on the browser.

THE FUTURE BECKONS!

Enabling e-commerce by marketing and selling to customers over the Internet (a la Amazon or General Electric) is merely the tip of the iceberg in terms of the transformational power of digital technologies. The real revolution will occur when every aspect of the company's operations runs on the Web, when companies move beyond e-commerce and embrace e-business. As Lou Gerstner, IBM's recently retired CEO, noted, "The end-game is not about company ABB becoming ABB.com. Some of the most important net-based transactions are not very visible. These include transactions between employees within businesses, transactions across supply chains, and online procurement."[25]

Some of the companies that were born netcentric (a leading example would be Cisco) are not just creating the tools that will transform the established global enterprises by running every aspect of their own extended operations on the Internet, they are also creating role models for how the global corporation of tomorrow might be organized and managed. To the extent that being big does not automatically equate with being able to capture economies of scale, we are inclined to agree with John Chambers, Cisco's CEO, when he proposes that in the Internet Age the race will be won not by those who are big but by those who are fast.[26] Of course, the interesting question then becomes: What happens when everybody is trying to be both big and fast? Over the coming decade, it should be a lot of fun to watch that race!

NOTES

CHAPTER ONE

1. Thomas A. Stewart, "A Way to Measure Worldwide Success," *Fortune*, 15 March 1999, p. 196.
2. *World Economic Outlook 1997*, The International Monetary Fund.
3. *World Investment Report 1999*, UNCTAD.
4. *Globalization of Industry: Overview and Sector Reports*, OECD 1996.
5. "Marks & Spencer: Black Marks," *Economist*, 6 November 1999, p. 66.
6. *World Investment Report 1996*, UNCTAD.
7. Thomas A. Stewart, "See Jack. See Jack Run Europe," *Fortune*, 27 September 1999, pp. 124–136; "The House That Jack Built," *Economist*, 18 September 1999, pp. 23–26.
8. *From Plan to Market: World Development Report 1996*, World Bank.
9. "Global Economic Prospects and the Developing Countries: Beyond Financial Crisis," World Bank, 1998/99; Ted Bardacke, "Thailand Quietly Eases Rules Governing Foreign Ownership," *Financial Times*, 23 June 1998, p. 6; John Burton, "Korea Returns to Privatisation," *Financial Times*, 23 June 1998, p. 6; Ted Bardacke, "GE Capital Acquisitions Build on Thai Operational Platform," *Financial Times*, 29 September 1998, p. 22; Gillian Tett, "GE Capital Creates a Stir Becoming Big in Japan," *Financial Times*, 23 February 1999, p. 20.
10. Stephen Fidler, "Dollarise or Die," *Financial Times*, 19 January 1999, p. 17; Ken Warn, "Argentina Edges Forward in Its Project to Embrace the Dollar," *Financial Times*, 21 May 1999, p. 9.
11. Quoted in G. Pascal Zachary, "Let's Play Oligopoly! Why Giants Like Having Other Giants Around," *Wall Street Journal*, 8 March 1999, p. B1.
12. "Globalization in Historical Perspective," *World Economic Outlook—May 1997*, International Monetary Fund.
13. "Globalization in Historical Perspective"; David Hale, "A Second Chance," *Fortune*, 22 November 1999, pp. 189–190.
14. *World Development Report 1998/99*, World Bank.
15. "FT Guide to Telecoms," *Financial Times*, August 1999.
16. "Nokia Delivers Upbeat Mobile Outlook, Countering Concerns Among Investors," *Dow Jones Newswires*, 5 December 2000.
17. Quoted in Paul Hofheinz, "What Now?" *Wall Street Journal Reports: A Survey of World Business*, 27 September 1999, p. R25.
18. "FT 500," *Financial Times*, 4 May 2000.
19. "Big Is Beautiful," *Wall Street Journal*, 30 April 1998, p. R9.
20. Quoted in J. Harding, "Siemens Optimistic on China Despite Difficulties Ahead for Foreign Investors," *Financial Times*, 29 December 1998, p. 12.
21. Krishna Guha, "India's Online Meritocracy," *Financial Times*, 25 October 1999, p. 14.
22. *The I.T. Software and Services Industry in India: Strategic Review 2000*, New Delhi, India: Nasscom.
23. Jonathan Karp, "New Corporate Gurus Tap India's Brainpower to Galvanize Economy," *Wall Street Journal*, 27 September 1999, p. A1.
24. Thomas L. Friedman, "Globalization, Alive and Well," *New York Times*, 22 September 2002.

CHAPTER TWO

1. Daniel Bernard, *Financial Times*, 12 December 1998, p. 14.
2. In developing the conceptual framework for this chapter, we have benefited from the research of many scholars, including F. R. Root, *Entry Strategies for International Markets*, Lexington, MA: Lexington Books, 1987; S. Zaheer, "Overcoming the Liability of Foreignness," *Academy of Management Journal*, 1995, *38*(2): 341–363; S. J. Chang, "International Expansion Strategy of Japanese Firms: Capability Building Through Sequential Entry," *Academy of Management Journal*, 1995, *38*(2): 383–407; J-F Hennart and Y-R Park, "Greenfield vs. Acquisitions: The Strategy of Japanese Investors in the United States," *Management Science*, 1993, *39:* 1054–1070; J. Li, "Foreign Entry and Survival: Effects of Strategic Choices on Performance in International Markets," *Strategic Management Journal*, 1995, *16:* 333–352; X. Martin, A. Swaminathan, and W. Mitchell, "Organizational Evolution in the Interorganizational Environment: Incentives and Constraints on International Expansion Strategy," *Administrative Science Quarterly*, 1998, *43*(3): 533–601; and H. G. Barkema and F. Vermeulen, "International Expansion Through Start-Up or Acquisition: A Learning Perspective," *Academy of Management Journal*, 1998, *41*(1): 7–26.
3. Vijay Govindarajan, "Note on the Global Paper Industry," Tuck School of Business Administration, Dartmouth College, 1999.
4. Marriott annual reports.
5. Authors who have discussed globalization imperatives include J. P. Jeannet and H. D. Hennessy, *Global Marketing Strategies*, Boston, MA: Houghton Mifflin, 1998; S. Ghoshal, "Global Strategy: A Conceptual Framework," *Strategic Management Journal*, 1987; G. Hamel and C. K. Prahalad, "Do You Really Have a Global Strategy?" *Harvard Business Review*, July-August 1985; and George S. Yip, *Total Global Strategy*, Upper Saddle River, NJ: Prentice Hall, 1995.
6. Based on interviews with company executives.
7. See, for example: G. Steinmetz and C. J. Chipello, "Local Presence Is Key to European Deals: Bombardier Finds Business Goes to Firms on the Scene," *Wall Street Journal*, 30 June 1998, p. A15.
8. "When Even a Rival Can Be a Best Friend," *Financial Times*, 22 October 1997, p. 12.
9. T. Khanna, R. Gulati, and N. Nohria, "Alliances as Learning Races," *Proceedings*, Academy of Management Annual Meetings, 1994, pp. 42–46.
10. Benjamin Gomes-Casseres, "Xerox and Fuji Xerox," Harvard Business School Case #9-391-156.
11. Ken Iverson and T. Varian, *Plain Talk: Lessons from a Business Maverick*, New York: Wiley, 1997.
12. Sandra Sugawara, "Japanese Shaken by Business U.S.-Style," *Washington Post*, 9 February 1999, p. E4.
13. Robert Anthony, "Euro Disney: The First 100 Days," Harvard Business School Case #9-693-013, p. 12.
14. Anthony St. George, "Mercedes-Benz in Alabama: Lessons from the Field," Harvard Business School Case #9-199-028, p. 2.
15. Krzysztof Obloj and Howard Thomas, "Transforming Former State-Owned Companies into Market Competitors in Poland: The ABB Experience," *European Management Journal*, August 1998, *16*(4): 391.
16. Douglas A. Blackmon, "A Factory in Alabama Is the Merger in Microcosm," *Wall Street Journal*, 8 May 1998, p. B1.
17. "Just How Hard Should a U.S. Company Woo a Big Foreign Market? Planes at the Forbidden City," *Wall Street Journal*, 1997.
18. "In Global Drive, Nike Finds Its Brash Ways Don't Always Pay Off," *Wall Street Journal*, 5 May 1997, p. A1.
19. "Whirlpool Expected Easy Going in Europe, and It Got a Big Shock," *Wall Street Journal*, 4 October 1998, p. A1.
20. Richard Lambert, "An Essential Component," *Financial Times*, 29 October 1998, III.
21. "Asia's Retailing Titan Hits a Great Wall," *Wall Street Journal*, 17 January 1996, p. A10.

CHAPTER THREE

1. Wal-Mart, 1999 Annual Report.
2. This chapter has benefited from discussions with John Menzer, president and CEO, International Division, Wal-Mart Inc.
3. Merrill Lynch, "Wal-Mart Stores Report," 6 March 1998, p. 11.
4. Merrill Lynch, p. 12.
5. Wendy Zellner, "How Well Does Wal-Mart Travel?" *BusinessWeek*, 3 September 2001.
6. These observations are based on *The Wal-Mart Encyclopedia*, Volume III, Salomon Brothers, October 1995, p. 32; and Merrill Lynch, pp. 18–19.
7. Zellner, "How Well Does Wal-Mart Travel?"
8. These observations are based on Merrill Lynch, p. 47; and "Wal-Mart International Reshapes the World Retailing Order," *Discount Store News*, 20 January 1997.
9. These observations are based on "Target Europe," *Chain Store Age*, March 1998; "Wal-Mart Seeks U.K. Supermarket Firm," *Wall Street Journal*, 15 June 1999, p. A3.
10. "Mutual Admiration Society Bonds Together," *Financial Times*, 15 June 1999, p. 30; "Wal-Mart Seeks U.K. Supermarket Firm."
11. These observations are based on Merrill Lynch, p. 34; and "Wal-Mart International Reshapes the World Retailing Order."
12. "Wal-Mart International Reshapes the World Retailing Order."
13. "Business This Week," *Economist*, 4 September 1999, p. 11; "Two French Chains Merge into No. 2 Retailers in the World," *New York Times*, 31 August 1999, p. C1.
14. C. K. Prahalad and K. Lieberthal, "The End of Corporate Imperialism," *Harvard Business Review*, July-August 1998, pp. 68–79.
15. *Financial World*, 13 October 1992.

CHAPTER FOUR

1. Tony Jackson, "Keep the Home Fires Burning," *Financial Times*, 9 January 1998, p. 25.
2. Authors who have discussed similar value creation opportunities include C. A. Bartlett and S. Ghoshal, *Managing Across Borders*, Cambridge, MA: Harvard Business School Press, 1989; B. Kogut, "Designing Global Strategies: Comparative and Competitive Value Chains," *Sloan Management Review*, 1985; M. E. Porter, *Competition in Global Industries*, Cambridge, MA: Harvard Business School Press, 1986; and C. K. Prahalad and Y. L. Doz, *The Multinational Mission*, New York: Free Press, 1987.
3. "As Business Goes Global, So Does *BusinessWeek*," *BusinessWeek*, 1 July 1996.
4. "For Coca-Cola in Japan, Things Go Better with Milk," *Wall Street Journal*, 20 January 1997, p. B1.
5. Remarks by John Pepper, chairman and CEO of Procter & Gamble, to MBA class at Tuck School, Dartmouth College, May 1995.
6. "Midwest Giant Struggles to Find Forward Gear," *Financial Times*, 4 January 1999, p. 22.
7. "Texas Instruments' Global Chip Payoff," *BusinessWeek*, 7 August 1995.
8. Paul Ingrassia, "Industry Is Shopping Abroad for Good Ideas to Apply to Products," *Wall Street Journal*, 29 April 1985, p. 1.
9. Gurcharan Das, "Local Memoirs of a Global Manager," *Harvard Business Review*, March-April 1993, p. 46.
10. Geoffrey Smith, "A Dark Kodak Moment," *BusinessWeek*, 4 August 1997, pp. 30–31.
11. Stefan Wagstyl and William Hall, "ABB to Cut Jobs in Western Europe," *Financial Times*, 9 June 1997, p. 1.
12. "Furnishing the World," *Economist*, 19 November 1994, pp. 79–80.

13. Remarks by John Pepper.
14. William Taylor, "The Logic of Global Business: An Interview with ABB's Percy Barnevik," *Harvard Business Review*, March-April 1991, pp. 93–105.
15. Remarks by John Pepper.
16. Taylor, "The Logic of Global Business."
17. Remarks by John Pepper.
18. "Driving Change: An Interview with Ford Motor Company's Jacques Nasser," *Harvard Business Review*, March-April 1999, p. 85.
19. Disguised names. This example comes from the consulting engagement of one of the authors. Some data elements have been altered in order to preserve the confidentiality of the companies.

CHAPTER FIVE

1. Quoted in Joseph B. White, "Global Mall," *Wall Street Journal*, 7 May 1998, p. A1.
2. See C. Argyris and D. A. Schön, *Organizational Learning*, Reading, MA: Addison-Wesley, 1978; A. Newell, *Unified Theories of Cognition*, Cambridge, MA: Harvard University Press, 1990; H. A. Simon, "A Behavioral Model of Rational Choice," *Quarterly Journal of Economics*, 1955, *69:* 99–118.
3. This chapter has benefited from comments by Milton Bennett.
4. As quoted in S. Wetlaufer, "Driving Change: An Interview with Ford Motor Company's Jacques Nasser," *Harvard Business Review*, March-April 1999, p. 80.
5. Reported in B. Dumaine, "Don't Be an Ugly-American Manager," *Fortune*, 16 October 1995, p. 225.
6. See J. P. Walsh, "Managerial and Organizational Cognition: Notes from a Trip Down Memory Lane," *Organization Science*, 1995, 6(3): 280–321, for a comprehensive review of the literature on managerial and organizational cognition that builds on the work of pioneers such as F. C. Bartlett, *Remembering*, Cambridge, MA: Harvard University Press, 1932; L. Festinger, *A Theory of Cognitive Dissonance*, Evanston, IL: Row Peterson, 1957; and U. Neisser, *Cognitive Psychology*, New York: Appleton-Century-Crofts, 1967.
7. See Simon, "A Behavioral Model of Rational Choice"; and W. H. Starbuck and F. J. Milliken, "Executives' Perceptual Filters: What They Notice and How They Make Sense," in D. C. Hambrick (Ed.), *The Executive Effect: Concepts and Methods for Studying Top Managers*, Greenwich, CT: JAI Press, 1988.
8. See R. Nisbet and L. Ross, *Human Inference: Strategies and Shortcomings of Social Judgment*, Upper Saddle River, NJ: Prentice Hall, 1980; and R. P. Schank and R. P. Abelson, *Scripts, Plans, Goals, and Understanding*, Hillsdale, NJ: Erlbaum, 1977.
9. See J. P. Walsh and L. C. Charalambides, "Individual and Social Origins of Belief Structure Change," *Journal of Social Psychology*, 1990, *130:* 517–532.
10. Walsh, "Managerial and Organizational Cognition," p. 282.
11. As quoted in "The Past, Imperfect," *Time*, 15 July 1996, p. 54.
12. See, for example, F. H. Allport, *Social Psychology*, Boston: Houghton Mifflin, 1924; M. Douglas, *How Institutions Think*, Syracuse, NY: Syracuse University Press, 1986; and E. Durkheim, *The Rules of Sociological Method*, New York: Free Press, 1938.
13. Walsh, "Managerial and Organizational Cognition," p. 291.
14. For research on how organizational level cognitive schemas can change, see J. M. Bartunek, "Changing Interpretive Schemes and Organizational Restructuring," *Administrative Science Quarterly*, 1984, *29:* 355–372; R. Greenwood and C. R. Hinings, "Organizational Design Types, Tracks, and Dynamics of Strategic Change," *Organization Studies*, 1988, *9:* 293–316; H. Hopfl, *Judgment and Choice: The Psychology of Decision*, New York: Wiley, 1992; and M. A. Lyles and C. R. Schwenk, "Top Management, Strategy, and Organizational Knowledge Structures," *Journal of Management Studies*, 1992, *29:* 155–174.

15. Here, we use the term *markets* broadly. Any particular country or region can potentially be a market for the sales of the company's products and services, for accessing technology and talent, for tapping into higher-quality or lower-cost labor, for the purchasing of raw material and components, and for the sourcing of capital.

16. Our dual emphasis on cognitive diversity as well as integrative ability is fully consistent with the perspectives reflected in the studies by T. P. Murtha, S. A. Lenway, and R. P. Bagozzi, "Global Mind-Sets and Cognitive Shifts in a Multinational Corporation," *Strategic Management Journal*, 1998, *19*(2): 97–114; and S. J. Kobrin, "Is There a Relationship Between a Geocentric Mind-Set and Multinational Strategy?" *Journal of International Business Studies*, 1994, *25*(3): 493 ff.

17. W. E. Taylor, "The Logic of Global Business: An Interview with ABB's Percy Barnevik," *Harvard Business Review*, March-April 1991, pp. 93–105.

18. These classifications parallel Perlmutter's (1969) notion of geocentric, ethnocentric, and polycentric organizations. See H. V. Perlmutter, "The Tortuous Evolution of the Multinational Corporation," *Columbia Journal of World Business*, 1969, pp. 9–18.

19. As quoted in J. L. Johnson, "Sears Questions Global Quest," *Discount Merchandiser*, February 1995, *35*(2): 10.

20. Letter to shareholders, 1994 Annual Report, Wal-Mart Stores, Inc.

21. Letter to shareholders, 1998 Annual Report, Wal-Mart Stores, Inc.

22. As quoted in "GE Capital in Asia," *Economist*, June 6, 1998, pp. 72–73.

23. See B. Newman, "Dutch Are Invading JFK Arrivals Building and None Too Soon," *Wall Street Journal*, 13 May 1997, p. A1.

24. Tim Stevens, "Managing Across Boundaries," *Industry Week*, 6 March 1995.

25. See J. S. Black and H. B. Gregersen, "The Right Way to Manage Expats," *Harvard Business Review*, March-April 1999, pp. 52–63.

26. See Alison Maitland, "New Paths to Global Thinking," *Financial Times*, 3 December 1998, p. 23.

27. See J. Ball, "DaimlerChrysler's Renschler Holds Job of Melding Officials into Cohesive Team," *Financial Times*, 12 January 1999, p. B7.

28. This conclusion is consistent with research findings by, among others, C. Eden, "On the Nature of Cognitive Maps," *Journal of Management Studies*, 1992, *29:* 261–265; R. Mitchell, "Team Building by Disclosure of Internal Frames of Reference," *Journal of Applied Behavioral Science*, 1986, *22:* 15–28; and Walsh and Charalambides, "Individual and Social Origins of Belief Structure Change."

29. See V. Govindarajan and A. K. Gupta, "Global Mindset of Samsung," a Tuck School case study, and A. Dragoon, "Samsung Electronics: Not Accidental Tourists," *CIO*, August 1996, p. 62.

30. Gurcharan Das, "Local Memoirs of a Global Manager," *Harvard Business Review*, March-April 1993, pp. 38–47.

31. G. Flynn, "Lilly Prepares Its People to Take On the World," *Personnel Journal*, January 1996, p. 58.

32. S. Baker, "Nokia," *BusinessWeek*, 10 August 1998, pp. 54–60.

33. P. Neff, "Cross-Cultural Research Teams in a Global Enterprise," *Research Technology Management*, May/June 1995, p. 15.

CHAPTER SIX

1. Letter to shareholders dated 12 February 1999, 1998 Annual Report, General Electric Company. Emphasis added.

2. "Strategies from the Bottom of the Pyramid," Presentation by John Ripley, senior vice president—corporate strategy, Unilever Ltd., Annual Meeting, Academy of Management, Chicago, August 1999; and communication with Unilever executives in India and Brazil.

3. E. Thornton, "At China's Gates: Microsoft Boss Conquers a Key Asian Market," *Far Eastern Economic Review*, 4 January 1996, pp. 54–55.

4. For a scholarly development of some of the ideas in this chapter, see also A. K. Gupta and V. Govindarajan, "Knowledge Flows and the Structure of Control Within Multinational Corpora-

tions," *Academy of Management Review*, 1991, *16*(4): 768–792; A. K. Gupta and V. Govindarajan, "Knowledge Flows Within Multinational Corporations," *Strategic Management Journal*, 2000, *21*(4): 473–496; Nitin Nohria and Sumantra Ghoshal, *The Differentiated Network: Organizing Multinational Corporations for Value Creation*, San Francisco: Jossey-Bass, 1997; J. Birkinshaw, N. Hood, and S. Jonsson, "Building Firm-Specific Advantages in Multinational Corporations: The Role of Subsidiary Initiative," *Strategic Management Journal*, 1998, *19*(3): 221–242; B. Kogut and U. Zander, "Knowledge of the Firm, Combinative Capabilities, and the Replication of Technology," *Organization Science*, 1992, *3*(2): 383–397; W. M. Cohen and D. A. Levinthal, "Absorptive Capacity: A New Perspective on Learning and Innovation," *Administrative Science Quarterly*, 1990, *35:* 128–152; R. L. Daft and R. H. Lengel, "Organizational Information Requirements, Media Richness, and Structural Design," *Management Science*, 1986, *32:* 554–571; M. Polanyi, *The Tacit Dimension*, London: Routledge & Kegan Paul, 1966; and D. J. Teece, "Technology Transfer by Multinational Firms: The Resource Cost of Transferring Technological Know-How," *Economic Journal*, 1977, *87:* 242–261.

5. For an extensive discussion of the pathologies that beset companies attempting to use knowledge existing within or outside their corporate boundaries, see also Jeffrey Pfeffer and Robert I. Sutton, *The Knowing-Doing Gap: How Smart Companies Turn Knowledge into Action*, Cambridge, MA: Harvard Business School Press, 2000.

6. "Otis Pacific Asia Operations (A): National Challenges," Harvard Business School Case #9-393-009, 1992.

7. Data on Nucor are drawn primarily from Vijay Govindarajan and Anil K. Gupta, "Nucor Corporation: A Case Study," Tuck School of Business, Dartmouth College, 1998.

8. Ken Iverson, cited in Ghemawat, 1992, pp. 8, 96.

9. Letter to shareholders, 1998 Annual Report.

CHAPTER SEVEN

1. As quoted by John A. Byrne, "21 Ideas for the 21st Century: Management," *BusinessWeek*, 30 August 1999, p. 88.

2. Tim Burt, "Volvo Cars May Build Next Range at Ford Plants in US," *Financial Times*, 2 June 1999, p. 1.

3. W. E. Taylor, "The Logic of Global Business: An Interview with ABB's Percy Barnevik," *Harvard Business Review*, March-April 1991, pp. 93–105.

4. Conference Board, "Organizing for Global Competitiveness: The Geographic Design," 1993; Conference Board, "Organizing for Global Competitiveness: The Product Design," 1994a; Conference Board, "Organizing for Global Competitiveness: The Matrix Design," 1994b.

5. In a broader treatment of the international dimensions of organizational behavior, Adler suggested that, notwithstanding such teams' necessity, the challenge of managing diversity would often render cross-cultural teams highly ineffective in achieving their goals. See Nancy Adler, *International Dimensions of Organizational Behavior*, Boston: Kent Publishing, 1986. More recently, Early and Mosakowski have reported that, at least in the early stages, culturally heterogeneous teams demonstrate poorer performance than do homogeneous ones. See P. Christopher Early and Elaine Mosakowski, "Creating Hybrid Team Cultures: An Empirical Test of Transnational Team Functioning," *Academy of Management Journal*, 2000, *43*(1): 26–49.

6. This chapter has benefited from comments by Vincent Duriau, Tapani Savisalo, and Craig Scheneier.

7. R. C. Mayer, J. H. Davis, and F. D. Schoorman, "An Integrative Model of Organizational Trust," *Academy of Management Review*, 1995, *20:* 712.

8. D. J. McAllister, "Affect- and Cognition-Based Trust as the Foundations for Interpersonal Cooperation in Organizations," *Academy of Management Journal*, 1995, *38:* 24–59.

9. See R. M. Kramer and T. R. Tyler, eds., *Trust in Organizations: Frontiers of Theory and Research*, Thousand Oaks, CA: Sage, 1996.

10. H. Hofstede, "Motivation, Leadership, and Organization: Do American Theories Apply Abroad?" *Organizational Dynamics*, Summer 1980, pp. 42–63. According to Hofstede, cultures can differ across four dimensions: power distance, the extent to which power is centralized; individualism/ collectivism, the extent to which people view themselves as individuals as opposed to belonging to a larger entity; uncertainty avoidance, the difficulty people have in coping with uncertainty and ambiguity; and masculinity/feminism, the extent to which people value materialism as opposed to concern for others. Although it is unlikely that a current writer would use the latter terms in this sense, the management literature still associates concern with things and concern with people with male and female approaches to business life.

11. Amos Tversky and Daniel Kahneman, "The Framing of Decisions and the Psychology of Choice," *Science*, 30 January 1981, *211:* 453–458.

12. These ideas are consistent with many scholarly studies on group effectiveness in general and on top management teams and multicultural teams in particular. See D. Ancona and D. Caldwell, "Demography and Design: Predictors of New Product Team Performance," *Organization Science*, 1992, *3:* 342–355; K. Bantel and S. Jackson, "Top Management and Innovations in Banking: Does the Composition of the Top Management Team Make a Difference?" *Strategic Management Journal*, 1989, *10:* 107–124; J. R. Hackman and Associates, *Groups That Work and Groups That Don't*, San Francisco: Jossey-Bass, 1990; D. Hambrick, T. Cho, and M-J Chen, "The Influence of Top Management Team Heterogeneity on Firms' Competitive Moves," *Administrative Science Quarterly*, 1996, *41:* 659–684; L. H. Pelled, "Demographic Diversity, Conflict, and Work Group Outcomes: An Intervening Process Theory," *Organization Science*, 1996, *7:* 615–631; S. Finkelstein and D. Hambrick, *Strategic Leadership*, San Francisco: Jossey-Bass, 1996; J. R. Katzenbach and D. K. Smith, "The Discipline of Teams," *Harvard Business Review*, March-April 1993, pp. 111–120; and Early and Mosakowski, "Creating Hybrid Team Cultures."

13. R. Bergstrom, "Global Issues Demand Global Teams," *Automotive Production*, 1996, *108*(2): 60–61.

14. K. G. Smith, K. A. Smith, J. D. Olian, D. P. O'Bannon, and J. A. Scully, "Top Management Team Demography and Process: The Role of Social Integration and Communication," *Administrative Science Quarterly*, 1994, *39:* 412–438.

15. K. M. Eisenhardt, J. L. Kahwajy, and L. J. Bourgeois, "How Management Teams Can Have a Good Fight," *Harvard Business Review*, July-August 1997, pp. 77–85.

16. Eisenhardt, Kahwajy, and Bourgeois, "How Management Teams Can Have a Good Fight," pp. 77–85.

17. M. N. Chaniu and H. J. Shapiro, "Dialectical and Devil's Advocate Problem Solving," *Asia Pacific Journal of Management,* May 1984, pp. 159–168.

18. D. B. Stoppard, A. Donnellon, and R. I. Nolan, "VeriFone," Harvard Business School Case #9-398-030.

19. John Pepper, chairman of the board, Procter & Gamble, remarks to an MBA class at the Tuck School, Dartmouth College, May 1995.

20. John Pepper, remarks to an MBA class.

21. These comments are based on our study of 39 country heads in Unilever; and on Floris A. Maljers, "Inside Unilever: The Evolving Transnational Company," *Harvard Business Review,* 1992, pp. 46–51.

22. Maljers, "Inside Unilever."

CHAPTER EIGHT

1. IBM Annual Report, 2000.

2. Amazon.com Web site; Company Annual Reports; "Amazon's Delta," *Economist,* 20 November 1999, p. 78.

3. This chapter has benefited from comments by Praveen Kopalle. In developing their ideas for this chapter, the authors have also benefited from Gary Hamel, "Strategy as Revolution," *Harvard*

Business Review, July-August 1996; Gary Hamel and C. K. Prahalad, "Competing for the Future," *Harvard Business Review,* July-August 1994; W. Chan Kim and R. A. Mauborgne, "Value Innovation: The Strategic Logic of High Growth," *Harvard Business Review,* January-February 1997; Charles Baden-Fuller and John Stopford, *Rejuvenating the Mature Business: The Competitive Challenge,* Cambridge, MA: Harvard Business School Press, 1994; and Constantinos C. Markides, *All the Right Moves: A Guide to Crafting Breakthrough Strategies,* Cambridge, MA: Harvard Business School Press, 1999.

4. Vijay Govindarajan and John K. Shank, "Value Chain Analysis: A Field Study," *Journal of Management Accounting Research,* 1991, *1:* 47–65.

5. Information on Dell Computer Corporation was obtained from the following sources: Annual Reports and 10-Ks; Dell Computer's Web site, http://www.dell.com; Joan Magretta, "The Power of Virtual Integration: An Interview with Dell Computer's Michael Dell," *Harvard Business Review,* March-April 1998, pp. 73–84; "Whirlwind on the Web," *BusinessWeek,* April 7, 1997, p. 132.

6. "Dell Tops Compaq in U.S. Sales," *Wall Street Journal,* 28 October 1999, p. E6.

7. Louise Kehoe, "Online Sales Drive Dell up 41%," *Financial Times,* 12 November 1999, p. 15.

8. "Whirlwind on the Web," p. 132.

9. Magretta, "The Power of Virtual Integration," p. 75.

10. "Whirlwind on the Web."

11. Magretta, "The Power of Virtual Integration," pp. 78–79.

12. "Dell's China Sales in Black After One Year," *Wall Street Journal,* 29 September 1999, p. 22.

13. "The Push for More User-Friendly Boxes," *Forbes,* 11 January 1999, p. 150.

14. This section draws upon the following sources: "Tetra-Laval," Company Brochure, 1999; Tetra-Laval Web site; H. G. Jones, "Tetra Pak—A Model for Successful Innovation," *Long Range Planning,* 1982, *15*(6): 31–37; "Boxed In," *Forbes,* 29 October 1990, pp. 102–103; "Tetra Pak: The Inside Story," *Financial Times,* 16 December 1998, p. 28; "Leader of the Pak," *Marketing Week,* 8 July 1994, pp. 36–37.

15. Jones, "Tetra Pak."

16. "Conquest of the Carton," *Marketing,* 26 November 1987, p. 40.

17. This section draws on the following sources: John Dessauer, *My Years with Xerox,* New York: Doubleday, 1971; Gary Jacobson and John Hillkirk, *Xerox,* Collier Books, 1986.

18. Jacobson and Hillkirk, *Xerox,* p. 61.

19. Jacobson and Hillkirk, *Xerox,* p. 56.

20. Benjamin Gomes-Casseres, "Xerox and Fuji Xerox," Harvard Business School Case #9-391-156, p. 10.

21. Gomes-Casseres, "Xerox and Fuji Xerox," pp. 10–11.

22. Gomes-Casseres, "Xerox and Fuji Xerox," p. 12.

23. Gomes-Casseres, "Xerox and Fuji Xerox," p. 142.

24. Gomes-Casseres, "Xerox and Fuji Xerox," p. 148.

25. Gomes-Casseres, "Xerox and Fuji Xerox," p. 148.

26. Gomes-Casseres, "Xerox and Fuji Xerox," p. 71.

CHAPTER NINE

1. Esther Dyson, *Release 2.0: A Design for Living in the Digital Age,* New York: Broadway Books, 1997, p. 9.

2. "The Future: Tomorrow's Internet," *Economist,* 13 November 1999, p. 35.

3. "FT Guide to Telecoms," *Financial Times,* August 1999.

4. "Nokia Delivers Upbeat Mobile Outlook, Countering Concerns Among Investors," *Dow Jones Newswires,* 5 December 2000.

5. "The Future," p. 30.

6. Quoted in "The Future," p. 30.

7. We thank Judy Olian and Sandy Boyson for coining the parsimonious concepts "netcentricity" and "netcentric organizations." See Judy Olian and Sandy Boyson, principal investigators for a Robert H. Smith School of Business study titled "Harnessing the Power of Netcentricity: A National Research Agenda," 2000. The study was sponsored by DARPA (the U.S. Defense Advanced Research Projects Agency). DARPA is widely regarded as one of the prime catalysts in the development and emergence of the Internet.

8. "Internet Retailing: A New Leaf," *Economist,* 23 October 1999, pp. 72–74.

9. Christopher Cooper and Stephanie Gruner, "U.S. Internet Firms Must Hustle to Catch Up in Europe," *Wall Street Journal,* 15 November 1999, p. A25.

10. Quoted in Cooper and Gruner, "U.S. Internet Firms Must Hustle to Catch Up in Europe," p. A25.

11. Ashling O'Connor, "Harrods to Launch Online Shopping Service," *Financial Times,* 7 September 1999, p. 10.

12. Antony Thorncraft, "Ex-Rugby Player to Tackle Christie's Drive at the Future," *Financial Times,* 13 January 2000, p. 8.

13. Larry M. Greenberg, "Canada Banks Try Web to Win U.S. Customers," *Wall Street Journal,* 28 October 1999, p. A18.

14. Warren Brown, "Ford, GM Drive onto Information Highway," *Washington Post,* 15 January 2000, p. E1.

15. Peter Marsh, "Honing a Nimble Structure," *Financial Times,* 15 November 1999, p. 16.

16. Fred Barbarsh, "The Business of Business Is Net's Future," *Washington Post,* 2 January 2000, p. H1.

17. Rod Newing, "Internet Rain Puts a Bloom on the Business-to-Business Marketplace," *Financial Times,* 18 October 2000, Special section, p. 1.

18. S. Karene Witcher, "Family Garment Business in Hong Kong Uses Internet to Gain Access to Global Customer Pool," *Wall Street Journal,* 24 November 1999, p. B15C.

19. Cisco Systems Inc., Annual Report 1999, pp. 12–13.

20. This example is described in an article by FedEx's CIO, Dennis H. Jones, "The New Logistics: Shaping the New Economy," in Don Tapscott, Alex Lowy, and David Ticoll (eds.), *Blueprint to the Digital Economy,* New York: McGraw-Hill, 1998, pp. 221–235.

21. John Burgess, "An E-Commerce Market Puts Borders to Test," *Washington Post,* 7 November 1999, p. H1.

22. Andy Rienhardt, "The Man Who Hones Cisco's Cutting Edge," *BusinessWeek,* 13 September 1999, p. 140.

23. "Cisco@speed," *Economist,* 26 June 1999, A Survey of Business and the Internet, p. 12.

24. Quoted in "Cisco@speed," p. 12.

25. Quoted in Sarah Parkers, "Global Online Communities Will Replace Old Structures," *Financial Times,* 24 November 1999, Section 2, p. 1.

26. Quoted in *Financial Times,* 3 March 1999.

BIBLIOGRAPHY

Adler, N. *International Dimensions of Organizational Behavior.* Boston: Kent, 1986.

Allport, F. H. *Social Psychology.* Boston: Houghton Mifflin, 1924.

Ancona, D., and Caldwell, D. "Demography and Design: Predictors of New Product Team Performance." *Organization Science,* 1992, *3,* 342–355.

Argyris, C., and Schön, D. A. *Organizational Learning.* Reading, Mass.: Addison Wesley, 1978.

Baden-Fuller, C., and Stopford, J. *Rejuvenating the Mature Business: The Competitive Challenge.* Cambridge, Mass.: Harvard Business School Press, 1994.

Bantel, K., and Jackson, S. "Top Management and Innovations in Banking: Does the Composition of the Top Management Team Make a Difference?" *Strategic Management Journal,* 1989, *10,* 107–124.

Barkema, H. G., and Vermeulen, F. "International Expansion Through Start-Up or Acquisition: A Learning Perspective." *Academy of Management Journal,* 1998, *41*(1), 7–26.

Bartlett, C. A., and Ghoshal, S. *Managing Across Borders.* Cambridge, Mass.: Harvard Business School Press, 1989.

Bartlett, F. C. *Remembering.* Cambridge, Mass.: Harvard University Press, 1932.

Bartunek, J. M. "Changing Interpretive Schemes and Organizational Restructuring." *Administrative Science Quarterly,* 1984, *29,* 355–372.

Birkinshaw, J., Hood, N., and Jonsson, S. "Building Firm-Specific Advantages in Multinational Corporations: The Role of Subsidiary Initiative." *Strategic Management Journal,* 1998, *19*(3), 221–242.

Buckley, P. J., and Casson, M. *The Future of the Multinational Enterprise.* New York: Holmes & Meier, 1976.

Caves, R. E. *Multinational Enterprise and Economic Analysis.* Cambridge, England: Cambridge University Press, 1982.

Chang, S. J. "International Expansion Strategy of Japanese Firms: Capability Building Through Sequential Entry." *Academy of Management Journal,* 1995, *38*(2), 383–407.

Chaniu, M. N., and Shapiro, H. J. "Dialectical and Devil's Advocate Problem Solving." *Asia Pacific Journal of Management,* May 1984, pp. 159–168.

Cohen, W. M., and Levinthal, D. A. "Absorptive Capacity: A New Perspective on Learning and Innovation." *Administrative Science Quarterly,* 1990, *35,* 128–152.

Daft, R. L., and Lengel, R. H. "Organizational Information Requirements, Media Richness, and Structural Design." *Management Science,* 1986, *32,* 554–571.

Douglas, M. *How Institutions Think.* Syracuse, N.Y.: Syracuse University Press, 1986.

Durkheim, E. *The Rules of Sociological Method.* New York: Free Press, 1938.

Early, P. C., and Mosakowski, E. "Creating Hybrid Team Cultures: An Empirical Test of Transnational Team Functioning." *Academy of Management Journal,* 2000, *43*(1), 26–49.

Eden, C. "On the Nature of Cognitive Maps." *Journal of Management Studies,* 1992, *29,* 261–265.

Eisenhardt, K. M., Kahwajy, J. L., and Bourgeois, L. J. "How Management Teams Can Have a Good Fight." *Harvard Business Review,* July-Aug. 1997, pp. 77–85.

Festinger, L. *A Theory of Cognitive Dissonance.* Evanston, Ill.: Row Peterson, 1957.

Finkelstein, S., and Hambrick, D. *Strategic Leadership.* San Francisco: Jossey-Bass, 1996.

Galbraith, J. R. *Designing the Global Corporation.* San Francisco: Jossey-Bass, 2000.

Ghoshal, S. "Global Strategy: A Conceptual Framework." *Strategic Management Journal,* 1987.

Govindarajan, V., and Shank, J. K. "Value Chain Analysis: A Field Study." *Journal of Management Accounting Research,* Fall 1991, *1,* 47–65.

Greenwood, R., and Hinings, C. R. "Organizational Design Types, Tracks, and Dynamics of Strategic Change." *Organization Studies,* 1988, *9,* 293–316.

Gupta, A. K., and Govindarajan, V. "Knowledge Flows and the Structure of Control Within Multinational Corporations." *Academy of Management Review,* 1991, *16*(4), 768–792.

Gupta, A. K., and Govindarajan, V. "Knowledge Flows Within Multinational Corporations." *Strategic Management Journal,* 2000, *21*(4), 473–496.

Hackman, J. R., and Associates, *Groups That Work and Groups That Don't.* San Francisco: Jossey-Bass, 1990.

Hambrick, D., Cho, T., and Chen, M-J. "The Influence of Top Management Team Heterogeneity on Firms' Competitive Moves." *Administrative Science Quarterly,* 1996, *41,* 659–684.

Hamel, G. "Strategy as Revolution." *Harvard Business Review,* July-Aug. 1996.

Hamel, G., and Prahalad, C. K. "Do You Really Have a Global Strategy?" *Harvard Business Review,* July-Aug. 1985.

Hamel, G., and Prahalad, C. K. "Competing for the Future." *Harvard Business Review,* July-Aug. 1994.

Hennart, J-F., and Park, Y-R. "Greenfield vs. Acquisitions: The Strategy of Japanese Investors in the United States." *Management Science,* 1993, *39,* 1054–1070.

Hofstede, H. "Motivation, Leadership, and Organization: Do American Theories Apply Abroad?" *Organizational Dynamics,* Summer 1980, pp. 42–63.

Hopfl, H. *Judgment and Choice: The Psychology of Decision.* New York: Wiley, 1992.

Hymer, S. H. "The International Operations of National Firms: A Study of Direct Foreign Investment." Ph.D. dissertation, Massachusetts Institute of Technology, 1960.

Iverson, K., and Varian, T. *Plain Talk: Lessons from a Business Maverick.* New York: Wiley, 1997.

Jeannet, J. P., and Hennessy, H. D. *Global Marketing Strategies.* Boston: Houghton Mifflin, 1998.

Jeannet, J-P. *Managing with a Global Mindset.* London: Financial Times Prentice Hall, 2000.

Katzenbach, J. R., and Smith, D. K. "The Discipline of Teams." *Harvard Business Review,* Mar.-Apr. 1993, pp. 111–120.

Khanna, T., Gulati, R., and Nohria, N. "Alliances as Learning Races." Proceedings, Academy of Management Annual Meetings, 1994, pp. 42–46.

Kim, W. C., and Mauborgne, R. A. "Value Innovation: The Strategic Logic of High Growth." *Harvard Business Review,* Jan.-Feb. 1997.

Kogut, B. "Designing Global Strategies: Comparative and Competitive Value Chains." *Sloan Management Review,* 1985.

Kogut, A., and Zander, U. "Knowledge of the Firm, Combinative Capabilities, and the Replication of Technology." *Organization Science,* 1992, *3*(2), 383–397.

Kramer, R. M., and Tyler, T. R. (eds.). *Trust in Organizations: Frontiers of Theory and Research.* Thousand Oaks, Calif.: Sage, 1996.

Li, J. "Foreign Entry and Survival: Effects of Strategic Choices on Performance in International Markets." *Strategic Management Journal,* 1995, *16,* 333–352.

Lyles, M. A., and Schwenk, C. R. "Top Management, Strategy, and Organizational Knowledge Structures." *Journal of Management Studies,* 1992, *29,* 155–174.

Markides, C. C. *All the Right Moves: A Guide to Crafting Breakthrough Strategies.* Cambridge, Mass.: Harvard Business School Press, 1999.

Martin, X., Swaminathan, A., and Mitchell, W. "Organizational Evolution in the Interorganizational Environment: Incentives and Constraints on International Expansion Strategy." *Administrative Science Quarterly,* 1998, *43*(3), 533–601.

Mayer, R. C., Davis, J. H., and Schoorman, F. D. "An Integrative Model of Organizational Trust." *Academy of Management Review,* 1995, *20,* 712.

McAllister, D. J. "Affect- and Cognition-Based Trust as the Foundations for Interpersonal Cooperation in Organization." *Academy of Management Journal,* 1995, *38,* 24–59.

Mitchell, R. "Team Building by Disclosure of Internal Frames of Reference." *Journal of Applied Behavioral Science,* 1986, *22,* 15–28.

Neisser, U. *Cognitive Psychology.* New York: Appleton-Century-Crofts, 1967.

Newell, A. *Unified Theories of Cognition.* Cambridge, Mass.: Harvard University Press, 1990.

Nisbet, R., and Ross, L. *Human Inference: Strategies and Shortcomings of Social Judgment.* Upper Saddle River, N.J.: Prentice Hall, 1980.

Nohria, N., and Ghoshal, S. *The Differentiated Network: Organizing Multinational Corporations for Value Creation.* San Francisco: Jossey-Bass, 1997.

Obloj, K., and Thomas, H. "Transforming Former State-Owned Companies into Market Competitors in Poland: The ABB Experience." *European Management Journal,* 1998, *16*(4), 391.

Pelled, L. H. "Demographic Diversity, Conflict, and Work Group Outcomes: An Intervening Process Theory." *Organization Science,* 1996, *7,* 615–631.

Pfeffer, J., and Sutton, R. I. *The Knowing-Doing Gap: How Smart Companies Turn Knowledge into Action.* Cambridge, Mass.: Harvard Business School Press, 2000.

Polanyi, M. *The Tacit Dimension.* London: Routledge & Kegan Paul, 1966.

Porter, M. E. *Competition in Global Industries.* Cambridge, Mass.: Harvard Business School Press, 1986.

Prahalad, C. K., and Doz, Y. L. *The Multinational Mission.* New York: Free Press, 1987.

Root, F. R. *Entry Strategies for International Markets.* Lexington, Mass.: Lexington Books, 1987.

Schank, R. P., and Abelson, R. P. *Scripts, Plans, Goals, and Understanding.* Hillsdale, N.J.: Erlbaum, 1977.

Simon, H. A. "A Behavioral Model of Rational Choice." *Quarterly Journal of Economics,* 1955, *69,* 99–118.

Smith, K. G., Smith, K. A., Olian, J. D., O'Bannon, D. P., and Scully, J. A. "Top Management Team Demography and Process: The Role of Social Integration and Communication." *Administrative Science Quarterly,* 1994, *39,* 412–438.

Starbuck, W. H., and Milliken, F. J. "Executives' Perceptual Filters: What They Notice and How They Make Sense." In D. C. Hambrick (Ed.), *The Executive Effect: Concepts and Methods for Studying Top Managers.* Greenwich, Conn.: JAI Press, 1988.

Teece, D. J. "Technology Transfer by Multinational Firms: The Resource Cost of Transferring Technological Know-How." *Economic Journal,* 1977, *87,* 242–261.

Tversky, A., and Kahneman, D. "The Framing of Decisions and the Psychology of Choice." *Science,* 30 January 1981, *211,* 453–458.

Vernon, R. *Storm over the Multinationals.* Cambridge, Mass.: Harvard University Press, 1977.

Walsh, J. P. "Managerial and Organizational Cognition: Notes from a Trip down Memory Lane." *Organization Science,* 1995, *6*(3), 280–321.

Walsh, J. P., and Charalambides, L. C. "Individual and Social Origins of Belief Structure Change." *Journal of Social Psychology,* 1990, *130,* 517–532.

Yip, G. S. *Total Global Strategy.* Upper Saddle River, N.J.: Prentice Hall, 1995.

Zaheer, S. "Overcoming the Liability of Foreignness." *Academy of Management Journal,* 1995, *38*(2), 341–363.

NAME AND SUBJECT INDEX

COMPANY INDEX